Undivided Love

What people are saying about
Undivided Love

In a time in history when the term "gender" is fraught with confusion and uncertainty, Gina's work here pierces through with great wisdom and clarity. Undergirded with the powerful landmark Apostolic Letter from St. John Paul II, *Mulieris Dignitatem*, Gina empowers women to realize who they are and be who they were meant to be in the world today.
-Jim Beckman, Executive Director for ImpactCenter, a ministry to ministers

Undivided Love bridges the gap between traditional values and an ultra-modern world. A potentially life-changing read for those wishing to rediscover their very nature, dignity, and purpose!
-Jacob M., Graduate in Business Admin and Marketing

This book couldn't have come at a more important time! In an age when many people are questioning their identity, value, and purpose, Gina Bauer exhorts women to step up and be who God has called them to be! Drawing on her thirty years of experience teaching, training, and speaking, Gina offers practical and inspiring wisdom that provides a clear roadmap for how women can fulfill their God-given vocation in the family, society, and Church. Read this book!
-David Rinaldi, President of NET Ministries

My life for twenty-eight years as a mother has been completely giving myself to my children and their needs. On surface level, I often have to ask myself, "Am I fulfilling what God is asking of me? Who am I when all I have done is sacrificed for my children?" I haven't completed any grandiose tasks. After reading Gina's words, I learned that God has already given me my "dignity and worth." I did not have to do anything to earn it. I can only find myself by giving love to others. Through all the challenges in my daughters' lives, God has given me the grace to love them and help them through each trial. I know now that I have fulfilled what God wants for me. I now know who I am. Thank you, Gina, for reminding me of who I am as a woman in God's unwavering love for me.
-Kelli Edwards, wife and mother

Gina Bauer's words have a way of piercing my soul and healing old wounds. Growing up, I struggled with loving myself and finding my identity in God. This is the book I needed, and as a youth minister, it will be such a good resource for helping build up teenage girls in the Church.
-Mary Lindsey Edwards, Youth Director (daughter of Kelli)

Gina's book, *Undivided Love*, left me utterly amazed! In a world where so many women are settling for unfulfilled lives, Gina shines a light on our true worth and identity as beloved daughters of God. Her message of love and fulfillment is exactly what we need in this pivotal moment in history. Through her insightful writing, she reveals the unique role that women have been called to play in healing a hurting world. If you're looking for a powerful message of hope and inspiration, I highly recommend this book. It's a true gift!
-Amy Cummings, Executive Director of Partnership for Youth & Leadership Coach with Cummings Coaching

Undivided Love is an accessible guide to St. John Paul II's Apostolic Letter to women. I have always found his writing style challenging, but Gina's book allowed me to study and receive the beautiful truths he shared with us nearly thirty years ago. Gina candidly expounds on his letter using real life examples that anyone can relate to and learn from. This book is a gift from the Holy Spirit that provides the opportunity for both women and men to gain insight into their own hearts and the hearts of the women in their lives.

I have grown tired of the "God's docile princess" narrative that Christian women are taught from a young age, when I know the truth is that my role in the Church is profoundly more exciting and substantial! Gina's book encourages us as men and women to dive deeper into the core truths of who we are as God's beloved children and reveals that we are called to follow Him in ways that I have rarely heard discussed elsewhere.
-Mary Therese P., Graduate from University of Mary, RN

A book for new beginnings

Undivided Love

You Are Worth the Fight

Gina Bauer

Little Pencil
Publishers

Copyright © 2023, 2024 Gina Bauer
All rights reserved.

Published by
Little Pencil Publishers
Marion, Iowa

Nihil Obstat	***Imprimatur***
Dr. John Froula	**The Most Reverend Bernard A. Hebda**
Censor librorum	**Archbishop of St. Paul and Minneapolis**
January 23, 2024	**January 25, 2024**

The *Nihil Obstat* and *Imprimatur* are official declarations that a book is free from doctrinal or moral error. No implication is contained therein that those who have granted the *Nihil Obstat* and *Imprimatur* agree with the contents, opinions, or statements expressed.

The Scripture quotations contained herein are from the *Revised Standard Version of the Bible—Second Catholic Edition (Ignatius Edition)* Copyright © 2014 National Council of the Churches of Christ in the United States of America. Used by permission. All rights reserved worldwide.

Cover photography by Collette LaRue. Used by permission. https://www.collettelarue.com/

Because of the dynamic nature of the internet, any web addresses and QR codes contained in this book may have changed since publication and may no longer be valid.

Paperback ISBN: 979-8-9872545-4-7
Ebook ISBN: 979-8-9872545-5-4

To my daughters,
Katie Rose and Genna Gabrielle,
as well as all of the daughters of God.
May you always know that you
do not have to earn your worth;
it has already been given to you!

Contents

Forward…………………………………………xi
Acknowledgements……………………………...xiii
Author Note……………………………………..xiv
Introduction……………………………………..xvi

Chapter 1—God Believes in You…………………………...1
   (Introduction)
   Supreme Calling
   The Exceptional Link (The Marian Year)

Chapter 2—You Are Enough with Grace…………………15
   (Woman-Mother of God)
   To Believe and to Belong (Union with God)
   God in a Bod™ (Theotokos)
   Yes, to the Yes (To Serve Is to Reign)

Chapter 3—You Are like God……………………………...37
   (The Image and Likeness of God)
   God Is Calling You (The Book of Genesis)
   How Big is God? (Person-Communion-Gift)
   God Is Like Man (The Anthropomorphism of
      Biblical Language)

Chapter 4—In Mary, Every Eve Has a New Beginning…..67
   (Eve-Mary)
   Those Darn Apples (The "Beginning" and the Sin)
   Evil Inheritance ("He Shall Rule over You")
   The New Beginning (First Gospel)

Chapter 5—Jesus Christ Is Talking to You................97
(Jesus Christ)
God Is on the Move ("They Marveled That He Was Talking with a Woman")
A New Beginning (Women in the Gospel)
Entrusted to His Heart (The Woman Caught in Adultery)
Women on a Mission (Guardians of the Gospel)
Who Will Move the Stone? (First Witnesses of the Resurrection)

Chapter 6—The Holy Spirit in You...........................135
(Motherhood-Virginity)
Another Little One for Heaven (Two Dimensions of Women's Vocation)
It's All About Love (Motherhood)
Mama Bear (Motherhood in Relation to the Covenant)
Radical Love (Virginity for the Sake of the Kingdom)
Heaven Bound (Motherhood According to the Spirit)
Another Little One for Heaven (My Little Children with Whom I Am Again in Travail [Labor])

Chapter 7—Will You Be Mine?................................177
(The Church the Bride of Christ)
Take Your Place (The Great Mystery)
Game Changer (The Gospel "Innovation")
God's Love (The Symbolic Dimension of the Great Mystery)
Heaven on Earth (The Eucharist)
I do! I do! (The Gift of the Bride)

Chapter 8—"The Greatest of These Is Love"................221
Light and Power (In the Face of Changes)
What's Love Got to Do with It? (The Dignity of Women and the Order of Love)
Grace Is the New Strong (Awareness of Mission)

About the Author................................237
End Notes...239

Forward

" 'If you knew the gift of God' (Jn 4:10), Jesus says to the Samaritan woman during one of those remarkable conversations which show his great esteem for the dignity of women and for the vocation which enables them to share in His messianic mission." – from *Mulieris Dignitatem*

In 2009, while attending a Council of Catholic Women's retreat entitled "Embracing Our Call: Dignity and Vocation of Women" in Fort Dodge, Iowa, I was so impressed with the presentation of a dynamic and obviously faith-filled woman who spoke about the irreplaceable role of women in the Church. The presenter, Gina Bauer, was well-read on Pope St. John Paul II's 1988 Apostolic Letter, *Mulieris Dignitatem,* and communicated its message with joy and enthusiasm to those present.

I told the faithful that I hoped the "Embracing Our Call" retreat would truly make a difference in their lives, pointing out that Gina's presentation gave them much to reflect upon. It encouraged me, still in the early years of my episcopacy in the Diocese of Sioux City, to know that my work as Bishop was supported by an impactful lay speaker like Gina.

In gratitude for her words of inspiration to the women of our diocese, I offered a blessing for Gina after my homily and encouraged her to continue her important work in ministry.

Gina has been a blessing to the women of our diocese for many years. She returned to inspire the faithful at several diocesan women's conferences in the Diocese of Sioux City.

Gina also spoke at our first "Rekindle" youth conference and made her mark on our younger Catholics. One eighth-grade student attending the conference said her presentation to the youth related to "real life." Gina reminded our young Catholics and the women of our diocese that "everyone is essential" and that we all have to take our place in the Church.

I am so grateful for Gina's message to encourage women to

take their place in the Church and to find their place in the Body of Christ, following the example of Mary, Mother of God. Gina encourages women to do more in the spirit of the Lord and to embrace their vocations.

I am so pleased that a wider audience will be inspired and encouraged by Gina to come forward and take their place in the Church through reading this book. Gina's 30-plus years in youth ministry and years of speaking about the vocation and dignity of women give her the voice to educate and empower women. She demonstrates to the readers the love Christ shows to women throughout the Scriptures.

Prayerfully read this book and meditate upon the message of your role and value in the Church. By the last chapter, you will be transformed and energized as Christ's workers in the vineyard of today's world. The Church needs you to take your place, now more than ever.

Your brother in Christ,

Most Reverend R. Walker Nickless
Diocese of Sioux City

Acknowledgements

Thank you, Duane, for your encouragement and support. Early in our marriage you often said, "You should write a book." Well, here it is! Thank you to our children, especially Michael, who believed it was all ready to be written down, and David for all of his encouragement, prayers, and joy. Thank you to my sister Lisa who listened to each chapter being read. Thanks, thanks, thanks to Theresa Endris, the Editors, Theresa Alt, Cheryl McCarthy, Collette LaRue, Father Scott Carl, Leslie Coons and all the people who prayed for the book's arrival. You are enough with grace!

Author's Note

I have a few signature phrases that I have often used over the years in my talks that drive the point home while entertaining the audience. "Whack-whack" refers to the power of the Holy Spirit to wake us up, convincing us of God's love and truth. "God in a Bod™" refers to the joy of Christmas, Jesus Christ the Son of God becoming incarnate.

The Samaritan woman who encountered Jesus at the well left her bucket there, signifying her choice to leave the old life behind, transformed by the love of Christ. Throughout the book, I highlight key sentences, placing them in buckets. These buckets are your invitation to allow Jesus's love to transform your life.

Finally, there are many stories of heroic people who give witness to their faith in my book. These stories help us all grow in our personal awareness of faith. If you would like to share your story of faith to help others grow, please go to my website at ginabauer.com. Keep swimming!

Scan the QR code to visit my website.

Introduction

As a theology student, I remember raising my hand and asking my professor, "So, what exactly is the role of women in the Church?" The answer given was not satisfactory to me, although it was true. I was told, "Most women are called to be wives and mothers." I remember thinking, "There has to be more to my life than being a wife or mother." The something more or the "something bigger" that I and so many women are looking for is the *meaning of being created as a woman*. What is the *meaning* of being a woman in the order of love? Does this meaning exist? If so, how does this meaning affect every aspect of my life as a woman? How does it impact the various roles I have within marriage and the family, the workplace, society, and the Church?

My professor pulled me aside after class that day and said that he did not have the answers to the questions that I was seeking. He suggested that I pray and study to help bring light and answers to the many questions being raised about the role of women in the Church. Around the same time I was asking questions about women's role in the Church, St. John Paul II was writing an Apostolic Letter to women on their dignity and vocation. When I read this letter, I just cried. I could not believe anyone would write such a letter as this for women. I also could not believe that person was the pope!

In his work *On the Dignity and Vocation of Women* (*Mulieris Dignitatem*), St. John Paul II reminded us that a Synod of Bishops in October 1987 called for further study on the meaning of being a woman or a man both from a theological and anthropological level. He invites us to a clearer understanding of women and the vital role they are called to play in Christ's mission within the family, society, and Church, *for "women imbued with a spirit of the Gospel can do so much to aid humanity in not falling."*[1]

Since the original fall from grace, the human person has constantly been in danger of falling. In the modern age things are no different as seen in men and women's diminished ability to relate to each other, as well as to govern the earth. The tragic results of sin can be found in our families, societies, governments, and even the Church herself. Women especially, across many different nations and cultures, are denied education, employment, and freedom. Women and children have been denied their rights, made the property of others, used in sex trafficking and pornography, and victimized by the abortion-on-demand mindset (i.e., abortion is the best answer to your problem).

St. John Paul II's Apostolic Letter *Mulieris Dignitatem* is a reminder to women that they are responsible to God for their most high calling. Being endowed with what St. John Paul II calls the feminine genius, woman has been created to be a gift of love to man. Woman's dignity and vocation, **"can and must be received in the 'light and power' which the Spirit grants to human beings, including the people of our own age, which is marked by so many different transformations."**[2] Each human person is especially entrusted to a woman's heart by the Creator. Woman can and must become a dwelling place of the Holy Spirit. Only in this way can she "acquire in the world an influence, an effect and a power never hitherto achieved."[3] This is what God is asking of her, particularly at this time in history.

St. John Paul II believed in women. In this Apostolic Letter, he is summoning the women of the Church to take the place God has prepared for them. This means that women, inspired and guided by the Holy Spirit are being called to step it up, to be a part of the answer to the many dangers that humanity is facing. It is not enough to have coffee and talk about all the problems. St. John Paul II is directing all women to influence human change as the grace is given to them through the power of God the Holy Spirit, Who guides and directs humanity to its supreme calling.[4]

Women and men together reflect God best, so when we talk about women taking their rightful place, we are talking about the place that God has for them *side by side with men*: *"male and female he created them"* (Gen 1:27).[5] While this book focuses on God's plan for women, men will benefit from reading it too!

For it was that first sin that divided Adam and Eve from God and each other. If prideful disobedience could divide, then surely humble divine love can heal and unite us. "On that Cross," Christ the divine Bridegroom fought for us, shedding His blood: Jesus loved us to the end. Christ's death proves the definitive worth of the human person. Christ loved us with a human heart but a divine love, powerful enough to save us. Powerful enough to unite us as men and women in *Undivided Love. You are worth the fight.*

Scan this QR code to access the document, *Mulieris Dignitatem*.

God Believes in You
(Introduction)

> The hour is coming, in fact has come, when the vocation of women is being acknowledged in its fullness, the hour in which women acquire in the world an influence, an effect and a power never hitherto achieved. That is why, at this moment when the human race is undergoing so deep a transformation, women imbued with a spirit of the Gospel can do so much to aid humanity in not falling.[6]

Supreme Calling

One night, I was at church praying in front of the Blessed Sacrament. It was dark and peaceful with only one candle glowing. I could see the beautiful crucifix and statues of Mary and Joseph. I, however, was not at peace. I was anxious about many things both at home and with my job. It all seemed so overwhelming. Then as the Scripture teaches us to pray in 1 Kings 19:11-12, I discerned the "still small voice" of God that seemed to say, *I believe in you.* A deep peace went through me. Despite everything that was happening, I knew it would be all right if Jesus believed in me. Jesus knows who we are and what we are capable of with grace. If you are a follower of Jesus, many times in your life you will simply need to have faith in Him, but Jesus also wants you to know that He *believes in you!*

St. John Paul II believed in women. In his Apostolic Letter *Mulieris Dignitatem* (*On the Dignity and Vocation of Women*), he summons the women of the Church to take the place that God has prepared for them. In this letter, St. John Paul II encourages women to be more responsible for their high calling in God, lest humanity fall. Women who are inspired, which means permeated with grace, can and are being called to step it up, to be a part of the answer for what is troubling the world. This is what it means to be "imbued with a spirit of the Gospel."[7] It is not enough to have coffee and talk about all our problems. Jesus has answers and wants the Church to look to Him for the wisdom and guidance to address life's most difficult questions and problems. St. John Paul II is summoning all women to inspire and influence human change as grace is given to them through the power of God the Holy Spirit, Who guides and directs humanity to its *supreme calling.*[8]

In other words, this is **Go** time; however, it must be **God** who directs the **Go** so that the change that is brought about is truly the good that is necessary for the human person who is in danger of falling. I was beginning my work in youth ministry when, in a dream, I saw a hammer pounding on a roof. Shingles were flying everywhere. Suddenly a big hand came down from heaven and took hold of the hammer and started carefully pounding and putting the shingles back into place. When I woke up, I knew that the Lord was telling me, "You are working awfully hard, however, you are only making a bigger mess of things." If we turn to the Lord and allow His grace to direct us, we will not only get more done, but it will be what truly needs to be done! You and I can acquire this influence, power, and effect only by saying "yes" to God.

Together we are called by God from the beginning. Men and women together reflect God best, so when we talk about women taking their rightful place, we are talking about the place that God has for them alongside men: *Side by side*, as God created them, "male and female" (Gen 1:27). Neither occupies a lesser place, nor is it a competition. While men and women are not the same, they are equal in dignity. St. John Paul II wants us to remember that it is a matter of both women and men, together in Christ, becoming what the Creator meant us all to be from the beginning: an Undivided Love.

This eternal *truth about the human being*, man and

woman—a truth which is immutably fixed in human experience—*at the same time constitutes the mystery which only in 'the Incarnate Word* [God made man] *takes on light…(since) Christ fully reveals man* [and woman]¹ *to himself and makes his supreme calling clear.*'⁹

Christ fully reveals the truth of the great dignity of men and women, who both share equally in the *"supreme calling"* to life and the light of understanding that can only come from God (Jn 1:4). St. John Paul II wrote the Apostolic Letter *On the Dignity and Vocation of Women* because it is difficult for us as women and men to understand ourselves, alone. We do not make sense by ourselves. God made us this way. I heard it said that after writing the Apostolic Letter on women, some men asked when he would write an Apostolic Letter on men. The pope responded simply by pointing to the letter on women. How we relate to one another as men and women, brothers and sisters, husbands and wives, and in all our human relationships, unmarred before the fall of original sin, is compared to the inner life of God. Within the Holy Trinity is found a profound love and unity that is totally divine and undivided. It is what we as human beings are made for and is the greatest power. The power of love, to love and be loved, is what it means to be human, made in the image and likeness of God who created us.

---

[1] The word "woman" is added to aid the reader in understanding that the word "man" is intended to be inclusive of both man and woman. "And woman," enclosed in brackets, will be used as needed to reinforce this meaning.

Embracing and living this call is worth the fight. Take, for example, my parents. It was not always easy raising a bunch of little kids. My mother could not swim. My dad could swim a little. They had eight children who all became little swimmers. One day at their cabin my mother sat on the dock, watching her kids swim, afraid to death that one would drown. She finally said to my dad, "I think we should go to the YMCA and take swimming lessons." Mom's fear of water had kept her from learning how to swim. She was, however, more concerned about protecting her children from the possibility of drowning.

This is what St. John Paul II is essentially saying: "It's time to learn how to swim. It is time to equip yourself for the fight that is going on over your life! Look at the world. Look and see how many people are really not doing well. People's relationships with each other are in danger of drowning. Everyone is so busy going after what they think is important, what they think will bring them happiness, instead of focusing on who they are and Who they are made for. With all the business of trying to buy our stuff, stuff, stuff and have our pleasure, pleasure, pleasure, and then success and more success, it's never enough. Add to all this the explosion of technology—Quicker! Faster! Better! Life becomes a whirlwind that can leave us empty and unfulfilled. Men and women, teens as well as children, often feel overwhelmed. So much suffering comes from failed relationships and the breakup of the family. Many people want good, strong families but are less and less willing to sacrifice for them. St. John Paul II put it this way:

> **Family communion can only be preserved and perfected through a great spirit of sacrifice. It requires, in fact, a ready and generous openness of each and all to understanding, to forbearance, to pardon, to reconciliation.**[10]

The truth about the human person is that we are made for love, and we are created to find happiness in giving and receiving love from the people God puts into our lives. We cannot figure out who we are except through this ability to make a *sincere gift of ourselves*.

All the suffering of humanity is the direct result of the failure to love in this way. So Jesus says, "Come on! Follow me or you will not get this right!" Yet we do not always listen and do what we should. It might be that we are afraid, or we don't know where to start, or we do not believe God. In truth, the real problem is we really do not know who we are. If we continue to merely focus on ourselves, we will never know who we are. So St. John Paul II says, *"Start then, with what I'm asking you to do. Follow Christ!"*

Inspired women are called by God to step it up by overcoming their fears. And so, my mom went with my dad down to the YMCA and took swimming lessons. They both learned how to swim. A few years later Mom was alone at the cabin. No kids were with her, which was very unusual. She was down at the dock when she saw a man chasing a ball, swimming. It was one of those beach balls that was red, yellow, and white. As she was watching she started to think, "Oh boy, he's swimming slower and the ball's going faster." All of a sudden, she realized, "He's trying to get the ball because he's too tired to swim back." When he did finally get to the ball, he grabbed the ball so tight, what happened…? It popped! And then he started struggling.

Now, Mom had had only two seasons of swimming lessons, but she was an inspired woman. She knew how to equip herself, so she said a prayer and grabbed her flippers and a noodle lying on the dock to act as a life preserver. She jumped in the water and went after him. And what was her mission? To save the drowning man! With her swimming lessons, flippers, and noodle, she paddled toward him. When she got to him, she said, "Grab this!" She pushed the noodle toward him, saying, "Do not touch me! I cannot swim!" She gave him a direct command because she knew she was in danger; this was a big guy—he had popped the beach ball! But correctly equipped, she paddled in with confidence, dragging the man behind her, and she saved him.

> **"Within Christianity, more than in any other religion, and since its very beginning, women have had a special dignity . . . ; it is evident that women are meant to form part of the living and working structure of Christianity in so prominent a manner that perhaps not all their potentialities have yet been made clear."**[11]

Because Mom had prepared and equipped herself, she was able to save the drowning man. The definition of potential is having the capacity to become more developed into something in the future. My coaches in high school loved this word *potential*. They would often say to us, "You have great potential to be a successful gymnast or volleyball player, but potential is not enough. You will have to train and work very hard if you are going to fulfill all that you are capable of becoming!"

Each woman in Christ has been called and gifted with a unique vocation that only she can fulfill during the time that God has given her on earth. On planet Earth, everyone is drowning, and all are in need of the Savior's love and redemption. Women who are inspired—that is, filled with the grace of the Holy Spirit—can, like my mom, come to the aid of persons who are desperate for a Savior. This is our great mission: to bring people back to God. It is also what God is asking of us at this time. At the end of our lives, we want to come before our heavenly Father with no regrets, knowing that we did our best to come to the aid of humanity. Jesus Christ is the answer for weak and sinful humanity. We do not want to stand before Him finding out that it was all true and that we missed our life's meaning and purpose on earth:

> **In the hour of our agony, in that hour of truth, when, at the moment of our appearance before God, we perhaps review in our memory our whole life, with so many miseries and weaknesses, so many failings and falls, I hope that with contrite hearts but immense confidence we shall say to Jesus, "All this, all this I give to you. Did you not come to earth to seek out my sins and take them upon yourself? In exchange, give me the price of your blood, the treasures of your Redemption, all your merits; they are mine."**[12]

Despite our "many miseries and weaknesses" with so many "failings and falls," as women we can confidently bring humanity back to its origin if we lean into our Savior and rely on His grace.

It was Mary's love for her Son that compelled her to stand with Him in His suffering. Her love and presence strengthened Jesus and the rest of His followers. Sometimes when evil is so overbearing, we simply must stand as Mary did with Jesus and our brothers and sisters. A close friend asked me recently, "How can you still support that institution [the Church] with all the scandals that have happened?" I gently replied, "I follow Jesus, not human beings." Jesus did not have it easy, either. Remember, Jesus was crucified, and at that time most of His followers abandoned Him. Mary, His Mother, Mary Magdalene, John, and a few others in the distance stood with him at the Cross. That is what we must do as well. *We must help each other to stand with Jesus no matter what.* We must be faithful by rejecting evil and doing good, for the sake of love.

> **This also explains the meaning of the "help" spoken of in Genesis 2:18-25: "I will make him *a helper fit for him*." The biblical context enables us to understand this in the sense that the woman must "help" the man—and in his turn he must help her—first of all by the very fact of their "being human persons."**[13]

Being a human person means that we are created by God to help each other. God created a helper fit for Adam, and if Eve was fit for him, he was also then fit for her. They were created in God's plan to help each other. This means that everyone is essential in God's plan. Your life matters because someone out there needs you to make it, maybe even to survive, whether they realize it or not.

It was my mom's love for her children that helped her to overcome her fear and learn how to swim. That is what Jesus was asking her to do. My dad helped my mom to overcome her fear of swimming by going with her to encourage her in taking swim lessons. He also became a better swimmer. He took the time to help her. That is what Jesus was asking of him. *She herself, however, needed to jump in and learn how to swim.* Dad could not do that for her. Together they both became better swimmers.

Jesus is the lifesaver. He wants to save us from drowning; secure us on the rock, the Church; and then guide us, which means we must be willing to follow Him. Jesus is the one Who is asking women and men to come together in an Undivided Love that God desires for all of humanity. He is calling all women and men back to the original unity planned from the beginning. The source of this unity is God; we must learn to recognize and see each other's dignity as Jesus does. *Why? Because we need each other now more than ever.*

In a particular way, St. John Paul II summons the women of the Church to rise up in Christ and take their rightful place within the Body of Christ, the Church, and society. To carry out God's plan, it is good for all women to be equipped as Christ's followers, which means developing their potential to aid in the rescue of humanity.

"Everyone is essential in God's plan."

The Exceptional Link (The Marian Year)

It is important for women to realize that Mary's role as Jesus's mother came before Peter's role as the pope. The link to the *new beginning* was not a pope, but a woman. Mary is *the exceptional link* between God and humanity for by her "yes," a woman opens the way for God's grace to restore humanity's dignity, the fundamental inheritance of being the "children of God." It is Mary, a human woman, who, full of grace, cooperates with God's mysterious plan to become one of us in order to save us: "And the Word became flesh and dwelt among us, full of grace and truth." (Jn 1:14). The "Word" is "Jesus Christ incarnate"—I like to say, "God in a Bod™." God gave Mary, a human woman, all the graces she needed to take her place and fulfill her mission of becoming the Mother of God. Impossible! Yet nothing is impossible with God (Lk 1:37). We too are called by God to take our place and to fulfill our mission. This is the supreme calling of each woman and each human life. Will God not also give to you and to all of His daughters, the grace and help needed to fulfill your mission, your supreme calling in life?

  I remember as a little girl, maybe seven or eight, playing out in the field that was a part of the school playground next to our house in Wisconsin. I was all by myself, and I decided to lie down on my back and check out the clouds. It was a beautiful summer day, and I thought to myself, "Well, God is not washing His floors or moving His furniture!" This is what Mom had said God was doing when it was raining and thundering. At that young age, I already realized that God had created me, as well as the beautiful sky filled with clouds, birds, and sunshine. I knew that God was good and that He loved me very much.

> **It is a question here of every man and woman, all the sons and daughters of the human race, in whom from generation to generation a *fundamental inheritance* is realized, the inheritance that belongs to all humanity and that is linked with the mystery of the biblical "beginning": "God created man in his own image, in the image of God he created him; male and female he created them" (Gen 1:27).**[14]

All of creation is made by God for humanity. The human being, however, is created by God, for God. How do you know you are made in God's image and likeness? When you see a beautiful sunrise or the ocean with dolphins swimming and seagulls soaring, you are filled with wonder and awe at the beauty with which the whole world is made and of which you are a part. God has given you this capacity to think and reason so that you can know who you are. As beautiful as this world is, you are even more beautiful and precious to God. You are created in God's image with memory, intellect, and free will so that you can choose goodness and love. You and I can cooperate with God's grace to become the person we are created to be, *like God.* This is the means of finding your way back to your first beginning, your first love, the Author of your life: GOD.

This is the inheritance that has been kept for you to discover and claim. "The lines have fallen to me in pleasant places; indeed, my heritage is beautiful to me" (Ps 16:6). Your inheritance is to be with God, the God Who loves you and calls you to Himself. Your life itself is a gift. It has been given to you for a purpose. At the base or core of who you are, you are and always will be a daughter of God, and nothing can ever change that truth. God knows who you are, your name, your address, what you think about, and what matters most in your life! "I have called you by name and you are mine" (Is 43:1). *God believes in you.*

God knows us, believes in us, and calls us each by name. When someone knows our name and says it, it helps us to recognize who we are. Our dignity is discovered in our relationships with other people, our family and friends, and most importantly in our relationship with God. In the garden after the resurrection, Mary Magdalene did not realize that the man she was talking to, who she thought was the gardener, was actually the risen Lord Jesus, until "Jesus said to her 'Mary.' She turned and said to him in Hebrew, 'Rab-boni!' which means teacher" (Jn 20:11-18). Only after Jesus said her name did she recognize Jesus. Yes, Jesus knew her and remembered her name. Jesus knows you. Jesus gets you. Jesus is always there for you.

One summer I was on a pilgrimage with a group of about one

hundred teenagers. At one point I asked all the teens and adult leaders to sit down in a big circle in the gym. To help them get to know each other better, I asked them to take turns standing up and saying their full names. Then everyone else was supposed to repeat their full name. I still smile when I think about the amazing change that took place in that gym. It was hard for many of them just to stand up in front of the group, let alone to say their own name out loud, showing everyone, "This is who I am." But when the group responded at full volume with much love and enthusiasm, each teen would stand a little taller, breaking into a grin or even laughter.

It is so important for each person to be seen and to be known. It is difficult, even frightening, to become the person you are meant to be in a world where so many are ignored or overlooked. God remembers you and all the little details of your life from your very beginning in your mother's womb until now. God knows everything about who you are and why you do the things you do—both the good and the not-so-good choices. God knows the true measure of your worth and is the source of your life. "For in Him we live and move and have our being" (Acts 17:28). God wants to reveal to you who God is, who you are, and who His mother is.

> **In this "revealing of man to himself," do we not need to find a special place for that "woman" who was the Mother of Christ?**[15]

When my daughter Katie was about four years old, playing in our living room, she opened a cabinet to discover a statue of Mary that I had stored there. I heard her exclaim, "Mary! What are you doing in there?" She came out holding the statue and looked at me and said, "Can I have her?" I said "Yes," to which she replied, "Good. Now I won't be so scared!" Katie promptly took her new friend up to her bedroom, finding a special place for Mary in her heart.

As Mary Magdalene found her special place close to the hearts of Mary and Jesus, we are invited to find that special place with her and her Son. It was the Blessed Mother who showed Mary Magdalene and the others how to stand with love under the Cross, which was the clearest revelation of God's love for humanity. That Cross of Christ teaches us that all which is evil and scary is diminished and shows it in its true colors. It is nothing, for in Jesus all evil has been overcome. That overcoming begins today, right now, for each and every woman who is searching to find her true self, her identity, no matter where she is in her life.

Mary Magdalene is a great example for women today of how to love courageously. She courageously stayed with Jesus during His darkest hour. This staying at the Cross with Jesus revealed her deep belief and belonging. According to the Scriptures, Mary Magdalene was the first person that the risen Christ came to after the crucifixion. Dead men are not supposed to rise from the dead, so you can only begin to imagine what Mary Magdalene experienced that day! Yes, spiritually she had already tasted the power and goodness of Jesus who had healed and delivered her from her affliction with seven demons. Jesus set Mary free from the one thing that she could not break from by herself—her past and the devil's grip on her life (Lk 8:1-2). No wonder she believed in Jesus! No wonder she stood by Him in His tragic hour. Only Jesus was able to reveal to her who she was, a beloved daughter, "Mary." "I have called you by name and you are mine!" (Is 43:1)

"I believe in you." Jesus wants you to know that He knows who you are and what purpose He has created you for. Despite everything that has happened in your life and in the world, everything will be all right if you can keep believing in Jesus. If you are a follower of Jesus, many times in your life you will simply need to have faith in Him. Jesus also wants us to find a special place for the woman, Mother Mary, who teaches us how to believe, so that we too might belong to Christ. In doing so, we can find a new beginning as women of grace. With grace, you are enough!

Questions for Reflection
Chapter 1
God Believes in You

1. What are one or two takeaways from this chapter?

2. Who is someone that believed or believes in you? Why is it so hard to believe in ourselves? How does it make you feel to know that God believes in you?

3. What is the supreme calling of humanity? What is your personal calling?

4. How does the Blessed Mother fit into your life right now? Do you see her as a strong advocate/support for your life and personal calling?

Notes

You Are Enough with Grace (Woman-Mother of God (*Theotókos*))

"When the time had fully come, God *sent forth his son, born of woman.*" [Gal 4:4] ...The Son, the Word, one in substance with the Father, becomes man, born of a woman, at "the fullness of time." This event leads *to the turning point* of man's history on earth, understood as salvation history.[16]

To Believe and to Belong (Union with God)

The woman St. Paul is referring to in this passage is Mary the Mother of Christ. Mary, full of grace, is the archetype, the model of the original plan that God had in mind when first creating woman. It is significant that St. Paul does not call the Mother of Christ by her own name, "Mary," but refers to her as the "woman" which points to Genesis 3:15, where God promises the great hope of a new beginning. Mary is that new beginning. She brings hope to each woman who longs for a new beginning. That hope can inspire and empower each woman who strives to bring life and love to those she cares for and those she defends against the negativity, sickness, and crimes of our times. The "woman," Mary, says to all women of every generation, "Do not fear. You are enough with grace!"

When the angel comes to Mary, a young Jewish woman, she accepts readily God's gift. She does so with faith. Mary believes God. Mary, who is chosen and called by God from her very beginning, her conception, is full of grace. Grace gives Mary the capacity to *believe and belong to God.* By saying "yes" to God's gift, Mary is the first to receive the gift of the given Son, Jesus Christ. She receives Him into her heart, a heart full of grace. So, what exactly is grace and why is it necessary for the human being?

> **Grace is the gift of God which contains all other gifts, the giving of His Son (R 8,32). But grace is more than just the gift. It is the gift which radiates the generosity of the giver and envelops with this generosity the creature who receives His gift. It is through grace that God gives, and he who accepts God's gift finds grace...**[17]
> **Grace is *favor*, the *free and undeserved help* that God gives us to respond to His call to become children of God, adoptive sons [and daughters], partakers of the divine nature and of eternal life.**[18]

Grace was given to Mary from the moment she was conceived in her mother's womb. With grace, Mary is enough. For through grace, Mary is able to come to know her identity as a daughter of God, her dignity, and her purpose. The grace she receives is itself the great gift of God to her which envelops her whole being, preparing her heart to receive Jesus Christ and also to *become His Mother*. Before Mary ever said "yes" to God, God said "yes" to Mary. God's "yes" means God created her exactly how He willed her to be, full of grace and ready to do her job on earth. God had a great plan, a great role that, if she responded to God's "yes" with her own, would impact the entire human race. She would become the mother of His only begotten Son, Jesus Christ, the Savior of the world. Would she say "yes"? Would she believe? Would she belong? Would she become the Mother of God? Yes, she would, for

> **she is that "woman" who is present in the central salvific event which marks the "fullness of time": this event is realized in her and through her. Thus, there begins *the central event, the key event in the history of salvation*: the Lord's Paschal Mystery.**[19]

One little woman together with one great God ushers in the central salvific event that would change the course of human life forever. Mary accepts the gift of God, taking her place, her spot, in God's mysterious plan, bringing to fulfillment the promise of a Messiah given long ago to fallen Adam and Eve: **"I will put enmity between you and the woman, and between your seed and her seed; he shall bruise your head, and you shall bruise his heel"** (Gen 3:15). This word of God is a promise that God makes to deliver humanity from sin and Satan. God will make the woman and her offspring enemies of Satan. Mary is the woman; her offspring is Jesus Christ. God will allow Satan to bruise fallen humanity with its sin and consequent suffering for a time, but ultimately God will destroy sin and death forever in Jesus Christ.

By Mary's "yes" to God's plan for her life, she is saying "yes" to becoming the image of the person that God thought of when creating her. She is also saying "yes" to the biggest calling a woman could ever have: she will become the Mother of God. So, what can Mary's life teach us about a life lived full of grace?

The bigger question is, what is it that you and so many others throughout history are looking for? What are you seeking to accomplish with your life? Pay attention to that, for you never know when an angel might be knocking at your door!

> **"People *look to the various religions for answers* to those profound mysteries of the human condition which, today, even as in olden times, deeply stir the human heart: What is a human being? What is the meaning and purpose of our life? What is goodness and what is sin? What gives rise to our sorrows and to what intent? Where lies the path to true happiness? What is the truth about death, judgment, and retribution beyond the grave? What, finally, is *that ultimate and unutterable mystery which engulfs our being,* and from which we take our origin and towards which we move?"**[20]

Mary's life of grace teaches us that the answers to all of these questions are found ultimately in believing in and belonging to God. This is the greatest need of the human person, to believe and to belong. We search for meaning, purpose, and identity. Who are we? Why are we here? What is our purpose? God created us to believe in and to belong to Him. God is the "something bigger" that we are searching for, whether we realize it or not. In all of the other religions of the world, it is man who searches for God. Only in Christianity does God come looking for man. *God is searching for me and for you.* By becoming one of us, Jesus the Son of God reveals to us God's own heart filled with divine love for us. Jesus also reveals to each of us our real identity as a daughter of the Father. We receive our real identity through the gift of grace given to us by Christ Who brings us into a relationship with His Father, Who is also our Father. This relationship allows us to live a life of grace on earth, becoming the person we are destined to be eternally. St. Thomas Aquinas tells us:

The good of grace in one is greater than the good of nature in the whole universe; for grace is the germ of eternal life, incomparably superior to the natural life of our soul or to that of the Angels.[21]

We came into existence because God wanted us. We can discover our true identity, dignity, and purpose in our relationship with God. Grace makes our real life possible; it does not mean there will not be difficulties and challenges.

I remember the first day of school when I was six years old. I was a little nervous about walking into my first-grade classroom. What was it going to be like? Would there be a place for me? Would I fit in, belong? What a relief it was when I finally found the desk that had my name on it, my spot. This experience happens throughout our lives; we land in one place only to discover later that it is not the right fit, and for one reason or another it is time to move on. It could be an educational opportunity, a job change, or a new role helping aging parents. Whatever it is, life keeps moving us forward, presenting new opportunities or challenges that can be exciting or scary depending on our mindset. Ultimately, we are all on our way back to God. I heard it said once that each and every human being living on the face of the earth is at the doorstep of eternity and everyone should get ready. Imagine you are visiting the ocean, you see the sandy beach with the waves and sunshine. The sandy beach is our life on earth and the ocean is God. The young are at the beginning of the sandy beach and the old are close to the water. Whether we are young or old, the whole beach is still just a short distance from the ocean. Are you ready?

> **Against the background of this broad panorama [of religions], which testifies to the aspirations of the human spirit in search of God—at times as if it were "groping its way" (cf. Acts 17:27)—the "fullness of time" spoken of in Paul's Letter emphasizes** *the response of God himself,* **"***in whom we live and move and have our being***" (cf. Acts 17:28). This is the God who "in many and various ways spoke of old to our fathers by the prophets, but in these last days has spoken to us by a Son" (Heb 1:1-2).**[22]

Everyone looks for an answer to the meaning of their existence at some point in their lives especially when approaching death. An elderly man made this comment, "I've been thinking about dying and what it will be like. I cannot help but wonder, 'where did all the people go that have lived before us?' That's a lot of people!" The greatest consequence of the loss of grace due to original and personal sin is that we suffer an immense absence in our relationship with God as our Father. In this great loss, it's no wonder that we often can feel isolated, alone, or confused about our lives especially when we suffer. Every choice made apart from our relationship with God as our Father results in disorder, pain, and ultimately death. So then, why did God send His only Son through Mary? Because God did not go anywhere. Our first parents did. They left God through the choices that they made. God sent Jesus, the second Person of the Trinity, the Word made flesh, into this world to reveal ultimately His immense love. Jesus desires to save us from all the chaos and confusion of sin and death that has resulted directly from the first original sin.

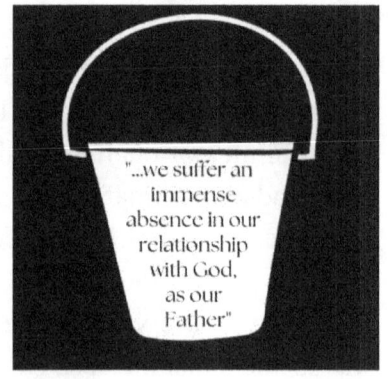

"...we suffer an immense absence in our relationship with God, as our Father"

> **The sending of this Son, one in substance with the Father, as a man "born of woman," constitutes the culminating and *definitive point of God's self-revelation to humanity*.**[23]

Jesus, the Son of God is "born of a woman;" from her, Jesus receives His human body. "God in a Bod™." He is one of us. Yet He is God, full of grace and truth (Jn 14:27). Jesus came to us as a tiny baby so we would not be afraid of Him. Who is afraid of a baby? Humble and sweet in a lowly manger, God reveals the secret of His love which is so tender and irresistible to humanity. Jesus, the Son of God, becomes a baby so that you and I can pick Him up, hold Him close to our hearts, and never ever let go. This is what Mary did and her life full of grace teaches us to do the same. Mary found her real life lived in union with Christ and once she found it, she never ever let go of it. We should do the same.

> **Hence *Mary* attains *a union with God that exceeds* all the expectations of the human spirit. It even exceeds the expectations of all Israel, in particular the daughters of this Chosen People, who, on the basis of the promise, could hope that one of their number would one day become the mother of the Messiah. Who among them, however, could have imagined that the promised Messiah would be "the Son of the Most High"?**[24]

So often we simply take the meaning of Christmas for granted. Until Jesus came with the authority to heal and restore our lives to grace, there was no clear solution to the tragedy of human sin and death. When I read this quote for the first time, I was surprised. The people of Israel had no idea that the Messiah would actually be the "Son of God." The women of Israel never even imagined that one of them might one day be the Mother of God.

So why do we need grace? It is how we discover our identity, worth, and life's purpose. This is your real life; you do not want to miss it! Yet so many doubt the very existence of God. How are they going to get the answers to life's big questions without God? What is it that they and so many others throughout history are looking for? When faith is reduced to a mere human institution or man-made religion, it is not going to inspire or motivate people to believe. I remember teaching a group of high school students about the Holy Spirit in preparation for their upcoming Confirmation. After a few minutes, it was clear I was not connecting with the kids, so I stopped the class and asked, "What's going on?" A young man sitting in the back stood up and said, "Hey lady, we don't even believe in God!" I replied to the challenge, "That's okay, God still believes in you!" I was grateful for his honesty.

Many people today struggle to believe in God. I knew that St. Thomas Aquinas teaches that we can prove through reason that God exists, so I quickly changed up the lesson and began a discussion on the question, "Why is it so hard to believe in God?" The discussion amongst the teens took off; finally, a connection was made. As I listened to them explain their doubts and fears about the existence of God, I was able to share with them proofs of the existence of God that St. Thomas Aquinas teaches. Slowly they opened up to the possibility of the existence of God.

One of the proofs we explored was history itself. How could so many people be wrong? People have testified to the reality of God's existence from the God of Israel in the Old Testament to Jesus Christ in the New Testament. Many saints, ordinary people, and even children have laid down their lives for their belief in God. There have also been countless miracles over the centuries, as well as many people whose lives were transformed by grace. This discussion of the existence of God eventually opened the door to the possibility of the existence of the Holy Trinity as unfolded before us in the Annunciation at Nazareth, where Mary, who believes in God, is able to say "yes," conceiving the Son of God in her womb by the power of the Holy Spirit. For,

> **the self-revelation of God, who is the inscrutable unity of the Trinity, is outlined *in the Annunciation at Nazareth.*[25]**

What would have happened if the woman, Mary, had not believed what was told to her? What if she had said "No thank-you" to God's request? Or, what if she'd said, "Get someone else, such as Elizabeth; she has been waiting a long time to have a baby." We will not know until we get to heaven the answers to many of these questions. However, we do know that God was pleased with Mary's attitude of faith, for she trusted in God. Mary, by her audacious "yes," her willingness to risk it all, put her faith in God, giving Jesus His first home, her heart.

> **Do we not find in the Annunciation at Nazareth the beginning of that definitive answer by which *God himself "attempts to calm people's hearts"?*[26]**

Through Mary, God himself is born into the world. God sends Jesus to us in an attempt to calm our hearts. This is what Christmas is all about. Mary teaches us that God is trustworthy; we are safe in His hands. By her example we are encouraged to do the same, to put our faith in God, to risk it all, and to say "yes" to His plan for our lives. Like Mary, we will never regret it.

"God in a Bod™": in becoming one of us, God attempts to calm our hearts. What do you need to calm down about in your life right now? Whatever it is, God your Creator already knows about it. All of it! *God has the answers to all of your problems.* God also has all the solutions for the problems of the world. His thoughts about you and reasons for creating you are decisive. God created you with a thought of who you would be and what good your life would bring to the world. That does not mean that you will not have troubles or difficulties.

There was a time when I was very discouraged. It was a particularly difficult time in my life. I was simply miserable and unsure what the next step was. With great emotion, I prayed to God, "So why did you make me if you knew this was all going to happen?" In prayer, I understood the "still small voice" to say, *I wanted you anyway.* As I continued to pray, I came to a deeper conviction that I was wanted, wanted by the very God Who created me. Well, what could I say to that? God wants you too. God believes in us, and God wants us with Him forever. To God, the pain and suffering is worth it as long as it brings us all back together with Him.

God in a Bod™ (Theotokos)

Jesus, the unspeakable gift of God, came down from His lofty place in heaven to earth. He was sent on a mission to reconcile the world with God. Mary is elevated to a supernatural union with God in order to bring about the promised Savior (Gen 3:15). Together Mary and Jesus begin God's plan to take back humanity, one person at a time, from death, sin, and a futile life that has no point and no meaning. Since the fall, all of the children of Adam had been cut off from their fundamental inheritance, which is their union with God, their Creator. Now God would intervene with His plan. God's plan is the New Covenant, and it "begins with a woman, the 'woman' of the Annunciation at Nazareth."[27]

> **Thus the "fullness of time" manifests the extraordinary dignity of the "woman." ... this dignity consists *in the supernatural elevation to union with God* in Jesus Christ, which determines the ultimate finality of the existence of every person both on earth and in eternity.**[28]

What does this plan, which "determines the ultimate finality of the existence of every person both on earth and in eternity," mean for us? I was up late one night, worried and unable to sleep due to the civil unrest in the city. I remember thinking, "If my dad were charge of the universe, he would have a plan." Dad always had a plan. I prayed, "Father in Heaven, I know that you must have a plan." As I prayed for this plan of God's to succeed, a sense of deep peace flowed through me, from the top of my head to the bottom of my toes. I knew with certainty that yes, indeed, *God has a plan.*

Peace is God's signature…this means you have been heard. It is also a promise Jesus made to those who put their trust in God. Clearly, God wants us to be at peace, but it can be a challenge to keep ourselves calm and trust God in all things. To be overly concerned or fearful about our future is a sign that we are leaning on ourselves instead of putting our faith in God's providence. God still has the plan, and quietly, persistently it is being carried out in His Son Jesus Christ; nothing can stop it. "I know that You can do all things, and that no thought or purpose of Yours can be restrained or thwarted" (Job 42:2). So, what does this plan mean for you and me?

God having a plan for us means that this is a big deal, and we should listen. It is Mary who teaches us how to have a relationship with God. By listening to God's call and opening her heart, she let Jesus in. It really mattered. It also really worked. For Mary's "yes" made your "yes" possible. Jesus Christ is the very means to your union with God. Wow! What a call and what an elevator.

> **From this point of view, the "woman" is the representative and the archetype [perfect example] of the whole human race: she *represents the humanity* which belongs to all human beings, both men and women.**[29]

St. John Paul II is telling us to look to Mary. She is our representative and the archetype. Her human life was real. Her supernatural life was real too. She lived and experienced many of the same joys, sorrows, and mysteries in life as you and me. Mary's "yes" to God in everything remained unwavering despite the many highs and lows she experienced throughout her life. It had to have been quite an amazing experience for Mary even having the Angel Gabriel in her midst, let alone being asked to be the Mother of God.

The Virgin of Nazareth truly becomes the Mother of God.[30]

Think about it. Mary finds out she is going to be the mother of the promised Messiah. Immediately after, she goes to visit her relative Elizabeth who is also to have a baby, despite the fact that she has been barren and now is very old. Mary and Elizabeth affirm each other's callings as they joyfully anticipate the births of their babies, Jesus and John the Baptist. Both have principal roles in God's unfolding plan. While this is happening, Mary also becomes subject to scrutiny and the possibility of Joseph quietly divorcing her. This is real-life drama. After the joyful birth of her baby, followed by the visits of shepherds and the three wise kings, the little family is forced to flee to a foreign land to save Jesus from death. Herod, the jealous, wrathful king, wants to kill the baby. Thirty-three years later Mary will experience the violent death of her Son. Mary gets it. Mary gets human life. Mary also gets supernatural life. That is why she is our representative and our archetype. Mary shows us how to live human life well. She can teach us how to live our life on earth with supernatural grace and hope, for she saw and experienced the worst and the best of human life.

In the early Church, Nestorius held that Mary was only the mother of Jesus as a man. This would mean that Jesus was in some way two separate persons and not fully God while in Mary's womb. However, the Council of Ephesus in AD 431 refuted this notion. Jesus is fully human and fully God but one divine person. It would be wrong to divide Him into parts.

At the moment of the Annunciation, by responding with her "*fiat*" [her "yes"], Mary conceived a man who was the Son of God, of one substance with the Father. Therefore *she is truly the Mother of God, because motherhood concerns the whole person*, not just the body, nor even just human "nature."[31]

Mary, therefore, experiences a union with God that has never been experienced before by a human person or an angel. So, what does this mean for our lives? I will never forget a young woman who suddenly turned to me and said, "What is up with God putting so much work into a human being?" She was asking the most important question of her life: "Who am I, that God would put so much effort into me?"

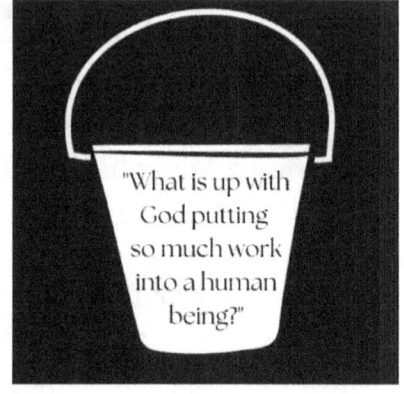

"What is up with God putting so much work into a human being?"

What is it about Mary and her life that gives humanity such hope? At times, human life can be so brutal. The experience of sin, betrayal, sickness, and death can harden hearts, making it difficult and often quite impossible to believe in a God of love. As Pope Benedict XVI taught in reference to Psalm 136,

Our danger is that the memory of evil, of the evils suffered, may often be stronger than the memory of the good. The Psalm's purpose is also to reawaken in us the memory of good as well as of all the good that the Lord has done and is doing for us, which we can perceive if we become deeply attentive.[32]

When it comes to God's goodness, it is important to stop and think about what that means. Everything good we have in our life is a gift from our Creator. When our boys were little, as we were praying at dinner, my husband concluded the prayer, "God is good," to which the boys responded, "all the time." Then my youngest son David quickly added, "David is not." We, of course, all started laughing at our rambunctious little troublemaker who was all boy in the best way possible. We are only able to be good with God's help. The angel proclaims to both Mary and all of us: "Nothing is impossible with God" (Lk 1:37). If you say "yes" to grace, God makes the impossible possible.

Mary is a constant reminder of the truth that God is good and loves us all. God kept Mary's heart open, free from sin and full of grace, that through her love and openness to God, we might have a second chance at life. She gives us Jesus Christ, the only return ticket to the Father's house. For us, it is not easy to believe in or to belong to God. Mary did what we could not. She brought us the great gift of grace, Jesus, the light of the world. This is why Mary is often called the Star of the Sea. When it is the darkest, she is a beacon of light pointing humanity back to her Son.

"Mary is often called the Star of the Sea."

Sadly, human selfishness, lust, and pride still often block the way for our humble newborn King. God, who is infinitely great, becomes humble and small, as a little baby born in a manger, in order to give us a share in the divine life. I thought of Jesus when I read this quote from Ralph Waldo Emerson: "A great man is always willing to be little." The greatest gift God could ever give was His own Son, Who humbly came not to be served, but to serve. In this way, Jesus reveals the truth about humble love and service, for in God's kingdom to serve is to reign.

Yes, to the Yes (To Serve Is to Reign)

St. John Paul II wants us to pay close attention to the significance of the personal interaction Mary has with the angel. It is a supernatural event that reveals a deeper truth about her dignity as the potential

Mother of God. It also reveals the truth about the dignity of human persons, especially women, since Mary is a woman.

> **The *"fullness of grace"* that was granted to the Virgin of Nazareth, with a view to the fact that she would become *"Theotokos"* [Mother of God], *also signifies the fullness of the perfection of "what is characteristic of woman," of "what is feminine."* Here we find ourselves, in a sense, at the culminating point, the archetype, of the personal dignity of women.**[33]

The Archangel Gabriel comes to the Virgin of Nazareth, with a personal invitation from the Most High God. There is to be a New Covenant, an agreement that will bring about a new beginning, a new relationship between God and humanity. Mary alone must give her response to God's request. The specific calling to be the Mother of God is given to Mary along with the "fullness of grace" in view of her role. St. John Paul II highlights for us that Mary was given this "fullness of grace" in view of the fact that she would become the Mother of God. Mary's gift of the "fullness of grace" also signifies for woman herself the fullness of beauty and perfection that the feminine genius is capable of with grace and her own "yes". Each woman must reflect on the meaning of her own life of grace. For each woman is called to make her own personal "fiat," her "yes" to God's personal call and the role she is called to fulfill. This is the "something bigger" for her life! Mary, like us, is a human creature who, when called by God, makes her own personal "fiat," her "yes." In saying "yes," Mary expresses her personal relationship with God, her gratitude to God, and her love for God in response to the gift of the Son.

> **When Mary responds to the words of the heavenly messenger with her "fiat," she who is "full of grace" feels the need to express her personal relationship to the gift that has been revealed to her, saying: *"Behold, I am the handmaid of the Lord"* (Lk 1:38). ... In the expression**

"handmaid of the Lord," one senses Mary's complete awareness of being a creature of God.[34]

Mary, who is a human creature like you and me, *believes*, and, because of that faith, in the freedom of her own will she makes her "fiat," her "yes." In doing so she takes her spot, her place in God's plan. Mary *belongs*. In belonging, Mary finds her identity as well as her life's purpose. Mary *becomes* the Mother of God; she lives her unique calling by helping God in His plan to universally restore the world one "yes" at a time. Mary reveals to everyone—and especially to women—the importance of saying "yes" to God. She reveals simultaneously the love of God in giving the world Jesus Christ and the sacredness of motherhood. Motherhood, which always includes spiritual motherhood, is a gift given to women. Woman's role involves great service to Christ in laying the foundations of the Kingdom of God, where to serve is to reign.

> *Mary takes her place within Christ's messianic service.* **It is precisely this service which constitutes the very foundation of that Kingdom in which "to serve ... means to reign."**[35]

To serve is to reign. Mary is God's big "yes," not only for her own sake but also for Jesus and ultimately for the good of the whole world. For Mary's "yes" meant Jesus could come; her life of loving service to God made way for Jesus to come for each one of us. Jesus is the big "yes" to you from God. Jesus Christ, the "Servant of the Lord," came into the world and into your life to love and serve you. Jesus came to show you the truth, to reveal God's unconditional love for you and for broken, sinful humanity. Humanity is healed and redeemed only through His loving service.

> **Christ, the "Servant of the Lord," will show all people the royal dignity of service, the dignity which is joined in the closest possible way to the vocation of every person.**[36]

We are called by our dignity as human persons to give a big "yes" to God—a "yes" to the vision God had when creating us. The vocation of every person is God's purpose and plan for that person's life. It is the way to find true happiness. This is what it means to say "yes" to God. When we say "yes," God will give us all that we need to fulfill what we are called to do and who we are called to serve. Every life has a beginning and end in God. What we accomplish in our life is our gift back to God.

The very fact that we exist has meaning. Each of us is called into existence for our own sake but we are also called into existence to become a gift for God and the world. We have a purpose, an important job that only we can do. Everyone is essential and every "yes" matters when it comes to God's plan. God's plan is to deliver us from all human harm, ruin, and loss—but not without our help. No matter where you have been in your life or what has happened to you in this crazy, at times seemingly out-of-control world, God has a unique plan, a vocation for your life that only you can fulfill. Your service means that others will be helped. It is also your path to fulfillment. *It's what you were born to do!*

Why do we need grace? Because we need hope. Many times, women themselves are simply not aware of their supreme calling in God, often discounting their personal worth, their value in the bigger scheme of life. The true dignity and calling of each woman can be found ultimately in a relationship with God. It is also the key to her success and ultimate fulfillment. So many women are not aware of this or, if they do say "yes," are unsure of the next step. This is why we need grace and guidance if we are to grow in wisdom.

Life can often feel like a boxing match, for no one, because of our fallen state, is free from struggle and temptation on planet Earth. In other words, we and the world have been compromised. This compromised state is referred to as concupiscence, which historically "can refer to any intense form of human desire."[37] Intense human desire has infected us all. It can get the best of us since we are often tempted to do the very things that we do not want to do (Rom 7:15). From a Christian perspective, it refers to a type of rebellion of the flesh against the Holy Spirit.

One day as I was driving to work, I saw a semi-truck driving across the road. On the side of the truck, there was a big picture of a man guzzling a bottle of booze. The caption beneath the picture read, "You Will Not Find Your Life at the Bottom of this Bottle." I remember thinking, "That is so true." We are told to stay "sane and sober so you can pray" (1 Pt 4:7). This is why Jesus came, so we could be sane and, by grace, bring peace and purpose to our lives: our "real life."

The big question is, what is it that you are seeking to do with your life? *Are you living your "real life"?* If you are seeking a human life without grace, you will live a worldly life according to the flesh (Rom 7). As one woman who used to live a "fleshy" life stated, "Oh, I hate that kind of life!" Grace gives us the strength and the tenacity to persevere in the struggle against the "fleshy life" and temptations that deter us from our life's calling.

When I was in college, I stayed in touch with a classmate from high school who was then studying law. I was studying theology. I commented to her that, if I ever needed a lawyer, I would call her because I knew she would be a great lawyer. I then told her if she ever wanted to talk about her faith in Jesus Christ and the Catholic Church, she could call me because I had studied it for as long as she had studied the law. With a full smile and laugh she agreed that she might take me up on it. Years later she did take me up on it. She had many questions about her life and ultimately about God. She was looking for answers.

"Let's go back to Christmas...." As I shared with my friend the truth about God's great love for us, becoming a little baby like us, entering into our lives to bring us hope, I could tell she was listening with such intensity. She also spoke about her own life: her failures and also her attempts to do what was right. She was very confused and unsure of the next step. I reassured her that she was not alone. No one but God is perfect and none of us can find our way in life without God.

I remember as I was preparing for marriage, a wise older woman saying to me, "Always remember that your God is your God, and your husband is your husband. Do not get the two mixed up! If you do, your life will be quite difficult." At the time I did not understand her, but later I did. Yet so many of us do this; we try to define our lives by our human relationships and our accomplishments. If we are successful in our relationships, accomplishments, and careers we think we are doing great. But if we fail for any reason, then we are nothing. The despair we can feel because we believe the lie that we are alone and that we will never be enough is very overwhelming. I say that "we are alone" is a lie because that is just what it is, simply a lie.

We are never alone. God is with us and has all the answers. God knows who we are and who He created us to be. God also waits patiently for us to engage with Him. So often we will settle for less, or like my friend, or perhaps someone you know, we forget who God is and who we are, so we need to start at the beginning and ask the right question. Who am I?

We are and will always be beloved children of God. When life is difficult and unforgiving, it is then that we need to look to God for the answers. Sister Margaret taught us as children in the second grade that no matter what, call out to Jesus when you are in trouble. Jesus will always come and help you, no matter what.

One night as I sat in the quiet, praying for my friend who was at the lowest point of her life, the words of an old Christmas hymn came to me…very slowly, "Oh Holy Night, the stars are brightly shining, it is the night of our dear Savior's birth. Long lay the world in sin and error pining, till He appears, and the soul felt its worth. A thrill of hope, the weary world rejoices…" As I listened to that hymn a wave of peace and hope washed over me. I knew that God was with her and that God would answer all of our prayers.

Jesus is the Son of God. He died for you and loves you the best. Jesus rose from the dead. His resurrection from the dead tells us that in the end, Love wins. Dead is dead for most of us, but for Jesus death is not a problem since Jesus is life.

God does not always let us know what is going to happen next in our life. We do not know the hour in which we will return to God. It is important to remember that whatever God asks you to do with the life He gave you, in the time He gave you, is possible. It is always for your good; it is always important!

Christ, the Servant of the Lord, invites you to be a partner in serving the Great Commission to bring hope and salvation to every human person (Mt 28:16-20). As Mary did, you and I are called to do. We are called to give our own "yes" to God. It is the most important "yes" you will ever give.

The dignity of every human being and the vocation corresponding to that dignity find their definitive measure in *union with God*. Mary, the woman of the Bible, is the most complete expression of this dignity and vocation. For no human being, male or female, created in the image and likeness of God, can *in any* way attain fulfillment apart from this image and likeness.[38]

We need to consider what the Lord of All would do in our current situation. *God's plans and solutions are not always going to be easy, but they always work.* We need to remember that God created the universe, and us, out of nothing. If our lives are going to amount to anything, they will need to be united to God's will for us. Mary shows us, as a woman, what God can do with the woman who is full of grace and willing to cooperate with God's plan. For we are all made in the image and likeness of God and can only hope to attain happiness and fulfillment as this image and likeness, in communion with our heavenly Father.

No one can ever replace the role that God has in your life, not your friends, coworkers, parents, or even a spouse. For no matter how good people are, they are not God. Our hearts are made to be in a relationship with divine love. Everything and everyone comes to us as a gift from God, who is the Giver of all the gifts. God's love is the best gift of all. The question is, which will you love more? The *gifts* of the Giver? Or the *Giver* of the gifts?

You are enough with God's grace. God's grace allows us and the people in our lives to accept the difficulties and sufferings of this life. God is with us and helps us, despite everything, to attain our ultimate human goal, which is God Himself. The key is that in every situation you have a choice. Saying "yes" to God means we invite God into all the different relationships and situations of our lives so that we can live our lives in union with God, now on earth, fully alive in the Holy Spirit.

God exists in the communion of three divine Persons, Father, Son, and Holy Spirit. They exist together in great spiritual happiness. Not only do Mary, the saints, the angels, and the rest of the supernatural order exist, but together with God and each other they live a supernatural life outside of human time. For the rest of us creatures on earth, supernatural life is a whole new way of looking at our little lives. I say "little" because that is just what your life is, extraordinarily little. (Whack-whack.) Yet, the Great God who made you in His own image and likeness can do so much with you and your little life, if you can learn how to say "yes" to the "yes." You can be like God!

Questions for Reflection
Chapter 2
You Are Enough with Grace

1. What are one or two takeaways from this chapter?

2. What is grace? Why is grace a big deal?

3. How did Mary live a life of grace? What can Mary teach us about grace?

4. What does a life without grace look like?

Notes

You Are like God
(The Image and Likeness of God)

> "God created man in his own image, in the image of God he created him; male and female he created them" (Gen 1:27). . . . Man is the highpoint of the whole order of creation in the visible world; the human race, which takes its origin from the calling into existence of man and woman, crowns the whole work of creation; *both man and woman are human beings to an equal degree*, both are created *in God's image.*[39]

God Is Calling You (The Book of Genesis)

From the beginning, all of creation is made for human beings. Human persons, however, are made for God. This is what St. John Paul II means when he says that the human race crowns creation. In the first biblical creation account found in Genesis 1:27, the focus is on the creation of the human race. If the human race is the crown of creation, then one could ask, what is the actual value of a human life?

"Could I ask for a volunteer?" It's hard to explain in finite terms how much a human being is worth, especially to God. The first time I asked for a volunteer to step forward, I was speaking to a group of moms and teens. A girl of about fourteen stepped forward. I said to her, "You have great dignity and worth in God's eyes. *God made all of creation for you.* You, however, have been created for God!" God loves you the best! Why? Because you are a person, created in God's own image to be like God:

> ***Man*—whether woman or man—is *the only being among the creatures* of the visible world *that God the creator "has willed for its own sake."*⁴⁰**

That means God wanted you just for you. You are worth more than the entire universe. More than all the world, with the sun, the stars, the mountains, all the gold and silver, all the beautiful animals, the oceans, and the little fishes.

How could this be true? God can make the universe and everything in it again; he will, however, never make *you* again! God created human beings with a body and a soul. You cannot see your soul but it's still there. Like your soul, you cannot see God. Your body is like a house to your soul. Your soul animates and brings your body to life. God created your soul to be immortal; this means you will exist forever. It is because of sin that our bodies experience death. After your body dies, you will return to God. You came into this world through God and will someday return to God. God loves you and calls you into life. Whether you realize it or not, the fact that you are alive at this time is because God wants you to exist. God created you as a unique person with a specific purpose, *your life itself is a gift and a calling.* Your life is worth more than you could ever imagine.

Let's talk about your life. It might be going rather well right now, or you might be facing great challenges. Many people experience difficulties during this life on earth depending on who they are and their life circumstances. There could be job loss with financial concerns, illnesses, drug addiction, family discord, and all sorts of other hard stuff. Whatever it is, God already knows and wants to help. Often, you might want to give up on life and on your dreams because your life gets so hard; it all seems like it's impossible. It's then that you must stop and listen to what God has to say. You just might be surprised.

Suppose I had two 100-dollar bills; one was clean, hot off the press, and the other bill was crumpled up, ripped, and faded. Which one would be worth more? That's right, both bills have equal value. Whether your life is all cleaned up, hot off the press, or a little crumpled and torn, the truth remains that your dignity as someone created in the image and likeness of God cannot ever be taken away or destroyed. No matter what your life has been, your ultimate destiny is God. Through your own humanity and who you are, you are called to

> **a unique, exclusive, and unrepeatable relationship with God himself.**[41]

This also means that no one can take your spot, your place. The young lady that volunteered just stood on stage in awe of what she was hearing and as tears began to well up, everyone started clapping. Later her mother came and expressed her gratitude saying, "She really needed to hear that right now." Her mother was right, her daughter did need to know the dignity of her own life. That dignity can only be discovered in a relationship with God. That's right! No one will ever treat you as well as God will, except for maybe your own mother! Yet, "even should she forget, I [God] will never forget you" (Is 49:15). Importantly, we need to believe in this love of God for us in our hearts in order to say "yes" to the God of love.

> **This image and likeness of God which is essential [absolutely necessary] for the human being, is passed on by the man and woman, as spouses and parents, to their descendants: "Be fruitful and multiply, and fill the earth and subdue it" (Gen 1:28).**[42]

The commandment to "be fruitful and multiply" is God's calling to women and men to marry and to continue to pass down both God's and their image together, by having children. This means filling the earth with children, who are like God and also like you. This makes sense since people are the reason God made the earth. Just as human beings are the crown of creation, so children are the gift given to the woman and the man as the crown of their marriage union.

The image and likeness of God is also passed on to us through the faith and beliefs of our parents and grandparents. My mother's and grandmother's attitude of faith, whether dealing with a disabled neighborhood boy or spiritually forming a grandchild, taught us about the goodness of God and the dignity and worth of all human persons.

Timmy was a developmentally challenged boy who lived several houses away from our home. Our house was frequently filled with kids from the neighborhood, and he, of course, was always included. If anyone ever attempted to pick on him because he was seen as "different," my mother quickly stepped in letting everyone know that he has dignity. "Timmy is sure to get the highest place in heaven," my mom would say. She insisted we keep that in mind when we were playing with him. "Remember," she taught us, "God sees all people with dignity and value just the way He made them. To God, different is good. From heaven's point of view, Timmy is a person with value and worth; his life teaches us all about our essential dignity as human persons." Since Timmy is not capable of sinning, my mother correctly stated he will go right to heaven. Timmy did, in fact, teach my family and, believe it or not, the whole town, what it means to value and care for others. Since he was unable to defend himself, we were called to care for and protect him, for that is what it means to be a human person created to be like God. We need the Timmy's of the world to teach us how to be human—how to love.

My sweet, rosy-cheeked, Irish Grandma Milton always talked about the "good Lord." She moved from Milwaukee, Wisconsin, to live closer to our family, moving in just one block away. One day when I was about eight years old, I stopped by Grandma's house for a visit. As she prepared me a snack, she said, "The good Lord would want—" I interrupted her and asked, "Why do you call the Lord 'good'?" She looked into my eyes and said with a twinkle, "Because the Lord *is* good," then she proceeded to tell me why the Lord is good. My grandma's way of speaking left an impression of the goodness of the Lord that has stayed with me my whole life. Grandma's faith and love for God was being passed down to me, and then through me to my children. This is one way that the image and likeness of God is passed down to our descendants, by the faith and fidelity of the family to God, generation to generation.

The image of God is essential to us as human persons and can never be totally destroyed. Sin, however, diminishes the likeness of God in us.[43] *Sin separates us from God and is the greatest threat to humanity.* In the beginning, our first parents were in the state of original justice. There was only a profound sense of love and divine unity that existed between God and them; they had no reason to turn against God. This divine intimacy allowed them to live in harmony with each other and all of creation.

> **…our first parents Adam and Eve, were constituted in an original "state of holiness and justice." This grace of original holiness was "to share in …. divine life." By the radiance of this grace all dimensions of man's life were confirmed. As long as he remained in the divine intimacy, man would not have to suffer or die. The inner harmony of the human person, the harmony between man and woman, and finally the harmony between the first couple and all creation comprised the state called "original justice."[44]**

My mother and grandmother lived their lives with the grace that was given to them by their faith in God. Strengthened by the Holy Spirit, they were able to teach their children by their example how to navigate life and how to value their own dignity as well as the dignity of all people. By doing so they cooperated with God, using their gifts and talents to pass on the image and likeness of God from their generation to the next. When we do this, we become more and more like God, fulfilling God's plan for creation.

> **God is the sovereign master of his plan. But to carry it out he also makes use of his creatures' cooperation.… For God**

grants his creatures not only their existence, but also the dignity of acting on their own, of being causes and principles for each other, and thus of cooperating in the accomplishment of his plan.[45]

In other words, God personally gives each woman and man a job to do. Called and uniquely gifted, you and I are called to order our lives by building homes and communities that reflect God's love for the good of each and every human person. That is what my mother was doing when she taught us kids how we were to treat Timmy as a person, made in the image and likeness of God with his own set of gifts and talents to bring to the world. We focus too often only on the human body with its need for proper housing, nutrition, and education in order to survive. Yet the body is created for a higher purpose: to house the soul. Since your body expresses your soul—your spiritual nature—it is important to care for and subdue it, quiet or bring it under control, for your own good. This means knowing and thinking about who you are as a human person and what gives your life purpose. This self-knowledge is necessary; it is what helps you to choose to act like God.

***Man is a person, man and woman equally so,* since both were created in the image and likeness of the personal God. What makes [them both] like God is the fact that—unlike the whole world of other living creatures, including those endowed with senses (*animalia*)—man [and woman] is also a rational being (*animal rationale*).**[46]

God is really saying, "If you want to be like me, think about me and then work on learning how to act like me." You are like God. You are made to think and act like God. Despite your faults and failures and those of other human beings, God wants to bless you and help you to become the best person that you can be. God is for you. Your life is happening for you. God blesses you with your own set of gifts and talents; your family, friends, and all the people around you;

His standards (the Ten Commandments and the Beatitudes); and most importantly, *grace*, so that you can be successful. Then God says, **"Go!"**

So often we limit God by our false thinking or imaginings. One day a woman approached me and said, "I would like my kids to be involved with their church, however, it seems like it is too spiritual." I smiled at her and said, "Yes, I guess God is very spiritual. So is heaven; heaven is going to be very spiritual, so what are you going to do when you get there?" She looked at me and started to laugh. Then she said, "I suppose that's true!"

We are not so far from heaven; the difference is that on this side we cannot see it with our senses. But it is still here. Heaven is with us on earth because of the Church that Christ established. Heaven is within us because of our baptism into Christ. This mother knew faith in God and spirituality were important, but she did not know how to connect with it.

Faith is not only strengthened in community building or in growing friendships but also in discovering and learning true authentic Christian spirituality. This is what Christ came to give us. Service and good works are not enough; they must be done through and in the Holy Spirit. All of these facets are given by God through His Church to nurture in us a healthy spiritual life, but the most important part of our faith is our relationship with God, who is personal and pure Spirit. That is pure love.

At the end of your life, you will give an account of your life to God, so try to keep your eyes on the prize. All that will matter is this: if we have loved. We cannot live without love. This is why it is so important to keep our minds and hearts on God because for us it is easy to get discouraged, even hopeless, when bad things happen. A good priest once said to me, "Only God can look at evil and not be changed." I never forgot that. We cannot help but see the evil in the world, but we must always keep our eyes fixed on the Lord, "the maker of heaven and earth" (Ps 121:2).

God is good. All the time. Are we good? In loving God, we show our gratitude for all God has done for us, for bringing us into existence and taking care of all of our spiritual and physical needs. *It is good to be good.* Thus, our being good means that we receive the goodness and grace of God and pass it on to others. It means we make good moral decisions, choosing to honor God by living a good life, which ultimately leads to happiness and fulfillment. This happiness that God wants for you might not take shape the way you would design it. Remember, God is the architect. The life you are building with God may require hard work. The endless days of sitting by the ocean with a good book and a margarita—that is for heaven!

Everything good in life God gives to you as a resource to enjoy, yes, but also for you to build a life that honors God and helps your neighbor. Think about Michelangelo or Mozart. They did what they loved, one painting the Sistine Chapel and the other creating beautiful music that lifts the mind and heart. In doing so, they honored and loved God. They also blessed countless people. It was hard work. You might be talented in music, art, photography, skiing, hiking in the mountains, playing basketball, or swimming in the ocean. Maybe you love cooking, eating ice cream and cheeseburgers with friends, or studying the stars. Whatever it is, it's your **Go**! Your life is your gift from God. Use your gifts and talents to build your life for others. Build it with God and for other people. Love God. Love people. This is why God made you. When we are doing what we were made to do, we are happier.

You are also given spiritual gifts to aid in your spiritual growth, as well as to help others in their spiritual growth. God freely gives all these gifts, material and spiritual, so that we might build up the life of God within all people. St. Catherine of Siena said that God put it this way:

> **For I could have supplied each of you with all of your needs, both spiritual and material. But I wanted to make you dependent on one another, so that each of you would be my minister, dispensing the graces and gifts you have received from me, so whether you will it or not, you cannot escape the exercise of charity ... All I want is love. In loving**

me you will realize love for your neighbors, and if you love your neighbors, you have kept the law [Mt 22:37-40].[47]

It's all about love. God did not give everyone all of the possible gifts and talents. He distributed them to different people so that we would need each other and thereby be forced to love and help each other. This way of loving and helping each other is what is most pleasing to God, it is also what makes us most like Him. What is easy for one person is more difficult or impossible for another.

I remember when we were making a move to another city. My husband rented a big moving truck, packed up all of our belongings together with our two little boys, and said with a big grin, "Let's go!" I was anxious and overwhelmed as he pulled out with everything I loved and owned in that truck. Meanwhile Duane and his boys were thoroughly enjoying the big move in the big truck. So often we can be overly anxious about what we think God is asking of us. It is important to let others do their own jobs. It was not until later that I realized that God was not asking me to drive that moving truck; that was Duane's job. Not only that but Duane was well-equipped to do his job and enjoyed sharing all the excitement with his boys.

…fill the earth and subdue it. (Gen 1:28)

God gives us a share in His authority and grace to live life, to order it, and to bring it under control. "Subdue" means "to bring under control." This does not mean controlling others. It means personal responsibility, self-control, or self-mastery. This is our responsibility. No one can do this for you. Remember, you cannot always drive the truck, meaning you cannot control what other people are doing. That is their job. We are only asked to love God and then to love others by helping them out when it is needed, as God asks us to do. Most of the time we need to focus on driving our own car, meaning getting our own life under control. It is only then that we will be ready to share our life with someone else. I love this verse: "I will walk with integrity of heart in my own home" (Ps 101:2). Integrity means to be whole and undivided. This is how God created man and woman originally. Integrity was lost in the garden, making human hearts divided and broken. This is why it is so difficult for us to subdue our lives.

In the beginning, Adam was alone in the garden, yet with God. Adam was alone in the sense that there was no other person like him. St. John Paul II refers to this concept as original solitude.

> **The concept of original solitude includes both self-consciousness and self-determination. He must consciously discern and choose between good and evil, between life and death ... Man is alone.**[48]

Solitude with God is knowing who you are as you stand before God. This is necessary for our identity. Each of us is a unique unrepeatable creation capable of self-determination. Adam was also alone in the sense that he alone could choose to accept God's offer of friendship and love, which calls for whole-hearted obedience to God's commands: "You may freely eat of every tree of the garden, but of the tree of the knowledge of good and evil you shall not eat, for in the day that you eat of it you shall die" (Gen 2:16-17). God is laying the ground rules for Adam's existence and his welfare. This is the way it must be for him to live. It is much like what I said to my little son as we would go out for a walk: "Take my hand, and do not run out in front of that car, or it will hurt you!" Adam's obedience is necessary for his existence as well as for the integrity of his heart, in a life shared with God. It is necessary for us as well.

> **The words of God-Yahweh addressed to man confirm a dependence in existing, such as to make man a limited being and, by his very nature, liable to nonexistence.**[49]

Could Adam have understood what the words "you shall die" meant? These words that are addressed to Adam at the very beginning of creation teach us the truth that you and I are dependent on God for everything, including our very own existence. From the very beginning, humans have experienced the tension between life and death. This is the dilemma of human life. It is important to think about and choose God since it is God alone who can give life to us. Nothing else can give us life. Nothing else even comes close.

> **Even though man's nature is mortal, God had destined him not to die. Death was therefore contrary to the plans of God the Creator and entered the world as a consequence of sin. "Bodily death, from which man would have been immune had he not sinned" is thus "the last enemy" of man left to be conquered.**[50]

God wants us to choose to do the good that lies before us every day. What other people say or do will not be your responsibility. God will only ask for an account of your life. Like Adam, we all stand alone before God with our "yes" or "no."

God's plan for the human race is not only that we would live our life as a man or a woman, but that we would also live together as men and women in unity. The second creation account, found in Genesis 2:18-25, is written **"to express the truth about the creation of man, and especially of woman."**[51] St. John Paul II wants us to know that there is much more to these Bible stories than you might think.

> **Then the Lord God said, "It is not good for the man to be alone; I will make him a helper fit for him." (Gen 2:18)**

Original solitude is necessary for self-knowledge. It also helps you to be able to enter into relationship with others. How? Adam discovers that he is lonely. After God says, "I will make him a helper fit for him," God begins to create every animal, bird, and sea creature that you can think of. It is as if God is showing Adam who he is, a human being, by showing him who he is not—an animal. Adam enjoys the animals, even naming them, yet he finds that he is still alone in the garden since there is not another being like himself, "a helper fit for him" (Gen 2:20).

So God casts him into a deep sleep, and from his side, he creates the woman. They are side by side, showing that the woman is another person like himself with whom he can live and do life.

> **From the very beginning, both are persons, unlike the other living beings in the world [around] them.** *The woman is another "I" in a common humanity.* **From the very beginning they appear as a "unity of the two," and this signifies that the original solitude is overcome, the solitude in which man does not find "a helper fit for him" (Gen 2:20).**[52]

At the first sight of the woman, Adam expresses joy, "even exaltation, for which he had no reason before owing to the lack of being like himself."[53] Finally, there was someone like himself, someone with whom he could share his life. The love and connection that Adam experienced with Eve were due to the source of their union, God the Creator. God Who is love, is the source of their unity. In the beginning, when Adam looked at Eve, he could see her the way God saw her, with "the peace and tranquility of the interior gaze."[54] In other words, he could see her in all of her elegant beauty—heart, soul, and body—the companion that God had created for him, to exist with him, to help him to be the human being he was created to be. To do life together. Side by side. Side by side is huge!

"He could see her... with the peace and tranquility of the interior gaze."

In the beginning, Eve was also able to look at Adam with the same peace and tranquility of the interior gaze, within her heart. She saw him as her companion, the one whom he really was created to be. She saw him the way God saw him, his heart, his soul, and the exquisite way God made him, just for her. It was Adam's experience of solitude that prepared him for his relationship with Eve, the companion God created for him, a lifelong friend to love and cherish. St. John Paul II calls this original unity. Anything that threatens Adam's relationship with God, threatens his unity with Eve.

> **Is it only a question here of a "helper" in activity, in "subduing the earth" (cf. Gen 1:28)? Certainly it is a matter of a life's companion, with whom, as a wife, the man can unite himself, becoming with her "one flesh" and for this reason leaving "his father and his mother" (cf. Gen 2:24).**[55]

A friend shared with me some insights given to her while she was praying about her relationship with her boyfriend. She told me, "I was alone with God in adoration, when I felt a joyful conviction that this was the man I would marry. I felt that God was preparing him and that I needed to begin preparing to be a wife and mother." She did, in fact, marry him and now is the mother of five beautiful children. She and her husband are united in a profound mystery, a one-flesh union, in which their bodies and their souls become one. In this way, God establishes marriage as the indispensable, absolutely necessary condition for the marital union, a union so profound that *sometimes*, nine months later, you can put a name on it.

Yes, bambinos! A new little person who looks like you and is also like God. The *gift* of a new life that comes from God and your "yes." Your child, willed by God for his or her own sake.

> **Thus, in the same context as the creation of man and woman, the biblical account speaks of God's *instituting marriage* as an indispensable condition for the transmission of life to new generations, the transmission of life to which marriage and conjugal love are by their nature ordered: "Be fruitful and multiply, and fill the earth and subdue it" (Gen 1:28).**[56]

Marriage is God's divine plan for the intimate love shared between spouses. God, the source of all life is the source of this marital union; it is *grace* that makes this love strong and permanent. In this loving union of husband and wife, a strong foundation is fashioned, so that the children can live and grow up together as a family, in a place they can call home. Yet today often God's plan for marriage and the family is threatened by great division and many trials.

I was asked to do a three-page autobiography about myself, including my marriage, family, and home. As I sat down to work on it a fly began to bother me. Then several more flies appeared. I got up to see if a window or door was open. After swatting them all and securing the house I went back to work. Suddenly there were more flies! I hate the little things. I kept writing and swatting. My husband came into the room and asked me, "What is going on?" I said that I did not know where all these flies were coming from, and they were making me crazy. Together we swatted a few more and swept them up. Then I sat down to try and finish my work. As I was writing, one more fly came walking slowly on the floor toward me. I could not believe it! I picked up my foot and struck a blow. The truth is that, in our culture, marriage and family life are seriously struggling to get the upper hand. Family life is often misunderstood, divided, and overwhelmed. Yet, God is bigger than these flies. With Duane's help I was able to conquer the flies; with God's grace the family can be victorious. St John Paul II urged the family to return to Christ, the author of human life and love.

I met my husband Duane when I was working for a large parish in Minnesota. I was busy subduing the earth, working as a youth director for middle and high school youth. I enjoyed working with the teens, leading retreats, taking canoe trips, and all the rest, but was also ready to begin my own life. I was lonely. Hoping to meet someone, I decided to sign up for a young adult retreat, called "Relationships Really Matter." It was there that Duane and I finally connected.

After signing up for the retreat I was asked to give a little talk for the retreat. Duane must have liked the talk because he asked me out at the end of the retreat. After a few dates, I asked him if he would be willing to pray with me. He told me he wasn't comfortable with that, but when I said, "That's too bad!" he asked, "Why?" and I said, "It's one of my prerequisites." On the next date, he agreed we could pray together. From that time forward, we prayed frequently, especially the rosary. Duane's prerequisite for me came up one day when he asked me, "So can you downhill ski?" I replied, "Yes. Why?" He said, "How good are you?" I said, "I am a decent B skier." He said, "Good enough, that is my prerequisite." We were engaged and then married about two years later.

Around the time we were planning on getting married, my dad asked me to take my sister who was struggling with multiple sclerosis to a Marian shrine in Europe. The pilgrimage was already set for a few days after our wedding day. It was agreed that all of us, my sister, her husband, Duane, and I, would go together. I remember as we were climbing the mountain, praying and sweating, asking my new husband, "So what does God have in store for us that we are starting our life off together on a pilgrimage?"

Years later, I think I can answer that question. We really needed our faith strengthened. It is so very difficult to be married and to raise a family. There are many highs and many lows in married life. After our wedding day, the most joyful times have been the birth of our four children. We also love to travel and have been able to go on some pretty awesome adventures: a Colorado ski trip; a trip to Italy, which included Rome and Venice; and a pilgrimage to the Holy Land. The most sorrowful or difficult times have included the loss of two of our babies, unemployment and job transitions, difficult pastoral situations, the priest scandals, loss of friends, deaths of loved ones, raising teenagers, and accepting disappointments in many, many situations. Yet, I see God's hand keeping us steady and filling our lives with many blessings, especially love for each other and our family's increased desire to serve the Lord.

I also now understand why God wants to draw us close to our Blessed Mother. Mary is a strong ally and support for all families. As our spiritual mother, she loves us and wants us to put our trust in

Christ. She has a lot of experience when it comes to putting one's faith in God. This is why she can help us throughout our lives, especially in times of trial and sorrow. I read an article recently which talked about how much suffering comes from homes that are broken. People want good, strong, healthy families but, left without hope and grace, they are less and less willing to put the sacrifice and work into building one. I know that family life can be crazy at times. Trusting in God has helped Duane and me to work and raise our kids together. Both of us became more aware of what our parents did for us after we had our first child. Sacrificial love and service, every day. Family means forgiveness, dedication, and loving acceptance of the other, despite the "flies." As St. John Paul II taught us:

> **There is no family that does not know how selfishness, discord, tension, and conflict violently attack and at times mortally wound its own communion: Hence there arises the many varied forms of division in family life. But, at the same time, every family is called by the God of peace to have the joyous and renewing experience of reconciliation, that is communion re-established, unity restored.**[57]

Thus, every person that comes into existence is a unique, unrepeatable gift with dignity and value that cannot be humanly measured. So often we can be overly anxious about what life is asking of us. Yet, God gave us our life. God is for us and is with us that we might have abundant life while becoming a sincere gift—that is, a gift of love—first to God, then to others. We find our real identity when we respond to God's invitation to live a life with grace. If we subdue our lives by loving and choosing virtue—that is, choosing moral excellence—we shall grow in our real identity; if we do not, we shall be diminished—that is, made smaller—by our poor moral choices.

The degree to which we choose to love is all that matters to God. Called into life, we are to work together to build up a civilization of love. In the end, love is all that will matter. The way we live our lives and the choices we make do make a difference for better or for worse. Each of us is called to strive to live in loving unity with God and people, which includes our spouses, children, parents, brothers, sisters, grandparents, aunties, uncles, cousins, neighbors, friends, and even our enemies. We belong to each other. This is true in each and every new generation.

How Big Is God? (Person-Communion-Gift)

Have you ever thought about how big God is? Years ago on a beautiful fall day, I was driving down a little road in northern Minnesota in my Pontiac T-1000. I began to think about how long it seemed to take me to get to the little town that I was heading to. As my mind began to wander, I started to think about how long it would take to drive my little car throughout the United States, then South America, Africa, Europe, and around the whole world. While I was thinking about how big the world actually is, I suddenly thought, "Well, how big is the being Who created it?" *God is soooo big!*

It is important for us to think about who God is and how big the mystery of God is. It is also important to think about who we are as human beings and how God made us. God made us for relationships. Relationships really matter. In the "unity of the two," we see from the beginning the divine plan for human love. When I first met my husband on our retreat, God was making it clear to both of us that relationships really do matter. Married relationships are especially significant to God. In this specific relationship, we, with grace, entrust ourselves to the other in a lifelong covenant of marital love. Done well, the marriage covenant points to the kind of love that God holds for each one of us. Married love reveals to us a glimpse of the love shared between the three Persons of the Trinity. All the faithfully departed experience this love now in heaven. We too will know this love someday if we choose wisely. The prelude to

"The degree to which we choose to love is all that matters to God."

heaven, our relationships on earth, especially those we hold most dearly, marriage and family, are but the whisper of what is to come.

> **Moreover, we read that man cannot exist "alone" (cf. Gen 2:18); he can exist only as a "unity of the two," and therefore *in relation to another human person*. It is a question here of a mutual relationship: man to woman and woman to man. Being a person in the image and likeness of God thus also involves existing in a relationship, in relation to the other "I." This is a prelude [introduction] to the definitive self-revelation of the Triune God: a living unity in the communion of the Father, Son, and Holy Spirit.[58]**

Married love in Christ calls both the woman and the man to live in a committed lifelong mutual relationship that is itself a prelude or introduction to something, or I should say, someone. *That someone is the Author of your existence.* Deep within every human heart, there is a longing, a homesickness for God that exists whether we are alone or not. The God-shaped hole in our hearts cannot be filled by the goods or relationships of this world, only by God. I can experience a taste of the Holy Trinity in my relationships and in my marriage when the other stands by me, and I by him, through thick and thin, side by side, one for the other. United.

> **In the "unity of the two," man and woman are called from the beginning not only to exist "side by side" or "together," but they are also called *to exist mutually "one for the other."* This also explains the meaning of the "help" spoken of in Genesis 2:18-25: "I will make him *a helper fit for him.*" The biblical context enables us to understand this in the sense that the woman must "help" the man—and in his turn he must help her—first of all by the very fact of their "being human persons."[59]**

Duane has been a best friend to me, especially when he prays and talks with me. His strong faith in God has been a constant in our marriage both to our kids and me. He also tends to stay calm in the storms of life, laughs a lot, forgives quickly, defends my integrity, and most importantly, likes to have fun with me. We enjoy just being together. We like to go on walks or kayak down a river. It only gets better when our kids are with us. Through all the ups and downs of our married life together, Duane and my kiddos have definitely helped me to heal and grow into the person I am today. If my husband Duane is a prelude to the life that we will both have together with God in eternity, I can only say that I am very grateful and excited.

> **Man and woman, created as a "unity of the two" in their common humanity, are called to live in a communion of love, and in this way to mirror in the world the communion of love that is in God, through which the Three Persons love each other in the intimate mystery of the one divine life.**[60]

For men and women, this means that God has called us from the beginning to live together as a "unity of the two," helping each other out in whatever happens in our lives together. It is because we share a common humanity that we are called by God to love each other and so reflect the communion of love that is in God, the Three Persons of the Trinity.

We have heard about God in the Old Testament—remember Moses who questioned God at the burning bush, "Who are you?" The answer is "I Am!" With the coming of Jesus in the New Testament, we get a better understanding of the mystery of the one true God as revealed in the unity of three divine Persons, the Father, Son, and the Holy Spirit, three divine Persons completely united in unfathomable love.

> **The whole Old Testament is mainly concerned with revealing the truth about the oneness and unity of God. Within this fundamental truth about God the New**

> **Testament will reveal the inscrutable mystery of God's inner life. *God*, who allows himself to be known by human beings through Christ, is the *unity of the Trinity:* unity in communion [friendship].**[61]

In Old Testament times, the mystery of the Holy Trinity was unknown. When St. John Paul II says that the mystery of God is "inscrutable," he means that it is impossible for us as created beings to understand the inner life of God. That is why, in the fullness of time, the Father sent the Son, "And the Word became flesh and dwelt among us, full of grace and truth; we have beheld his glory, glory as the only begotten Son from the Father. And from his fullness, we have all received, grace upon grace. For the law was given through Moses; *Grace and truth came through Jesus Christ"* (Jn 1: 14-16; emphasis added). We have the capacity to know God and love God because of the grace given to us in Jesus Christ. However, our capacity must be filled with God Who makes Himself known to us. That is why it is important to pay attention to the ways God reveals Himself to us every day. Sometimes it is quiet and hidden like the beauty of a sunrise or an inspirational song. Other times it is more startling and dramatic, such as in the case of a man who had an experience of God that had a profound impact on his life.

There was a man—a husband and father of two children—who was boating alone on the lake one beautiful summer day. Later in the afternoon, as he was idling about one hundred feet from shore, waiting to enter the boat landing, a sense of apprehension suddenly came over him. Turning around, he saw another boat, whose driver was not paying attention, heading right toward him. He was going to be hit. The collision threw him off his boat. As he was going down into the water, he remembered being fully conscious of everything that was happening to him. He was almost back up to the surface of the water when the boat ran over him a second time, the motor slicing a part of his left leg. Close to the landing, he could see people moving toward him. The first person to reach him held him and consoled him, telling him that everyone there was praying for him. He remembered thinking that was strange. How did this man who was holding him even know that he was a Christian?

In the ambulance, his leg was hurting badly. He recalls the severity of the leg pain, yet somehow he knew it was exceedingly small in comparison to what Christ suffered on the Cross. He suddenly saw three men talking with one another. When one turned to him, he realized that his life was just a tiny speck compared to the reality of God and eternal life. He knew that man was God. Then he could see himself sitting in the palm of God's hand and realized, "How secure I am" (Is 49:16).

While the man was being prepped for surgery to amputate his leg, one of the surgeons came in one more time and found a pulse in his foot. He immediately had him sent back to his hospital bed. After thirteen surgeries, he has his full limb and a full life, for which he is eternally grateful.

This spiritual experience greatly strengthened and reassured him. Yes, he was definitely secure in the palm of God's hand. When his life was out of his control, God let him know that a bigger hand was safely keeping him. Humbly our Creator waits for us to acknowledge our human limitations and our need for His love.

"Love is not loved!" proclaimed St. Francis of Assisi. God desires that we would return love for love, especially in always doing good for our neighbor. We often remove ourselves from God's hand, being super busy doing our own thing or things that harm both ourselves and our neighbor. This is especially true in nations where there is much wealth and consumerism. So many problems happen in our families and societies because we have distanced ourselves from God.

> **[M]any men have separated themselves from God and tried to organize intellectual and social life without Him. The great problems that have always preoccupied humanity have taken on a new and sometimes tragic aspect. To wish to get along without God, first Cause and last End, leads to an abyss; not only to nothingness but also to physical and**

> **moral wretchedness that is worse than nothingness. Likewise, great problems grow exasperatingly serious, and man must finally perceive that all these problems ultimately lead to the fundamental religious problem; in other words, he will finally have to declare himself entirely for God or against Him.... Christ Himself says: "He that is not with Me is against me" [Mt. 12:30].**[62]

Yet God reveals the truth to us personally. If we are open to Him, the divine communion and friendship that we long for can be accessed in Jesus Christ. You see, the Three Persons of the Holy Trinity are selfless. They're not about themselves; They are all about love, a divine love that both gives and receives while maintaining Their personal divine integrity. The Three Persons of the Holy Trinity work perfectly together, accomplishing the will of the Father because the Holy Trinity is completely whole, Undivided Love. The Father invites us to live our lives within this divine communion.

> **This "unity of the two," which is a sign of interpersonal communion,** *shows that the creation of man is* **also marked by a certain likeness to divine communion (*"communio"*). This likeness is a quality of the personal being of both man and woman, and is also a call and a task.**[63]

In other words, all relationships on earth can either be in the likeness or non-likeness of God. This is why it is so important that we hear our calling to be the people God created us to be while also acting in the service of our neighbor. This is true in all relationships but above all in marriage. We are called to be like God. It takes both our effort and God's grace. St. John Paul II says it is a "call and a task." You are an immortal person, which means you will live on forever in eternity. So working on your personal divine integrity is essential for you and for those you serve. Your life on earth carries over into the next. Either you are going to put effort into becoming a virtue-filled, excellent person or you will put time into being a vice-filled, morally depraved person. Either way, you become and influence others to become what you think about. What you think about is what you love and give yourself to.

A Catholic priest came to talk to me about some of the students he was working with. He was discouraged because they did not seem to be willing to leave vice behind: "They keep committing the same sins. I do not think I can help them." I said, "I hear what you are saying, but I disagree with you. Do not give up! What if Jesus would have given up on you and me? Keep helping them to discover the exciting life that God has called them to. This is our calling, our task." God is the Who we are created for, God sees all the possibilities for our life. Ignoring God's call is not an option. All sin and vice are really nothingness, compared to the greatness of God's love for us. St. Therese spoke of this before she died:

> **I ask Jesus to draw me into the flames of His love and to unite me so closely to Him that He lives and acts in me. I feel that the more the fire of love encompasses my heart, the more I shall say: "Draw me," ... for souls on fire cannot stay still. Like St. Magdalene, they may sit at the feet of Jesus, listening to His gentle yet exciting words. They seem to give Him nothing, yet they give much more than Martha who is anxious "about many things." Jesus does not, of course, blame Martha's work, but only her worrying about it.**[64]

The fire of God's love is calling each of us, drawing us closer to His mercy and forgiveness. God's love is revealed to you personally in Jesus Christ, so you can discover who you are: you are like God.

In this way new light is also thrown on man's image and likeness to God...[65]

You are more than what you think you are! Having an immortal soul with the faculties of a mind and will, sets you up for a really great mind-blowing future. Many people either think very little about heaven, or they think it will be boring, or they just do not think about it at all. They might be atheists or agnostics, or they might be part of a formal religion by birth but never really invest the time into understanding their religion or getting to know God personally. Wherever you are, God does not wish for you to live your life alone. Your Creator God knows who you are and how to lead you to the very best life you could ever have.

"Show me the way and I will follow You," is an excellent way to pray to God when you are trying to find your path. Jesus, the Son of God, came from heaven to earth to show us the way and to give us an example of how to pray with our hearts. We find personal divine integrity, wholeness, and our ultimate worth in a loving relationship with God and other people.

Think about it. Jesus did not live life for Himself, or even by Himself. Jesus lived His life on earth for His Father and with the Holy Spirit, for us, and for the Kingdom to come. Jesus never acted alone. For Him, it meant laying down His very life. First, for the Father, Who is worthy of all honor and love, and second, to save us, as brothers and sisters, from a broken, meaningless, empty existence by restoring us to grace. God promises us we will see His face one day (Ps 11:7) and that will be the best day of our lives.

> **"The Lord Jesus, when he prayed to the Father 'that all may be one...as we are one' (Jn 17: 21-22), opened up vistas [pathways] closed to human reason. For he implied *a certain likeness* between the union of the divine Persons and the union of God's children in truth and charity. This likeness reveals that man, who is the only creature on earth which God willed for its own sake, cannot fully find himself except through a sincere gift of self."[66]**

"Trust the experts." This is the advertisement I read on my way to Mass one day, displayed on the back of a moving truck. Immediately I thought about Jesus. Jesus wants us to know that He is the expert on human life. We can look to many others for wisdom and expertise, but in the end, we must follow our conscience which moves us to do good and avoid evil. In a world that sends so many mixed messages, what voice will we listen to? Now more than ever, if we want to discover who we really are, we need to listen to the voice of Jesus and trust that we too are called to become a sincere gift of self.

> **Being a person means striving towards self-realization [and self-discovery] ...which can only be achieved** *"through a sincere gift of self."* **... To say that man is created in the image and likeness of God means that man is called to exist "for" others, to become a gift.**[67]

Let me share an example of a man who went to Guatemala to help build a house for a family who did not have a proper home. He paid for all the materials and stayed to help out with the construction of the house. A special Mass of thanksgiving was celebrated upon the completion of the new home. When the father of the family stood up and gave thanks to God for their new home, the man who had given the material and time felt bad, wondering why he hadn't been acknowledged for his gifts of money and labor. The man did not realize that, when the father of the family gave thanks to God, it was actually the greatest compliment that could be given to him. In his actions, his self-gift reflected his Father in heaven.

God Is like Man (The Anthropomorphism of Biblical Language)

Anthropomorphism is a big word that means the giving of a human characteristic or behavior to a god, animal, or object. St. John Paul II wants us to know that there is a reason that the Scriptures use this technique. Anthropomorphism in Scripture helps us to understand God through human eyes. God often communicates to us in a human way, using a language, analogy, or action that we will be able to understand. Anthropomorphism is also found in other literary analogies, like the story of the Turtle and the Rabbit. Years ago, I was praying to God about my life as a mother. As I prayed to God, I said, "I started out like a racehorse, then I seemed to become a rabbit; now I am a turtle." As I sat and contemplated how my life as a mother had changed and slowed down, the "still small voice" seemed to say, *But who won the race?* I had to think for a moment, then I remembered the story. The turtle won the race by slowly, step by step, going forward. A smile came across my face. It seemed that God was letting me know that, with all the joys and difficulties of my life, marriage, and motherhood, I was to just keep going forward, step by step, even if they felt like baby steps some days.

> **God speaks in human language, using human concepts and images. If this manner of expressing himself is characterized by a certain anthropomorphism, the reason is that man is "like" God: created in his image and likeness. But then, *God too is* in some measure "like man," and precisely because of this likeness, he can be humanly known.**[68]

God can be humanly known because God, Who is pure spirit, knows how to communicate with His creatures. Remember Moses and the burning bush? The burning bush definitely got Moses's attention! The fiery flame of the bush drew Moses in, causing him to wonder why the bush was not being consumed. Then God spoke in a way that Moses was able to understand. God used a similar analogy when speaking to St. Catherine of Siena:

> **Just as the fish is in the sea and the sea in the fish, so am I in the soul and the soul in me, the sea of peace.**[69]

God compared the human person to a little fish and the sea to Himself. This little fish like Goldie, my family's goldfish, might not be aware of the sea while swimming happily about, yet the sea gives the little fish life. The big sea does not crush the little fish, nor does the fish take away anything from the sea, for the sea is complete and full in and of itself. You should be a goldfish!

You are created in the image of God, yet you are not able to fully know God, for the greatness of God is unsearchable (Ps 145:3). In other words, we are limited creatures and can only know so much about the God who "dwells in unapproachable light" (1 Tim 6:16).

This is why God sent Jesus: so that Adam and Eve could have a new beginning. By sending Jesus to us through Mary, God gave us a chance to begin again, to have a fresh start with God and each other. It is difficult to understand God and His bigger plan for the creation and salvation of human persons in Christ. It's like an ant trying to figure out who you are as a human being. (Whack-whack.) It is not going to happen. Yet the great mystery of God reveals that in Mary, every Eve has a new beginning.

"It's like an ant trying to figure out who you are as a human being."

Questions for Reflection
Chapter 3
You Are like God

1. What are one or two takeaways from this chapter?

2. You are created in the image of God, full of love and grace. What might happen if you started believing this?

3. "Bear with each other and forgive one another if any of you has a grievance against someone; forgive as the Lord forgave you" (Col 3:13). Who is difficult for you to love in your life? How can you learn to forgive more quickly?

4. Which areas in your life need to have some order or boundaries so that you can have a more fulfilling life?

Notes

In Mary, Every Eve Has a New Beginning (Eve-Mary)

"Although he was made by God in a state of justice, from the very dawn of history man abused his liberty, at the urging of the Evil One. Man set himself against God and sought to find fulfillment apart from God."[70]

Those Darn Apples (The "Beginning" and the Sin)

Those darn apples! One day I was speaking to a group of high school teenagers about their life's purpose and calling. We become what we think about, so the challenge was to get them to think about their lives from God's perspective. It's easy to go along with what everyone else is doing. But that might not be what is right for you. With prayer and faith, you might live your life differently, becoming the person you are meant to be. So, when it comes to your life right now you may want to ask: "God, what do you think about all this?" You also may want to ask yourself: "What is it that I need to do to take care of my life so that I can become the person I am called to become?" It takes courage to be different, remaining true to God and to whom you really are called to become.

To get the discussion going, I asked the teens to write down their top ten apples, their top temptations, those thoughts and things that might keep them from living a happy, fulfilling life that honored God. Is this kind of life with God even possible? Yes. It's why we are created and put on this earth. The teens came up with many apples, the top ones including negative influence from social media, family problems and divorce, social pressures, bullying, the desire for many material possessions of which they did not think God would approve, drinking and drugs, distasteful music that they enjoyed even though it felt wrong, and struggles with sexuality and porn. I was incredibly surprised to find the number one apple was "We do not want anyone telling us how to live our lives."

"Even God?" I questioned. "Yes, even God!" they replied. I said, "Well, I think we should go back to the beginning. I heard a story about a couple of other people who struggled with that apple as well." Adam and Eve did not want anyone to tell them how to live their lives. They decided to ignore God's warning, choosing no God, no rules. This choice led to their separation from God, causing much pain, sorrow, and ultimately their own death. These consequences affected them, their children, and all future generations. Someone asked, "Well, what did they actually do that caused so much trouble?" The book of Genesis says that they ate the forbidden fruit (Gen 3). In doing so they fully cooperated in an act of disobedience that cut off their relationship with God and greatly harmed their relationship with each other, which resulted in the loss of many extraordinary blessings.

> **The account of the fall in Genesis 3 uses figurative language, but affirms a primeval event, a deed that took place *at the beginning of the history of man*. Revelation gives us the certainty of faith that the whole of human history is marked by the original fault freely committed by our first parents.**[71]

The Scriptures teach us the true meaning of this story of Adam and Eve using figurative language that reveals the temptation and fall from grace of our first parents. This occurrence happened during the first age of humanity. Satan lied to Adam and Eve, telling them that if they ate of the forbidden fruit, they would be like gods, knowing good and evil (Gen 3:1-6). What the evil one hid from them is that they would be destroyed by that knowledge of evil. This is because to know evil meant that they would experience it. The experience of evil changed their lives forever. It did not, however, change God. For only God can look at evil and not be changed.

> **Scripture speaks of a sin of these angels. This "fall" consists in the free choice of these created spirits, who radically and irrevocably *rejected* God and his reign. We find a reflection of that rebellion in the tempter's words to our first parents: "You will be like God." The devil "has sinned from the beginning;" he is "a liar and the father of lies."**[72]

So let's look at it another way. Think of looking through the eyes of a little goldfish. My fish Goldie jumped out of his aquarium years ago. I had fed him before going to bed, and I must have left the tank lid open. God does, in a sense, leave the fishbowl open. As human beings, we have free will. If we choose to go against His will for our lives, we can jump out of the fishbowl and do our own thing. I do not know why Goldie thought life looked better outside the fishbowl. By the time I found him he was dead. After I told my younger sisters, we proceeded to give him a proper funeral and then—flush—down the toilet he went. His decision cost him his life. Life might look like it will be okay, good, or even better without God, but ultimately life without God leads to death. All sin separates us from God, leads to destructive knowledge, and

should be avoided at all costs.

We are created for more than this. God created the entire world for you and for me. God also created us for Himself: "Before I formed you in the womb I knew you, and before you were born, I consecrated you" (Jer 1:5). The life God gave you is a gift. Calling you into existence, God has a personal plan for your life. No one can ever give you your life again, and no one ever has the right to take it away; even you do not have that right. Your life itself is a gift and a calling to a greater life with God that brings supernatural happiness. This happiness can only be found in God. Think of one of the best gifts you have ever received or a time you experienced great happiness. Now multiply that experience by about a million. You will get a tiny glimpse of the supernatural happiness to be found in God. God's special gift to you and to me is that we can become like Him, holy; that is what it means to be drawn into the intimate life of God Most High.

> **This truth presents the creation of man [and woman] as a special gift from the Creator, containing ...** *the beginning of the call to both of them to share in the intimate life of God himself.*[73]

In creating Adam and Eve, God favors them with the special gift of being created in His image. This favor brings many blessings and responsibilities. The blessing of having free will comes with the responsibility to choose to do what is good and to avoid what is evil. Above all, God is their greatest good. Sadly, like Goldie the goldfish, Adam and Eve still decide to jump out of the plan that God has for their existence; it leads to their demise.

> **...God wills for them the fullness of good, or supernatural happiness, which flows from sharing in his own life.** *By committing sin man rejects this gift* **and at the same time wills to become "as God, knowing good and evil" (Gen 3:5), that is to say, deciding what is good and what is evil**

independently of God, his Creator.[74]

The fact that God created them immortal meant that they were like God (Gen 1:26), so the consequences of their actions had a greater impact. As immortal beings, our actions can have such ripple effects for good or for bad. When we choose to go with or against the good of God's divine will, it causes either positive or negative effects throughout the world. Our actions greatly help or wound our relationships with God and one another. I was not always aware of the effects of original sin, especially of how that first sin and all the rest of the sins to follow greatly wound and offend God, until I read this quote by St. John Paul II. It is something for us all to think about. Remember, what God has willed for us is that we would love Him and one another above all.

It must be admitted that God, as Creator and Father, is here wounded, "offended"—obviously offended—in the very heart of that gift which belongs to God's eternal plan for man [and woman].[75]

The "very heart" of God was wounded in the rejection of God's plan for humanity. The relationship that God offered Adam and Eve, and also us, was given in the hopes that we would choose with our freedom and free will to share in His love and life; each person was created with this intention. God's grace also makes it possible for us to love one another selflessly, which leads to our greatest happiness. By disobeying God and eating the forbidden fruit, they rejected God's love, which was their greatest offense. This caused a negative ripple effect of unhappiness, misery, and division on all of human life, but especially on the relationship between man and woman.

Most kids growing up challenge their parents in every way. My siblings and I were no different; thankfully in this incident no one got hurt. One night I woke up to the voices of my parents and the police who were at our door. My mother had gotten up during the night to take care of the youngest child, only to discover that her teenagers were gone. They had snuck out of the house in the middle of the night.

None of us had any idea where they were.

I was caught up in the excitement of it all: the police at the door, the flashing lights from their car, and everyone being questioned as to their whereabouts. One of my little sisters whispered, "Oh, poor dad." It was only then that I realized the seriousness of the situation and my poor parents' worry for their kids' safety. God, who is a loving Father, wishes only the good for you. If, however, you disregard His authority, heading out into the night, you open yourself up to dangers and many sorrows. You also break His heart.

The Genesis biblical story expresses the truth of the mystery of good and evil, how things came to be, and also how life got so messy on planet Earth. Remember, God in His goodness wants to share His own life and love with people. The fall from grace is a historical event in which our first parents used their freedom to disregard the love and authority of God who is a good Father. God set up the rules for their good. Like defiant teenagers, they opened themselves up to dangers that they were not prepared to handle. Deceived, Adam and Eve experienced the consequences of disobeying God which were serious not only for them but for all generations to come.

> **In that sin man *preferred* himself to God and by that very act scorned him. He chose himself over and against God, against the requirements of his creaturely status and therefore against his own good. Constituted in a state of holiness, man was destined to be fully "divinized" by God in glory. Seduced by the devil, he wanted to "be like God," but "without God, before God, and not in accordance with God."[76]**

In the beginning, the Garden of Eden was a paradise: you have Adam and Eve and they're enjoying their life with God. There is no sin, so there's nothing to divide them until the serpent comes along. Mmmhmm…and what does the serpent do? The serpent takes something that God has said and twists it. He tells Eve that God cannot be trusted by saying, "Did God really say that? This won't hurt you! In fact, God knows that the minute you do this you will become like gods, knowing good and evil" (paraphrase of Gen 3:1-6). He uses the same tactics and lies today! "Does God really say that? Where is that in the Bible? You do not need to read the Bible or listen to the Church. You can decide for yourself what is good and evil. This won't hurt you!" All lies, for immediately Adam and Eve experience the consequence of losing God and the grace that was the source of their existence and unity. But they were not left without hope.

Adam and Eve immediately lose the grace of original holiness. They become afraid of the God of whom they have conceived a distorted image— that of a God jealous of his prerogatives.[77]

Like Adam and Eve, the devil is allowed to tempt us in our thoughts. We must be on guard against these temptations to see God in a distorted way, checking our thinking against the truths that we have learned about God. For as you think so you believe. Remember, you have been created to think and act like God. Wisdom comes to us from God in many ways. Learning about our faith, reading the Scriptures, and listening to others who have gone before us can help us to grow in knowledge. All the sacraments of the Church, especially the Eucharist, give us the grace to know how to live our lives. Yes, it is true that we are enough with grace. Yet, the fight is real. It is up to you to struggle and fight against the various sins and temptations that present themselves. The devil does not want you to think and act like your Creator. The devil wants you to think and act like him, a prideful fallen angel. The devil is a liar, a cheat, a thief, and a murderer (Jn 10:10). So, by going against your human nature and the divine nature you participate in, you actually diminish your dignity and become less like the person God made you to be, and more like the devil after he fell from grace. You are made for more!

Sin in fact "diminishes" man.[78]

So this is what happens to Eve: she gets into this conversation with the devil like we do sometimes. The more we look at or think about a temptation, the better it looks. The next thing you know, she's eating apples! And she's likin' 'em! So often we do the same. We also call on our friends to join us. Sure enough, Eve calls out to Adam: "Adam, come on!" and the next thing you know, Adam's eating apples too and enjoying it! All of a sudden, boom. He's naked; she's naked; they are filled with shame, and they're running and hiding, from whom? God (Gen 3:6-7). Often Eve gets the bad rap for the fall, but the truth is that they both ignored what God told them and went against his divine will. As St. John Paul II puts it:

> **But there is no doubt that, independent of this "distinction of roles" in the biblical description, *that first sin is the sin of man*, created by God as male and female. It is also *the sin of the "first parents"* ... we call it "original sin."**[79]

Our first parents had different roles in this first offense, but the truth is that they both said no and went against God. They could have chosen to overcome the threat of the devil by sticking together and calling on God for help. Likewise, the first mistake Eve makes when tempted is that she starts talking to the serpent. When the devil comes around to tempt you, don't talk to him. Pray! Especially when there is confusion, fear, and anxiety. Ask God: "What is really going on here?" Then follow the guidance of the Holy Spirit who helps us to do the good we are called to do. All of this disobedience, along with the loss of grace, brought much suffering and chaos to planet Earth. We have been compromised.

> **The harmony in which they had found themselves, thanks to original justice, is now destroyed: the control of the soul's spiritual faculties over the body is shattered; the union of man and woman becomes subject to tensions, their relations henceforth marked by lust and domination. Harmony with creation is broken: visible creation has**

become alien and hostile to man. Because of man, creation is now subject "to its bondage to decay."[80]

God said "no," but they decided to do it anyway. Often, we choose to do the same. I was out shopping with a friend a while back when we came upon a stop sign that was just crushed to the ground. I turned to her and said, "Well, it looks like someone had a hard time following that rule." That's how it goes with us. God says, "Stop!" and we say, "We don't want to." Crash. That hurt. In second grade, Sister Margaret taught us about that first sin using a picture book. Adam and Eve looked so sad as they had to leave paradise, the Garden of Eden. Their relationship with God… changed. The sin that the serpent said would not harm them—well, it did—and yes, man would die.

Finally, the consequence explicitly foretold for this disobedience will come true: man will "return to the ground," for out of it he was taken. *Death makes its entrance into human history.*[81]

Death entered human history because Adam and Eve abused the gift of their freedom by violating their covenant with God: "You may freely eat of every tree of the garden; but of the tree of the knowledge of good and evil you shall not eat, for in the day that you eat of it you shall die" (Gen 2:16-17). By breaking their covenant with God, Adam and Eve lost God as they knew Him. They had to leave the Garden of Eden; they experienced nakedness and shame. Now they could no longer love each other freely as before. Adam had to toil and sweat to earn a living; Eve would bear their children in pain. On their own, they were quite miserable. Not only did they lose grace, but they also lost their inheritance, as well as their very identity as children who belonged to God. Just as God's love had united them, sin now divided them and made the lives of Adam and Eve and their children subject to death.

And all this is marked by the necessity of death, which is

> **the end of human life on earth.... "you are dust, and to dust you shall return" (cf. Gen 3:19).**[82]

I lost a close neighbor and friend in ninth grade to a fatal car accident. He was a year older than me. Since he lived down the street from us, we talked frequently. His death not only caused me much grief, it also caused me to ask many questions about the afterlife. I remember grieving him and thinking, "I just cannot believe he is gone. Where is he right now?" Many people have lived and died before us asking these same questions. Being made immortal and in the image of God, human beings were not created for sin and death. The peaceful harmony that filled the garden in the beginning was broken by sin. This original sin continues to cause more sin, selfishness, and an imbalance in the natural world even until today. The break in the original unity affected man's and woman's ability to love each other in all of their relationships as well as in everyday life in the external world of nature. We are broken without God.

> **Sin brings about a break in the original unity which man enjoyed in the state of original justice: union with God as the source of the unity...in the mutual relationship between man and woman *("communio personarum")* as well as in regard to the external world, to nature.**[83]

The break in the original unity of Adam and Eve is the direct result of the break they both experienced in being separated from God. Sin damaged and twisted their relationship because without God they were not able to love in the way they were made to love. Yet they both still wanted to have a relationship. So now, because of sin, Adam sees Eve not as a wife and beloved companion but as an object, someone he can take or use for his own pleasure. Adam falls, becoming a man of lust instead of the original man created in the divine image. Instead of being a self-gift to Eve, he is weakened and looks out for himself. He becomes a self-seeker.

Evil Inheritance ("He Shall Rule over You")

Left unchecked, Adam can now threaten Eve using domination, power, and control. This inclination sadly diminishes the man, for without grace, he cannot fulfill the nobility of his own masculinity which is to lay down his life in loving service of others, especially his wife and his children. For a man who is not married, it means the service of showing loving kindness toward women in all situations, but especially his family and those women he knows closely through his work or social connections. Even with grace, it remains a task and a fight for men to treat women with dignity and for women to take responsibility for their own lives. Yet the truth remains that whenever a man participates in anything that offends the dignity of a woman, he diminishes himself.

> **The overcoming of this evil inheritance is, generation after generation, the task of every human being, whether woman or man. For whenever man is responsible for offending a woman's personal dignity and vocation, he acts contrary to his own personal dignity and his own vocation.**[84]

I overheard a group of men talking about going downtown to see a "girlie show." I wanted to challenge them, so I said a quick prayer, turned toward them, and said, "Hello!" After making some small talk, I cut to the chase asking simply, "Do you guys believe in God?" Quickly the conversation turned to spiritual matters. Not knowing that I had overheard their after-dinner plans, they began to talk to me about God and their different experiences of faith. I then asked if any of them were married. Did they have kids, daughters? Yes, they were married and had daughters. Some even pulled out their wallets and showed me pictures. It was then that I asked, "How would you feel if it was your daughter up on that stage tonight?" There was such a look of shock on all their faces! I followed with, "And how do you think God the Father feels when His sons go in to watch His daughters acting in this way?" Silence. Then one of the men said,

"You're pretty good at this," to which my friend said, "Well, she does this for a living!" I don't know if they ever went downtown to that girlie show. I only know that what was said made them think about what they were doing. Somehow in their minds, they had separated the way they see their wives and daughters from the way they could see and act toward other women. All women are someone's daughters, and all belong to God.

> **...we discover a break and a constant threat precisely in regard to this "unity of the two" which corresponds to the dignity of the image and likeness of God in both of them. But this threat is more serious for the woman, since domination takes the place of "being a sincere gift" and therefore living "for" the other: "he shall rule over you."**[85]

St. John Paul II is teaching that the break and constant threat to the unity of man and woman is more serious for the woman. In all human relationships, no one likes to be pushed around or treated in an inhumane way. The answer to this problem is a return to the truth about the "unity of the two" in God. The integrity of being a woman or of being a man comes from the truth that we are created with equal dignity in the image and likeness of God. We are made to live in Undivided Love with God and each other, for this is what it means to be human. Is it possible for us to do better? Only in Christ. For as men and women we are called by God to be so much more. In the divine plan, human love is meant to imitate, in the body, the divine expression of the life and love held within the mystery of the Holy Trinity.

Men and women glorify God by loving each other in a mutual relationship of self-giving love. Sin throws all of this into a tailspin, causing an imbalance and constant threat to the unity of the two. This lack of unity and respect can only be overcome in Christ: "Be subject to one another out of reverence for Christ" (Eph 5:21). Be selfless. Love her. Love him. Do the right thing because it matters.

Eve must also face the consequences of her decision: "Your

desire shall be for your husband, and he shall rule over you" (Gen 3:16). Eve still desires the relationship with Adam that God intended for her to have from the beginning. Now, however, things have changed. Without her union with God, loving Adam is more difficult. She struggles to see Adam the way God had intended, as a beloved husband and companion, an equal. Have you ever heard the song, "I Want You to Want Me" by Cheap Trick? Eve experiences the imbalance of her own desires, such as a strong craving for attention, to be wanted. So strong that she might give herself away, placing a man in her life before God, in fact making him her god, while at the same time demanding that he make her his god. This too is the result of original sin.

St. John Paul II wanted to teach women and men that after the fall, fear from lack of trust and the desire to control the other threaten the ability to be a gift. This is as true today as it was from the beginning. Since the fall, sin has affected all relationships between women and men in marriage, educational opportunities, the workplace, and all aspects of society. Women's liberation came about from this imbalance between the sexes. Yet the difficulties can only be overcome with grace and a willingness to forbear, forgive, and work toward a more just and equal society where every person is treated with the dignity and respect deserving of a human being, created in God's image. The break and threat to the unity of man and woman must not be fought with more power and violence, for that will only lead to more destruction of humankind.

> **…"He shall rule over you" (Gen 3:16) must not under any condition lead to the "masculinization" of women. In the name of liberation from male "domination," women must not appropriate to themselves male characteristics contrary to their own feminine "originality."**[86]

With hard work and grace, it is possible for women to remain true to their original feminine design, despite the difficulties, sorrows, and injustices of life. Often a woman must fight like a man, yet we are called by God to be women, which means not becoming like those who dominate and threaten through violence. We are responsible for ourselves and being true to God, which is ultimately what is most important. God calls all human beings to a life of love and service.

This is both woman's and man's calling and great dignity. We are not responsible for how others treat us. We are responsible for our own conscience, the quiet voice of God which calls us to do the good we are created to do. Do it anyway, even if you are mistreated. God sees you. God wants you to become who you are created to be. God wants your life to reflect His own love for you. With your "yes" and His help you are unstoppable.

This comes about by your free decision to make a sincere gift of your life to God. St. Mother Teresa was already serving as a nun when God called her to leave her convent—where she had a bed, food, and a good teaching position—to go to the poverty-stricken streets of Calcutta, India. At the beginning of this work, she had no one but Jesus to help her. It was there in the streets, amongst the poorest of the poor, with the most abandoned and the dying, that she found her life's calling.

> **Hence a woman, as well as a man, must understand her "fulfilment" as a person, her dignity and vocation, on the basis of these resources, according to the richness of the femininity which she received on the day of creation and which she inherits as an expression of the "image and likeness of God" that is specifically hers.**[87]

Women are strong and are called to be strong, finding fulfillment in their own unique calling. Mother Teresa found her fulfillment as a person using the richness of her femininity to bring God's light and love into some of the darkest places of humanity. All women are called by God to love and bring light to those who are in their sphere of influence. It may be a struggling teenager, an alcoholic husband, or a struggling coworker. Each of us as women is given gifts and talents to share with others to help them. Our fulfillment as persons is found in making use of the rich resources God has given through our union with Him. It is up to us to courageously rely on God and the graces given for our personal calling and task. Many times, women will say, "This is just too much!" But when women say "yes" to God, God will make the way.

I was leading a women's retreat on *Mulieris Dignitatem* when one of the pastors from the parish came in and began to listen. As I worked to convey the teachings of St. John Paul II regarding the dignity and role of women, the women laughed often, nodding their heads in agreement. They responded well to such clear teachings on their dignity and calling, and the many difficulties for women because of original and personal sin. At the break, the pastor came up to me and kindly asked, "Do you really think they are ready for all of this?" I said with a smile, "Oh, Father, they have been living this!" to which he said, "Continue on."

Women are ready for St. John Paul II's teachings on their dignity and vocation. Many women see the troubles in their lives and simply want answers. One such woman shared some of the troubles in her life with me. She had experienced one failed marriage, and the one she was in was not doing well, either. Despite it all, she still longed for a real, lasting marriage. I asked her how her relationship with God was. It was not too good. She then proceeded to talk about her mother, who had a strong faith in Jesus. Her mother had prayed often and went to Mass on Sunday, even daily Mass when possible. Because of her mother's example, she did believe in God's love yet had left God both times she got married. She agreed that she was not happy about her life, the choices she was making, or the people she presently socialized with. The friends she socialized with lived a hook-up lifestyle and encouraged her to do the same. Although she wanted more for her life, she had no concrete goals; except she knew she wanted to be a healthy role model for her daughter.

I listened to her, quietly praying and hoping I might be able to say something helpful. When she was done, I asked her simply, "Do you want to go to heaven?" to which she responded emphatically, "Yes! Yes, I do!" I said to her, "Well you are going to have to get some new friends."

Who do we recognize in this story? Eve. She is broken and she wants a new beginning. She wants to find grace and unconditional love. She understands very deeply within her own heart that her fulfillment as a woman is based on this truth, even if she goes about it in the wrong way. The woman in this story was Catholic, so I asked her when she had last made a good confession. It had been a long time…

After making a good confession, she decided to ask her current husband if he would go to counseling with her and consider going to church. Regretfully, she shared that he really wanted nothing to do with saving the marriage. He said "no" to counseling and "no" to building a spiritual foundation for their marriage. "In fact, he just laughed in my face," she said.

For a marriage relationship to be successful, openness to grace and effort on the part of both the woman and the man are necessary. Both, as individual persons, must grow in their own sense of personal dignity and responsibility for themselves and then for each other. Without this, neither can truly love or become a sincere self-gift to the other. Unfortunately, the opposite too often happens, and the other person is reduced to an object or someone to possess or control. This, St. John Paul II says, cannot happen.

> **The matrimonial union requires respect for and a perfecting of the true personal subjectivity of both of them.** *The woman cannot become the "object" of "domination" and male "possession."*[88]

Sadly, this woman's second marriage also failed. It failed because she married someone who did not want the best for her as a person. She allowed herself to be used because she did not want to be alone. She accepted the lie that without a man she was alone. The truth was she was not alone. She had God and she had herself. That meant she was enough.

This woman went on with her life, putting God and her daughter in first place. She found the acceptance and confidence that she longed for in a relationship with Jesus. She promised herself that she would never leave God again, especially for a relationship that offered her no lasting future. She wanted God in her life as number one.

"She wanted God in her life as number one."

This was a whole new way of looking at her life. She did, in fact, meet someone several years later. After the third or fourth date, she asked him if he was willing to go to church with her. She also told him, quite nervously, where she was at with her faith. She was looking for someone who wanted to share that part of her life as well. After laying it all out on the table, she was surprised and quite filled with joy to find out that he was more than willing to take a look at the Catholic faith. He joined the RCIA program and did become Catholic. Their shared faith and mutual love for each other equipped them to equally enter into their married life. Together with grace, they were both able to say "yes" to God and to each other.

> **...equality...is both a gift and a right deriving from God the Creator... only the equality resulting from their dignity as persons can give to their mutual relationship the character of an authentic** *"communio personarum"* **[communion of persons].**[89]

In a true marriage, the woman becomes the best person she can be. This is true for both the woman and the man because they are free to become all that their Creator intends as persons. It is also by God's grace and their effort, *that their marriage relationship becomes an authentic communion of persons.* The unique gifts and talents that they each have are to be shared freely with each other and their family. Thus together, side by side, they develop and live life in a communion of friendship in which each is able to make a sincere gift to the other. In this personal gift of self, they do not diminish each other, but, in fact, do just the opposite. They affirm and build each other up, discovering fully who they are through their sincere gift of self.

> **A human being, whether male or female, is a person, and therefore, "the only creature on earth which God willed for its own sake"; and at the same time this unique and unrepeatable creature "cannot fully find himself except through a sincere gift of self."[90]**

Side by side, created as male and female, they are both willed by God for their own sake. Each, as a unique and unrepeatable creature, can only fully find themselves in becoming a gift to the other. The highest form of friendship is this type of self-gift, whereby a person desires and does what is truly the best for the other. This type of friendship is the foundation of Christian marriage. For Christ loved us and showed us what it means to love someone by laying down your life for them. This is the way we are to love each other, first in our marriage, then with our children, families, and all others. The couple mentioned above married a year later. They were able to have a really happy marriage because of the gift of their faith and the ability to practice the virtues of mutual respect and kindness toward each other. They also were committed to loving each other well. This type of love means that we are willing to be kind and tender, forgiving faults and weaknesses, as well as—and most importantly—putting the needs of the other first. So side by side, as man and woman, we can live our lives in a peaceful union that reflects Christ's love for his Church.

St. John Paul II's teaching not only encompasses marriage and family life but the life of the Church and all spheres of society.

> ***These words of Genesis*** **refer directly to marriage, but**

> **indirectly** *they concern the different spheres of social life:* **the situations in which the woman remains disadvantaged or discriminated against by the fact of being a woman.**[91]

St. John Paul II's teachings focus on any situation where the woman is at a disadvantage by the fact of being a woman. In many first-world nations, women have rights, so it may not seem that women are often at a disadvantage. However, there are still many problems that women face even in the more advanced nations, where abuse and discrimination often take place in the home, workplace, and society. In third-world nations, many more women also live in poverty and are not allowed an education or freedom to better themselves or their children.

The New Beginning (First Gospel)

God does not want your life to be destroyed by sin and evil. That is why God promised a Savior right away after the fall, to bring hope to the human race. God's promise says, "I will put enmity between you and the woman, between your seed and hers; He shall bruise your head, and you shall bruise his heel" (Gen 3:15). God makes "the woman" and her offspring enemies with the devil and his offspring. This means that there is going to be a fight. "The woman" and her offspring will suffer greatly, yet ultimately be victorious. Love always wins.

> **The Book of Genesis attests to the fact that sin is the evil at man's "beginning" and that since then its consequences weigh upon the whole human race. At the same time it contains** *the first foretelling of victory* **over evil,** *over sin.*[92]

So the question is, who is the woman of Genesis 3:15? It is Mary, "full of grace." Who is her offspring? Jesus Christ, who ultimately defeats sin and evil by shedding His blood. God never gave up on Adam and Eve. God never gives up on us either. Never. Mary is the first one to bear witness to this new beginning since it first takes place in her. Mary, who is conceived "full of grace," is a "new creation." We also see other significant times when emphasis is placed on "the woman." When Jesus begins his public ministry at the wedding feast of Cana, He says, "O woman, what have you to do with me? My hour has not yet come" (Jn 2:4). As Jesus is dying, He says, "Woman, behold your son" (Jn 19:26). Finally in the last book of the Bible, Revelations: "A great sign appeared in heaven, a woman clothed with the sun, with the moon under her feet, and on her head a crown of 12 stars" (Rev 12:1). This all takes place to show us the strong emphasis that God is placing on "the woman" and her mission to humanity. "The woman" is the Virgin of Nazareth.

> ***Mary is the witness to the new "beginning"*** **and the "new creation" (cf. 2 Cor 5:17), since she herself, as the first of the redeemed in salvation history, is "a new creation": she is "full of grace."**[93]

By the promise of God's word (Gen 3:15), Mary is conceived without sin; full of grace. She is like a spring of fresh water that will ultimately bring life back to fallen humanity. Herein lies the basis for the teaching of Mary's Immaculate Conception. Every other person born after the fall is born in a state of being separated from God by original sin. God kept Mary free from original sin in anticipation of her becoming the Mother of Jesus. The new beginning for humanity takes place in her and through her. Jesus, Who is God, comes to us through Mary, who is human, and "makes all things new." The new and definitive Covenant in the redeeming blood of Christ has its beginning in "the woman."

> **The Covenant begins with a woman, the "woman" of the Annunciation at Nazareth. Herein lies the absolute originality of the Gospel: many times in the Old Testament, in order to intervene in the history of his people, God addressed himself to women, as in the case of the mothers of Samuel and Samson. However, to make his Covenant**

with humanity, he addressed himself only to men: *Noah, Abraham, and Moses.* **At the beginning of the New Covenant, which is to be eternal and irrevocable, there is a woman: the Virgin of Nazareth. It is a *sign* that points to the fact that "in Jesus Christ"** *"there is neither male nor female"* **(Gal 3:28).**[94]

The New Covenant in Jesus Christ, made possible through Mary's motherhood, makes way for every Eve to have a new beginning. St. John Paul II wanted us to know that Eve and Mary are joined under the name of woman. Eve is that woman who, as the mother of all the living, was present at the beginning of creation. Mary is that "woman" who was present at the new beginning of the New Covenant between God and humanity, which is to be eternal and irrevocable. Mary gives us an insight into the dignity and vocation of women, for Mary takes us back to the original position of woman before sin entered into the picture. Mary is the beginning of the New Covenant, for through her obedience and cooperation with God, she welcomes the promised Messiah, Jesus Christ.

Today this battle continues on for "the woman" and her offspring which includes you and me and all who "keep the commandments of God and bear testimony to Jesus" (Rev 12:17). If we say "yes" to God, keep the commandments, and bear witness to Jesus Christ, we will become a part of the solution.

Your witness as a woman will affect others and their ability to say "yes" to God. If you say "no" to God's plan for your life, it will make it more difficult for other people to find God. In finding God, they will find their purpose and their place, their spot, in God's plan. God's plan is for the peace and salvation of the world, giving us certain proof from God that we are worth the fight.

God sends the Angel Gabriel to Mary in order to establish a New Covenant with humanity. St. John Paul II reminds us that all the Old Testament Covenants were made with a man. But the new and eternal Covenant begins with "the woman," re-establishing not only the relationship that humanity had lost with God after the fall but also the unity and friendship between man and woman that were lost with that first sin. With the coming of Christ, the possibility of a righteous, very good, excellent relationship with God is restored, along with a possibility of a new relationship between men and women. Jesus Christ came not only to save us from eternal death—Jesus came to deliver us from bad relationships.

In Christ the mutual opposition between man and woman—which is the inheritance of original sin—is essentially overcome. "For you are all *one* in Jesus Christ," St. Paul will write [Gal 3:28].[95]

Jesus Christ wants to establish you in right relationships. This includes your relationships with God and with all the people in your life. The Covenant that God began with Mary was also for you and for me, to help us to have a new beginning. Mary is the new beginning for each person because she is the first person that God called upon to help Him to get things turned around after Adam and Eve messed up. She is the new beginning for women because, as a woman, she shows us how God values and thinks about women. She also shows us how we can honor God by graciously allowing Him to have His spot in our lives—that is, in our hearts.

Forming a new identity is essential for everyone because how we think is how we act. If we believe in God's love for us, we can also come to accept our own dignity, worth, and value. This helps us to become the person that God created us to be, having a chance at a new beginning no matter where life has taken us. If we can come to accept our own dignity and value, we can come to accept the dignity and value of others as well. This brings hope and peace to a broken world.

God has high standards and calls all people to live life based on those standards, the Ten Commandments. Even if it seems impossible, God is patient and brings us along if we want to do the right thing. That's why it is so important to pray and lean into grace. We might mess up a bit, or a lot. Life is messy. But God is the expert at the cleanup job. That is why God sent Jesus to show us how to live. God believes in us.

It's easier to do the right thing if we believe it is worth it or, even more importantly, if we believe *we are worth it.* I remember working with a senior in high school, eighteen years old, who was struggling with the virtue of chastity. The man that she was having a bad relationship with was already married. She had let herself fall in love with him even though she knew it was all wrong. Finally, completely frustrated with herself and the situation she had fallen into, she came to me and said, "It is over—I mean it this time!" She had come to the point where she realized that this was not love: "I need to take control of my life, go to confession, end this relationship, and start my life over!" She did start over with the support of others, the grace of her faith in Christ, forgiveness, and hope that she could begin again. She found her new beginning.

> ***Mary* means, in a sense, a going beyond the limit spoken of in the Book of Genesis (3:16) and a return to that "beginning" in which one finds the "woman" as she was intended to be in *creation,* and therefore in the eternal mind of God: in the bosom of the Most Holy Trinity. Mary is "the new beginning" of the *dignity and vocation of women,* of each and every woman.[96]**

God gives you the self-worth and confidence to get through life doing the right thing if you let Him help. No one has the power to take you away from God's plan for your life unless you let them. Keep believing in God. Keep believing in yourself. One of the ways God works in your life to overcome sin and broken behavior is through other people who have worked on making good, healthy decisions in their relationships. God gives you these people who can become your friends and mentors, teaching you how to think about life and how to relate to others, especially if you want to find your purpose and become the person God calls you to be.

Are you more like Eve or Mary? I remember this story about a friend who was concerned about another friend's potentially hazardous dating relationship. Concerned for her well-being, he asked, "So when you are with him, are you more like Eve or Mary?" to which she simply blushed and said, "Well, that is a good question." Later, when out on a date with Mr. Potential Hazard, she asked, "What are your future goals?" He replied, "Um, I do not know. How about you?" "Well, I want to become a saint!" was her quick reply, to which he emphatically responded, "I cannot help you with that."

I love this story because it shows how this young woman wanted more for her life than a boyfriend on her arm. She wanted God and the life that was meant to be hers. She also knew that meant dating someone who shared her goals and values, who would help her to become the person God made her to be. God wants you and me to seek Him with all our hearts. If we do, God will let us find Him. The people and things we make important in our lives will impact who we become. It is the wisdom of God that helps us to make good choices in our relationships. Good relationships with others who share our beliefs and values are mutually encouraging to all but also set us up for success in living our lives with purpose and meaning.

The question is, who will you choose to be like? Mary, a woman of grace, or Eve, who disregarded the Creator's commands to follow an unknown, dangerous path?

The truth is most women want to be like Mary. We are attracted to her courage, honesty, and virtue. Mary is good. She is a true heroine. She is strong, kind, brave, and humble. Most of all she is full of grace, which means pure love, real love, God's love. Due to our fallen nature, we tend to think we are more like Eve and that it's certainly not possible for us to be like Mary. Like the statues of her, Mary is always well-behaved with her hands folded in prayer, wise, calm, and radiantly beautiful. She does not seem realistic or even possible for the modern woman.

Yet we want and desperately need her, our spiritual mother. Think about it. Mary is a woman like us, yet she truly received the gift of Jesus into her heart and being. What does she do right after this great miracle occurs? She immediately goes off to help her elderly relative Elizabeth. It is as if the gift she has received is too much for her to contain. She must go and share it with another.

When she arrives at Elizabeth's door, she is welcomed by Elizabeth who, filled with the Holy Spirit, confirms Mary's Motherhood by saying, "Blessed are you among women, and blessed is the fruit of your womb!" (Lk 1:42) Even the babe in Elizabeth's womb confirms this truth for he is jumping for joy: "For behold, when the voice of your greeting came to my ears, the child in my womb leaped for joy" (Lk 1:44). Mary's response to this joyful greeting is a rich hymn of praise, "For he who is mighty has done great things for me!" (Lk 1:49)

Mary joyfully praises God because she sees that she is a little creature for whom the mighty God has done great things. She is completely amazed! By her actions, Mary is saying to everybody, but especially to women, "This is the level that God raises a little creature to!" Impossible! In bringing the joy of her Son and Savior (Lk 1:47), to the human race, she also reveals her great belief and joy. Mary can be trusted with the gift. Elizabeth discovers and shares in the belief in and joy of what Mary herself has already discovered, her dignity as a woman and her vocation. She came to Elizabeth, and she still comes to us today with Jesus.

> *...this is the discovery all of the richness and personal resources of femininity,* all the eternal originality of the "woman," just as God wanted her to be, a person for her own sake, who discovers herself "by means of a sincere gift

of self."[97]

Mary discovers who she truly is by making her life a sincere gift to God. As she came to Elizabeth years ago, she now comes to us to help us discover our own dignity. As our spiritual mother, she knows the depth of desire we each have to be cherished and welcomed. She knows well the pain and suffering in each human life. She also knows the great blessings that God desires to give you. She knows who you are called through faith to become. She wants each of us to achieve that. Every good mother wants her child to be successful and great. Mary wants that too and yet even more she wants us to be whole—that is, holy. God has blessed each of us with many gifts and talents and a purpose. But the greatest blessing God gave us was Jesus. Mary clearly knows her worth and yours, for the cost of our lives is the death of her beloved Child:

> **At the foot of the Cross Mary shares through faith in the shocking mystery of this self-emptying. This is perhaps the deepest *"kenosis"* [self-emptying] *of faith* in human history. Through faith the Mother shares in the death of her Son, in his redeeming death; but in contrast with the faith of the disciples who fled, hers was far more enlightened. On Golgotha, Jesus through the Cross definitively confirmed that he was the "sign of contradiction" foretold by Simeon. At the same time, there were also fulfilled on Golgotha the words which Simeon had addressed to Mary: "and a sword will pierce through your own soul also."**[98]

We can do nothing to earn our worth; it is a gift that has already been given to us by God. God gave Mary her life of grace. God gives us our life full of grace too. Mary said "yes" to this gift, and it raised her up to the heights of divine love within the heart of the most Holy Trinity. Wow, what a gift! That gift is for us as well. At Baptism, the waters of life are given to you and me, making it possible for us to enter into that same heart of God. Total access.

Mary's life and example of relating to God beckon every Eve to find the new beginning, her dignity and vocation. For Mary's life of grace points to the true dignity and calling of every woman. A discovery for each and every woman to find again and again.

***In Mary, Eve discovers* the nature of the true dignity of woman, of feminine humanity. This discovery must continually reach the heart of every woman and shape her vocation and her life.**[99]

The blessings that God showered upon Mary revealed the true dignity of woman. Each woman is continually offered grace by God so that she might also discover her dignity, worth, and purpose in Jesus Christ. If you are open to receiving that blessing, you will not be disappointed. If someone does not have your back, meaning the ability to know and want what is best for you, they are a potential hazard—a danger or a risk—because without grace they can actually lead you away from your ultimate life destiny: God. It is your responsibility to care for the life you have been given and to discover your life by first giving it back to God, as a gift, and then giving it to others. This life is short and is passing; the next life will count forever. You will be enough with grace, both in this life and in the next! God is faithful to us all, so that, in Mary, every Eve can go beyond the limits of this fallen world to find herself at a new beginning. Jesus Christ is the new beginning for each and every woman. This is why Jesus came from heaven, and He wants to talk to you!

Questions for Reflection
Chapter 4
In Mary, Every Eve Has a New Beginning

1. What are one or two takeaways from this chapter?

2. Christ was presented by Joseph and Mary in the temple to Simeon, a holy prophet who predicted that a sword would pierce Mary's heart. What has pierced your heart?

3. What old Eve habits do you have that need to go?

4. What new beginning are you looking for in your life? What lies or limitations will you have to set aside in order to become the woman you believe God created you to be?

Notes

Jesus Christ Is Talking to You (Jesus Christ)

Man's Redemption, foretold in Genesis, now becomes a reality in the person and mission of Jesus Christ, in which we also recognize *what the reality of the Redemption means for the dignity and vocation of women.*[100]

God Is on the Move ("They Marveled That He Was Talking with a Woman")

In Jesus Christ, no matter what has happened in your life, you can have a new beginning. What does the reality of the Redemption mean for the dignity and vocation of women? It means everything. For in Jesus Christ every loss that women's dignity has suffered is found and restored. Like the Samaritan woman, most of us are searching for love and self-worth, unaware that we already have infinite love and self-worth in Jesus Christ. Belief in Him gives us hope that we too might belong to God. In belonging we might become the person God has created us to be. It's our chance for a new beginning.

At the beginning of the Gospel of John, we see the evangelist John expressing the powerful Word of God. The Word, the second person of the Trinity, becomes the Incarnate Word, fully God, fully man. Yes, God in a Bod™, so that you and I could talk to Him. Jesus Christ came to us so that, through Him, we could find our place, our spot, in Him and, like Mother Mary, find a new beginning.

> **In the beginning was the Word, and the Word was with God, and the Word was God. He was in the beginning with God; all things were made through him, and without him was not anything made that was made. In him was life, and the life was the light of men. The light shines in the darkness, and the darkness has not overcome it. (Jn 1:1-5)**

I was a sophomore in college going on a Catholic retreat weekend. I had heard that this was a good retreat experience to grow in your faith. So I decided to go. At one point everyone was singing the words, "Be not afraid, I go before you always." The song leaders had motioned for us to raise our hands in praise as we were singing. Not me! I was afraid, so I kept my hands tight by my side, looking at everyone and wondering, "What is going on here?" Later that evening, everyone had gone to bed, but I was restless. It was after midnight when I went down into the chapel and sat on the floor. I was looking for quite a while at a picture of Jesus that was in front of the altar. "Jesus, is this true, all that is being said about you?" I found myself questioning and praying deeply, as I had never prayed before. "Jesus, are you really here with us?" My questions continued. Did the Word become flesh, actually becoming a baby who grew up, lived, taught, worked miracles, and then died on that Cross and rose again? Was there really a Jesus Christ and did He want to talk to me? I spent a long time in the chapel that night.

I was up early the next morning before the sun rose over the city. I decided to go outside to get some fresh air. As I looked at the beautiful sunrise shining over the skyline, I knew that I would never look at my life the same way again. I believed with all my heart that God was real and that He loved me personally. I knew that I had always been looking for Him. I did not realize that Jesus had been looking for me. So often as a child and in my young adult years, life had overwhelmed me. Sometimes I just did some really stupid things, or I was so embarrassed in a situation and felt so alone. Trying to figure out life with friends, boyfriends, careers and especially trying to figure out why people did what they did…it was all so much to do on my own.

Jesus is real. Believing that Jesus died sacrificially for me to make up for my faults and sins, and hearing story after story of what He had done for others convinced me. I can have the life God wanted me to have on earth and eternally with God, which seems just so good and exciting. Life on earth is never going to be easy. Jesus said we would have to die to ourselves and carry our cross. At the time, I wasn't sure about that part. I like to have fun, and it seemed that faith in God could become so serious. Yet this is the whole purpose for which Christ came, to reveal the love of God through that Cross of His. The people on the retreat who had shared their stories all had crosses, yet with Christ they still seemed so happy. What they were giving up to follow the Lord definitely made them more happy than unhappy, so I was in. I said "Yes."

The greatest blessing I received was having the faith I was taught from childhood confirmed in the deepest part of my heart. At the end of the retreat, I was given a Bible verse to help me to remember God's promise to me: "Behold, I am with you always, to the end of the age" (Mt 28:19). What a promise. I was not alone; this promise reminded me that my life was a forever gift that came from God alone. I could not earn my worth or get it from anyone else. I also was responsible for my life. In choosing to follow God, I also accepted grace. To be a follower of Christ meant that I would honor and trust Him with my life. It meant that I would do life as best as I could, trusting that He would work it all out in the end. I would say that Jesus believed in me and my worth more than I or anyone else ever could have. That's because Jesus Christ is God, and He knows what He is talking about!

It is universally admitted—even by people with a critical attitude towards the Christian message—that *in the eyes of*

> ***his contemporaries Christ became a promoter of women's true dignity...* At times this caused wonder, surprise, often to the point of scandal: "They marveled that he was talking with a woman" (Jn 4:27).**[101]

Jesus, or as I like to say, "God in a Bod™," came to restore woman's true dignity. While Jesus was living His life on earth, He revealed the truth about who God is and who we are. In a particular way, Jesus revealed the truth about women by the way He interacted with them, by what He said and by what He did. He clearly went against the status quo of the time, where women had few rights and to even talk to a woman alone, as a man, would be frowned upon. Jesus's attitude and teachings changed everything for women, from His own Mother to the little girl whom He raised from the dead (Mk 5:21-43), the prostitutes (Lk 7:38), and the outcast (Jn 4:4-26). All, without exception, were treated as He made them, in His own image and likeness. These very women, influenced by grace, will become great disciples of Jesus Christ, powerfully bearing witness to the truth that in Jesus Christ, "there is neither male nor female; for you are all one in Christ Jesus" (Gal 3:28).

It might be hard to believe that Jesus Christ is really who He says He is and that He wants to talk to you. Yet this is why Jesus came from heaven, to talk to ordinary people like us. History shows Jesus Christ really lived, was crucified, and had a following. Historian Flavius Josephus wrote one of the earliest non-biblical accounts of Jesus. The best way to know Jesus and to learn to recognize His voice is to talk to Him. Conversation with Jesus Christ is called prayer. Prayer works.

Jesus wants us to believe in the God of love. Love has called each one of us into existence. Jesus suffered and died for us so that in Him we could overcome all sin and become the real persons we so much need and desire to be, full of life and purpose. Above all Jesus came so we could be at peace in our own skin, our inner being at peace.

Seem impossible? Keep reading...

Having faith in Jesus means that we will have to put effort into growing and maturing in that belief. Much like our bodies have to be nurtured to have optimal physical, mental, and emotional health, our spiritual life, our soul, also has to be nurtured and fostered so we can grow and authentically develop as the human persons we were created to be. What we need to understand is that we are so much more than just a body; we are unique, unrepeatable persons, created by God with a united body and immortal soul. Jesus knows what your body and soul united should look like. Jesus knows who you really are. Jesus wants to encounter you so that you can discover your true worth and become the real you!

A young lady with whom I worked is a good example of the impact that an encounter with Jesus Christ can have. Her heart was still open to faith in God, even though her life was a sea of misery that made it difficult for her to grow and mature. A junior in high school, she came from a home with both parents, yet was lacking the guidance and loving affection that teenagers especially need. She did not much like herself or anyone else, especially her siblings. She was miserable, incredibly angry, and often took it all out on her little brothers. She wanted to act in a better way and have a happier future, but she was having a hard time figuring it out. I had been working with her for some time, teaching her about God and His unconditional love for her. It is extremely difficult for people to believe in God's love when there is not much love in their lives.

One evening she came to find me after a youth program. She was frustrated, visibly upset, and basically done with God. When I asked her what happened, she said that she had gone to confession, but did not feel better. She said that she had given God a chance, but nothing ever seemed to get better in her life. She was quitting. I asked her if she would like to sit down and talk for a minute. As I tried again to reassure her that belief in God and oneself takes time, I knew I was not getting through to her. Despite all of my best efforts, we were going to lose her. Discouraged and tired, I was ready to give up as well, when I glanced up and saw the crucifix on the wall behind her. At that moment, I was suddenly inspired by what I hoped was the Holy

Spirit. I jumped up, walked around her, and grabbed the crucifix off the wall. Then I put it in her hands. She looked at me and said, "What? What are you doing?"

I looked at her and said, "This is how much God loves you. What else does He have to do for you?" She said, "What do you mean?" I said, "Jesus died on this Cross for you, His feet were pierced for all the times that your feet or the feet of another have walked all over you or hurt you. His hands were pierced for all the times that you have been pushed away or taken a hit in your life. His head was crowned with thorns for all the mind games, the negative thoughts you think about yourself or others, the times when you judge yourself as never good enough." Yes, for all of the hurt and pain that life brings us, especially in our broken relationships with others, Jesus was whipped and beaten, for the Word of God teaches us that "by his stripes [wounds] we are healed" (Is 53:5).

As she looked upon the Cross, I could tell she was thinking about what was being said. In the quiet, I waited for her response. I was amazed when she silently started to cry. She had been so tough, sarcastic, and angry. Now, as she looked at Jesus on the Cross, her heart began to soften. Jesus was talking to her about what really mattered to her. I will never forget when she took the cross and moved it close to her heart. We just sat together in silence as she received the Gospel, the good news of Jesus Christ: "In the world you will have trouble. But take heart! I have overcome the world" (Jn 16:33). Her suffering eased through love, as only Jesus Christ can give. That is why Jesus came into this world—to love us, to conquer what we cannot, and to show us the way back to the Father. By that Cross of His, Jesus conquered all of the problems you have and all those of everyone else in the world. He came into this world as the Son of God, searching for our love and our brokenness. He took it all to that Cross of His so that you and I could be free!

At that moment I witnessed a young woman accept Jesus into her heart, and her life was changed forever. As she wiped her tears and blew her nose, she asked me, "Now what do I do?" I said, "How about you go to confession?" She said, "Well, I was just there." I said, "I think you left out the big one, that you have not believed in the love of the Son of God for you!" It is not enough to believe in God's love for everyone. We need to believe and accept that God loves us personally. Acceptance of this truth is what is called conversion, the turning of our small, bruised, broken hearts to the great loving heart of God. God accepts us just as we are with all our doubts and fears. There is never anything that we can do to earn His love and acceptance. God will not ever reject His own creature but, in fact, as the story of the prodigal son teaches (Lk 15), He waits patiently with much tenderness for us to return.

Father was still at the parish and met with her right away. She was able, through the Sacrament of Reconciliation, to encounter Jesus, to speak to Him about her sorrow for not believing in Him or herself. Without faith, it is difficult to become the person that we deeply want to be. She then received forgiveness and the affirming truth that she was wanted and loved by God. She belonged. The Sacrament of Reconciliation set her free to begin again. This all happens through the priest of Jesus Christ. Jesus Christ came to talk to us, to forgive us, and to set us free. We can have a new heart, a new beginning through Christ.

Jesus wants to talk to us and help us with our life on earth. God blessed this young lady with many graces and gifts from His own heavenly storeroom. I saw her life transformed as she learned how to see herself in a new way, becoming more and more her true self, exactly as God intended.

That is the power of this sacrament. Sacraments are given by God to give grace. You are enough with grace. People, especially Catholics who do not use this sacrament, are like children who have huge bank accounts with their parents, but for many different reasons never access the cash (grace) that has been freely given to them by God the Father through Jesus Christ.

The gift of God's love in Jesus Christ is much greater than the sin of Adam and Eve or anything we will ever have to face in this life. This is because the gift is God Himself. All the love and grace that we will ever need flow from Jesus Christ and that Cross of His.

> **For if the many died by the trespass of the one man [Adam], how much more did God's grace and the gift that came by the grace of the one man, Jesus Christ, overflow to the many. (Rom 5:15)**

Jesus instituted the sacraments when He began the Church. You can find the scriptural foundation for the Sacrament of Reconciliation in the Gospel of John, where Jesus gives the Apostles the power to forgive sin:

> **On the evening of that day, the first day of the week, the doors being shut where the disciples were, for fear of the Jews, Jesus came and stood among them and said to them, "Peace be with you." When he had said this, he showed them his hands and his side. Then the disciples were glad when they saw the Lord. Jesus said to them again, "Peace be with you. As the Father has sent me, even so I send you." And when he had said this, he breathed on them, and said to them, "Receive the Holy Spirit. If you forgive the sins of any, they are forgiven; if you retain the sins of any, they are retained." (Jn 20:19-23)**

What would it be like if our sins weren't forgiven? This is why Jesus came, to forgive us and set us free so that we could fly again. Without the grace to love and forgive others, we cannot fly; we actually become bound up in bitterness, pain, and unforgiveness. Instead of learning how to love and to be compassionate to those who are weak and vulnerable, we learn how to hate and to destroy ourselves and one another. God wants more for our lives and the lives of those whom we are to influence. "Truly, I say to you, as you did it to one of the least of these my brethren, you did it to me" (Mt 25:40). Jesus came to forgive us and free us from life's greatest problem, sin and all the mess it has made.

Jesus wants us to have a bigger perspective in our "little life." God's perspective. Jesus is the Alpha and the Omega, the beginning and the end. This means Jesus sees everything and everyone. Jesus sees the Samaritan woman when she comes to the well that day (Jn 4). He sees her whole life from beginning to end and knows her better than she knows herself. Jesus wants to forgive her and set her free. Jesus wants to talk to her!

Jesus has been waiting for this encounter with her for a long time. In fact, since the foundations of the world: "as He chose us in Him before the foundation of the world…He destined us in love" (Eph 1:4-5). She is one of the reasons He has come from heaven. She has an incredible destiny and Jesus Christ wants to talk to her about it.

While Jesus is resting at Jacob's well in the heat of the day, she comes to get water. She has no idea Whom she is going to bump into. She has come to get water at the hottest time of the day when no other women would be at the well, most likely because of her poor reputation. She is an outcast. The disciples had gone into town to get food. Jesus Christ, the Word made flesh, is waiting for her. God is on the move.

Jesus Christ sees you and me. Jesus is talking to you now, to each of us personally, and He is on the move. It does not matter if we have been talking with Him for a long time or if we are just getting started. Just as a person grows and matures into adulthood, Jesus wants us to grow and mature spiritually. Like the Samaritan woman coming to the well to get water, Jesus meets us where we are and wants to teach us about the things of God. Jesus is kind, sweet, and humble, not arrogant or prideful. Jesus is also very handsome and smart, the most powerful man that ever lived, holding all authority in heaven and earth (Mt 28:18). Most importantly Jesus is love, so if you have spent your life looking for love you can stop now. Jesus has taken care of that for you. Jesus gently leads the Samaritan woman to the awareness of who she is in light of God's existence.

Jesus does not begin by telling her who He is or addressing her lifestyle. Jesus begins by simply asking her for a drink of water. This strikes her as odd. First, she is a woman, and second, she is a Samaritan. Jews did not talk to Samaritans because of different customs and laws that forbade it. A rabbi talking to a Samaritan

"Jesus does not begin by telling her who he is or addressing her lifestyle."

woman at this period in history—this is just not going to happen. So when she says, "How is it that you, a Jew, ask a drink of me, a woman of Samaria?" (Jn 4:9) she is really saying, "I am amazed, blown away, that you would even talk to me!"

Jesus remains calm and friendly. To the woman's surprised question, "Why are you talking to me?" Jesus responds, "If you knew the gift of God and who is saying to you, give me a drink, you would have asked him, and he would have given you living water" (Jn 4:10). She, not skipping a beat, begins to ask Him about how He thinks He can get this water when He does not have a bucket or jar to get the water.

She is totally unaware of Who she is talking to and what He can do for her. She is worrying about a bucket! He can make a bucket. He can make water. This is how we are, too. Jesus wants to talk to us about the things of God, the divine, the spiritual. We have such a hard time because we are looking at things from a natural or human point of view. We think about worldly things, such as buckets, clothes, money, and cars. It's easy for us to overlook our spiritual side, which is as real as our own human nature. Our spiritual life needs to be developed because, in fact, it is our immortal soul that gives life to and animates our body. It is our immortal soul, comprised of our mind and will, which gives us our ability to reason and guides us in all of our choices in life. If our bodies and senses are leading us to follow every impulse, we are not free to choose the highest good, which is to love.

While Jesus is talking to her, she continues to go on about the well: "Sir, you have nothing to draw with, and the well is deep; where do you get that living water? Are you greater than our father Jacob, who gave us the well…?" (Jn 4:11-12) She is curious now and is asking the right questions, such as, "Who are you?" An important point to remember is that it is Jesus who is initiating this relationship, and it is Jesus who is drawing her to Himself. Jesus continues by saying, "'Everyone who drinks of this water will thirst again, but whoever drinks of the water that I shall give him will never thirst; the water that I shall give him shall become in him a spring of water welling up to eternal life.' The woman said to him, 'Sir, give me this water that I may not thirst, nor come here to draw' " (Jn 4:14-15).

Her response shows that she is definitely interested. Now that Jesus has her attention, He begins to teach her about the goodness of God that is within her reach. She is created for more. Jesus says, "Go, call your husband and come back" (Jn 4:16). By doing so Jesus is intentionally bringing up the deepest longings and desires of her heart: to love and be loved. She simply says, "I have no husband" (Jn 4:17). He says back to her, "What you say is true, for you have had five husbands and he whom you have now is not your husband" (Jn 4:18).

> **He was a witness of God's eternal plan for the human being, created in his own image and likeness as man and woman. He was also perfectly aware of the consequences of sin, of that "mystery of iniquity" [immoral behavior] working in human hearts as the bitter fruit of the obscuring of the divine image.**[102]

Jesus knew all about this woman that He met at the well, her whole life, good and bad. In that moment at the well, Jesus loved her with a pure love that was so attractive to her, a true love that met with the deepest desires of her heart. In that powerful acceptance, she is set free from all her attempts to find love in the wrong places. She can see that Jesus is a prophet, one who is sent from God. Jesus then speaks to her about true worship of God and later reveals to her His identity as the Messiah (Jn 4:23-25). This revelation is an example of the radical way Jesus interacted with women. Jesus amazes and challenges the women who become His disciples. The men also were amazed and perplexed at Jesus and the way He chose women, especially women who were considered to be sinners, to be His disciples.

> **At times this caused wonder, surprise, often to the point of scandal: "They marveled that he was talking with a woman" (Jn 4:27), because this behavior differed from that**

> of his contemporaries. Even Christ's own disciples "marveled."[103]

When the Apostles came back from shopping, they saw that Jesus was talking with a woman. They were in a sense scandalized. This sinful woman became a follower, a disciple of Jesus Christ. She is known as St. Photini. Through her testimony, many came to believe in Him (Jn 4:39). Jesus the Messiah revealed to her God's eternal plan for her life. In her personal encounter with Jesus Christ at the well, her life took a turn for the better. This encounter altered her destiny and the destiny of those who, through her witness, came to believe in Him. This is unbelievable, yet it is true. The possibilities are as true for me and for you. God is still on the move.

The bitter fruit that all women have endured and suffered since the fall is still happening today. Many women live quiet, desperate lives that are not at all what their Creator intended. When women, men, and children are cut off from grace, the divine image in them becomes obscured and darkened. This makes it very difficult for people to see each other—see in the spiritual sense. For without grace, we cannot love as God loves; we cannot see as God sees in the spiritual sense. In our brokenness, we become selfish and miserable.

Jesus also challenged the Pharisees on some of the religious customs of the time that discriminated against women. When asked by some of the Pharisees a question about a man's right to divorce his wife, Jesus simply states, "Have you not read that he who made them from the beginning made them male and female; and said, 'For this reason a man shall leave his father and mother and be joined to his wife, and the two shall become one'? So, they are no longer two but one. What therefore God has joined together, let no man put asunder" (Mt 19:4-6).

> **The principle of this "ethos," which from the beginning marks the reality of creation, is now confirmed by Christ in opposition to that tradition which discriminated against women. In this tradition the male "dominated," without**

> **having proper regard for woman and for her dignity, which *the "ethos"* of creation made the basis of the mutual relationships of two people united in marriage.**[104]

Christ affirmed that, from the beginning, God's gift of marriage, the union between a woman and a man, is indissoluble (Gen 2:24), meaning incapable of being dissolved, undone, or destroyed. This is because the "unity of the two" is a one-flesh union of body and soul. It is God who joins them interiorly, meaning spiritually, as well as physically, with their bodies. This means that sex and human love are holy to God. They are holy because they are the path to all human life and existence itself. The marital union reveals God's life and power when a couple conceives and brings a new little one that comes from the self-gift of both the man and the woman, a little bambino! The intimate life and love intended for the couple to share in reflect, above all, God's own inner life within the Trinity.

Because of sin, human love struggles to be a communion of love as the divine plan of God intended. Throughout history, beginning with the fall, we see the marital relationship tossed about in the darkness of lust, in which a person takes from the other, using them instead of loving them. Lust destroys love because to take is the opposite of love. Historically, lustful sin and pride led to the development of unfair laws that discriminated against women, resulting in husbands divorcing their wives for any reason whatsoever. The husband would simply write a divorce decree and the marriage was done, leaving the woman with little or no income to provide for herself and their children. This hardness of heart (Mt 19:8) is the bitter fruit that resulted from original sin. When the Pharisees bring up the teaching of Moses and the rights of men to be able to divorce their wives, Jesus reminds them of the rights of women, the dignity that was given to them by God from the beginning.

> **It is truly significant that in his important discussion about marriage and its indissolubility, in the presence of "the Scribes," who by profession were experts in the Law, Jesus**

> *makes reference to the "beginning."* **The question asked concerns a man's right "to divorce one's wife for any cause" (Mt 19:3) and therefore also concerns the woman's right, her rightful position in marriage, her dignity.**[105]

Christ begins to shed light on why Moses permitted divorce: "Because of the hardness of your hearts" (Mt 19:8), which is caused by their own sinfulness. Then Christ points them back to the original plan of the Creator when creating them male and female (Gen 2:24). When the disciples hear Jesus speaking about marriage in this way they say, "If such is the case of a man with his wife, it is not expedient [convenient] to marry" (Mt 19:10). In other words, they thought that, if men could not divorce their wives, it would be more advantageous for them not to marry at all. This is how bad it was—marriage and intimacy with one woman seemed impossible for the men. When I told this to my husband, he just laughed!

Christ gives wisdom, strength, and grace to married couples to enable them to preserve their union throughout the years, learning self-mastery as well as how to love and forgive each other. You are enough with grace.

A New Beginning (Women in the Gospel)

Jesus taught through His words, actions, and miracles how women should be treated with respect and honor. In reflecting on the dignity and honor that Jesus Christ gave to the various women encountered along His path, I felt grateful for and happy about what I saw God doing!

> **In all of Jesus' teaching, as well as in his behavior, one can find nothing which reflects the discrimination against women prevalent in his day. On the contrary,** *his words and works always express the respect and honor due to women.*[106]

In the Gospel of Luke 13:10-17, we hear about a woman with a stoop; she has been bent over for eighteen years. She is at the synagogue listening to Jesus teach. Jesus sees her and calls her over to Him. He says, "Woman you are freed from your infirmity." Then Jesus lays His hands on her and immediately she is made straight, and she starts praising God.

Some of the Pharisees at the temple become upset with Jesus because he healed her on the Sabbath. Jesus heals her. He completely changes her life. The Pharisees are so small-hearted that they become indignant, calling Jesus out for working on the Sabbath, the day of rest. At the same time, everything has changed for this woman because of Jesus. Think about it! Physically she is healed, and mentally her whole outlook on life is different. Most importantly, she is healed spiritually. Her position as a woman, her very dignity, and her existence take on a whole new beginning.

Jesus Christ gives her a new identity as a "daughter of Abraham." God not only has compassion on her because she is bent over, but He also has compassion on her social status as a woman. How do we know that? Jesus calls her a daughter of Abraham. How sweet His words must have sounded in her ears. Jesus defended her honor, giving her a new identity that places her, a woman, as a person "side by side" with the men, the sons of Abraham. This "new beginning" in her life is totally orchestrated by God. It also sends a clear message to the Pharisees as well as the rest of humanity: God cares about little old women with stoops!

The woman with a stoop is called a "daughter of Abraham" (Lk 13:16), while in the whole Bible the title "son of Abraham" is used only of men. Walking the *Via Dolorosa* to Golgotha, Jesus will say to the women: "Daughters of Jerusalem, do not weep for me" (Lk 23:28). This way of speaking to and about women, as well as his manner of treating them, clearly constitutes an "innovation" [a new method, idea] with respect to the prevailing custom at that time.[107]

God cares about all women who have suffered from many

different forms of injustice. Jesus knows the truth about each person, and each life is ultimately in the care of God. In God's perfect timing (not ours), God will restore and re-establish each one of us, so it is important to remain vigilant. The woman with the stoop never lost hope, going to the synagogue for eighteen years. I am sure she is thankful she kept her hope.

Let's go back to Jesus, the Pharisees, and the prevailing customs of the time. The customs do not prevent Jesus from doing the right thing for the woman with the stoop. Because Jesus healed on the Sabbath, the religious leaders became angry and annoyed. They said, "There are six days when work ought to be done; come on those days and be healed, and not on the Sabbath day" (Lk 13:14). They missed what God was doing because their hearts were small. A heart full of love comes from God. Prayer is our relationship with God; it is the prayer of the heart that changes us and makes our hearts like God's. Prayer is also powerful, for it brings many blessings—even miracles—to those who believe. For the woman with a stoop, her heart, her reason for being at the synagogue brought about a big healing for her. Where were the Pharisees' hearts at?

Jesus calls them out on it! He says, " 'You hypocrites! Does not each of you on the Sabbath untie his ox or his donkey from the manger and lead it away to water it? And ought not this woman, a daughter of Abraham whom Satan bound for eighteen years, be loose from this bond on the Sabbath day?' At this, all of his adversaries were put to shame; and all the people rejoiced at all the glorious things being done by him" (Lk 13:15-17). Jesus is saying to them, "You care for your animals on the Sabbath, should you not care more for a woman, a daughter of Abraham? In fact, she is worth more than your animals, for she is a human being; she is a daughter, your sister, and most importantly, my child."

> **Christ is the one who "knows what is in man" (cf. Jn 2:25)—in man and woman. He knows *the dignity of man*, his *worth in God's eyes*. He himself, the Christ, is the definitive confirmation of this worth.**[108]

"Definitive" means done or taught decisively with authority. In becoming man, Christ confirms the worth of a human being. The Lord Jesus Christ alone, as the Son of God, possesses the true knowledge of the worth of each and every human being (Mt 28:18-20).

The question is, where are our hearts? Are we open to belief in God, and do we accept Jesus's authority as Lord? I was not sure why this was important or even stood out until one night at dinner with a colleague, I was questioned point blank, "Why do you call Him 'Lord'?" I said, "Who do you mean? Jesus?" She said, "Yes, Jesus. It sounds so exaggerated." I said, "Well, I call Him Lord because He is!" "Jesus is Lord" is an immensely powerful statement that can only be proclaimed by the power of the Holy Spirit. For "no one can say Jesus is Lord except by the Holy Spirit" (Rom 10:9-13).

Why was the woman with the stoop at the synagogue that day? Perhaps, despite all of her long sufferings, she still had faith and a deep hope in the Lord. What is so wonderful is that on that day, in God's perfect timing, Jesus sees her, calls her, and then heals her. Jesus Christ sees you too. Like the woman with a stoop, Jesus wants to talk to you, heal you, and set you free!

> **Jesus' attitude to the women whom he meets in the course of his Messianic service reflects the eternal plan of God, who, in creating each one of them, chooses her and loves her in Christ (cf. Eph 1:1-5). Each woman therefore is "the only creature on earth which God willed for its own sake."** *Each of them from the "beginning" inherits as a woman the dignity of personhood.*[109]

Each woman is willed for her own sake and is called to a unique, exclusive, personal relationship with God, from Whom each one inherits the dignity of personhood. This is what it means to be willed by God for one's own sake, as a person. When I was giving a retreat for men and women together, some of the men asked me what I was going to talk about. I said, "How Jesus Christ treated women." Then some of the women present also asked me what I was going to talk about, and I said, "How Jesus Christ treated men!"

Entrusted to His Heart (The Woman Caught in Adultery)

God did not create the woman to become a mere object or possession of the man. Yet, this often happens: the woman who is created by God to both give and receive love in a mutual relationship often becomes someone to control, manipulate, or use to gratify his needs. Instead of helping her to become the unique person she is created to be with her own unique gifts and talents, the man lords himself over her often in an unfair or selfish way. As one woman stated in reference to the harmful relationship she was caught up in, "This is not love!"

> **Consequently each man must look within himself to see whether she who was entrusted to him as a sister in humanity, as a spouse, has not become in his heart an object of adultery…an object of pleasure, of exploitation.**[110]

Men and women must look into their own hearts to see if their hearts are full of lust for power and control or filled with God's grace and goodness. It is very easy to take advantage of another person in order to get what you want. However, even God does not force us to do things against our will. To take someone as an object, using them or forcing them to do what you want, is not what the Creator intended for man or woman.

> **…in the light of the New Testament and Tradition, …Adam and Eve, were constituted in an original "state of holiness and justice." This grace of original holiness was "to share in…divine life." … As long as he remained in the divine intimacy, man would not have to suffer or die. The inner harmony of the human person, the harmony between man and woman, and finally the harmony between the first couple and all creation, comprised the state called "original justice."**[111]

After the fall of Adam and Eve, men could not relate to women the way they did at the beginning, when, without having sinned, Adam and Eve were able to live in harmony with each other and all of creation. Remember, sin diminishes the human person. After the fall they both experienced lustful (immoral, immodest) desires. These desires produced shame in both of them, as they were no longer in control of themselves. Simply put, their sensual appetites were out of control. For men, this sin can mean, "I want what I want, even if I have to take what I want. Even if it hurts the other who is supposed to be my entrusted companion, my sister, my wife." The man of lust sees her as an object, as something to possess or own for himself.

She would still long to be wanted, loved, and held in esteem as we see in the Scriptures: "Yet, your desire shall be for your husband, and he shall rule over you" (Gen 3:16). This consequence of the original sin and all following sin was especially harmful to women. For even today, in many countries and places, women and children are treated as less than human persons or even less than animals. Dominated and discarded by men and social structures, women can be easily dismissed or divorced, with no social status, education, or means to earn an income. They also can be brutally treated, even murdered, without anyone having to answer for it. Despite all of this, Jesus Christ enters into the historical situation of each woman and man.

Remember, God created women and men in His own image and likeness, as persons. Whatever you do to another person you do to God. This is something to think about. In the end, God will take care of every wrong, and everyone will have to give an account of themselves. This is why Jesus Christ came into the world. He came to save us from our sins and our bad relationships, to teach us how to act toward each other as God intended, and to teach us what it is to honor God by how we treat each other, as men and women, sons and daughters, brothers and sisters.

Jesus enters *into the concrete and historical situation of women*, a situation which is *weighed down by the inheritance*

> ***of sin.*** **One of the ways in which this inheritance is expressed is habitual discrimination against women in favor of men. This inheritance is rooted within women too.**[112]

Wow! When I read this for the first time, I just could not believe someone was saying it and that someone was St. John Paul II. The inheritance of sin is expressed in habitual discrimination against women in favor of men, and this inheritance is also in women themselves. This means that not only do men tend to favor other men before women, but even women themselves tend to favor men before women. Finally, someone has said it and has connected this fault to the inheritance of sin. The equality of human relationships has been compromised in favor of men. Habitual discrimination is rooted in both men and women. This is also why Jesus came to overcome discrimination in all its forms but especially between men and women.

A powerful example of this is found in John's account of the woman caught in adultery (8:3-11). Her accusers catch her, drag her out into the streets, and bring her to the temple where Jesus is teaching a crowd of people. They use this woman in an attempt to trap Jesus. She has been caught in the very act of adultery. First, let's remember that one cannot commit adultery alone. Yet she alone must die. If someone sins or neglects to do the right thing for another person, they contribute to the wrong being done. Second, even if they are blind to their fault, accusing the other while negating the part they played, God does not turn a blind eye. This is what was happening in this situation of the woman caught in adultery. Jesus will not be trapped, for He is the Son of God, and He sees everything. He will address the woman and her sin, but first He will deal with the accusers and their sin. Jesus defends her.

> **...first he *evokes an awareness* of sin in the men who accuse her in order to stone her, thereby revealing his profound capacity to see human consciences and actions in their true light. Jesus seems to say to the accusers: Is not this woman,**

for all her sin, above all a confirmation of your own transgressions, of your "male" injustice, your misdeeds? This truth is *valid for the whole human race*....[it] is repeated in countless similar situations in every period of history.[113]

This type of unfair treatment, at times the condemnation of women by men, has happened and continues to happen in different societies and cultures to different degrees throughout the world. The capacity for men, as well as women, to favor men is as true today as it was years ago. The eye-opener for me was coming to the understanding that the unfair and even harsh treatment of women is also directly caused by women themselves. It is especially important for each woman (and man) to understand that this tendency comes as a result of original sin and has been overcome in Christ. We must see the problem—sin—and embrace the solution—life in Christ!

The awareness of this tendency to treat women unfairly or to favor men before women is important for those who are on the quest to help build a civilization of unity, peace, and love. Unity is possible within every aspect of our lives, but not without a fight. With grace, each woman as a person is responsible to uphold her own dignity, for her thoughts and her actions belong to her, even if others disregard her. Yet, St. John Paul II is also saying that men as a whole are given the task of defending and protecting women's dignity. Women and men together are called by God to look out for and defend each other based on the dignity of their shared humanity.

On the basis of the eternal "unity of the two," *this dignity directly depends on woman herself, as a subject responsible for herself, and at the same time it is "given as a task" to man.*[114]

That is where the hope lies, in women's knowledge that God is for them and that they are responsible for their own lives. Each woman as a free person must ask the question, "What am I responsible to God for in this situation? What am I in control of in this situation?" Women must be formed to be aware of their fundamental worth and dignity, aware and free, understanding that they should make their choices with freedom and strength. Women need to choose the good for themselves and those they serve, not making up excuses: "Well I just can't help myself…it's just so hard…I do not know why I do this." Women must choose to act, doing the next right thing as grace guides, especially in times of turmoil and trial, for that is what God wants and even expects of His daughters.

"Do not sin again," Jesus says to the woman caught in adultery. This is what Jesus is saying to all women: "Do not let another's sin cause you to sin. Sin hurts you; it diminishes the real you." Jesus intends and wants you to live a life of integrity and wholeness. You are in command of your own ship (your interior soul) at all times. You always have a choice. So do not ever throw your life away, despair, or give up on yourself. Jesus wants you to know that you are given the gift of being a person made with great dignity. You are always responsible for yourself and your actions, even if others have harmed you or treated you unjustly. This is where freedom comes in. You always have a choice.

…and Jesus was left alone with the woman standing before him. (Jn 8:9)

How many times does this happen to a woman? She is left all alone with such great burdens, shame, and terrible regret. It seems at times that even God expects more from women because in many ways God made women strong—strong in faith and strong in love. Now all of her accusers are gone, and the woman caught in the very act of adultery is left alone with no one there…but Jesus. At the end of every day, we are left alone with Jesus. At the end of our lives, it will be the same—we will be alone with Jesus.

In another instance of being alone with Jesus, a strong-willed, beautiful young woman was attending college, living in the dorms with friends, and like most students, trying to figure out her future. She went out with her girlfriends one night and whether she drank too much or had something put in her drink, she doesn't really remember. Somehow she was separated from her friends and taken advantage of that night. As a result, she became pregnant. Not willing to end the life of her baby, she courageously carried her baby to term while attending school and working.

> **...but she alone pays, and she pays *all alone!* How often is she abandoned with her pregnancy, when the man, the child's father, is unwilling to accept responsibility for it? And besides the many "unwed mothers" in our society, we also must consider all those who, as a result of various pressures, even on the part of the guilty man, very often "get rid of" the child before it is born. "They get rid of it": but at what price? ...Normally *a woman's conscience does not let her forget* that she has taken the life of her own child...**[115]

All alone, she took responsibility for her life and the life of the child within her. She could have chosen to end the pregnancy, but at what price? She would never be able to forget that she had taken the life of her own child, a child that was conceived within her at such a price. To know that a life is within you is one of the greatest privileges of being a woman. Normally no woman alive can ever harm the child within her. It is this sensitivity to the dignity of human life that makes women strong. When the pregnancy was discovered, she freely chose the difficult path of giving life.

Her decision to protect the life of her child strengthened other young women who also found themselves with child. It also brought joy to her friends and family who held a baby shower for her during which her baby received more than thirty-two pairs of shoes. What a welcome to this new little one. Her plan was to keep her baby.

Once the baby was born and placed in her arms, she sensed God had another plan in which He gently seemed to say, "This is not your baby." It took her several days to come to terms with the reality of the demands of raising a child as a single mother. As adoption became the clear answer, finding the right family was all that mattered to her. She knew that it would have to be a family who would raise her child in the Catholic faith, not just in words, but with love and devotion—that was her number one! After that were all of the other essentials: family vacations, soccer, and good schools. In the whole line-up of couples looking to adopt a baby, only a few met her stiff requirements. An interview with one of the couples was set up. They were a faith-filled couple who were not able to have a child of their own. They had tried to adopt for many years. Her baby would become the answer to their prayers and their longing for a child of their own.

The man who took advantage of her, a woman with the potential of motherhood, at the same time also diminished his own manhood and potential for fatherhood. He diminished his manhood by going against the very dignity of what it means to be a man, a husband, and a father. This definition of what a man or woman should be comes from God, Who has the attributes of both fathers and mothers.

> **…the woman was entrusted to the man with her feminine distinctiveness, and her potential for motherhood…The man was also entrusted by the Creator to the woman—they were *entrusted to each other as persons* made in the image and likeness of God himself. This entrusting is the test of love, spousal love…This test is meant for both of them—man and woman—from the "beginning."**[116]

It was God Who brought the child into existence. God, Who is good, does not ever make mistakes. God has entrusted the motherhood of women to women themselves and to men. Women and men are entrusted to one another and are both responsible before God for themselves and each other. This is the test of love. Will we do the right thing for the sake of the other person who is like us, a person? When the baby was conceived, the young woman did what was right in a very wrong circumstance: she defended her motherhood by protecting the life of her child. In giving life she found her own dignity, for to go against her nature would have only brought more pain and destruction.

When women and men choose to "get rid of it," they and their child pay an extremely high price. God always loves and forgives us when we ask for forgiveness. The remorse and regrets in life can be so overbearing; that is why we need God's mercy and peace so that we can go on. Jesus can and will defend you in every circumstance. It does not matter who you are or how far along in life you have come. With God's help, you can find the grace and strength to overcome weakness and begin again to take responsibility for your life.

We are created for love and to give love. The potential for life is always present in the gift that God has given woman and man in their capacity for motherhood and fatherhood. It is this very gift that reminds us that we are responsible for ourselves and each other. Brokenness and sin are not what God wanted for our human relationships. When God created them, male and female, it was with the potential to love each other selflessly and heroically as this young woman loved her child, even willing to consider adoption if that was best for her child. She cooperated with God in bringing a new life into the world. A life that would be lived on earth and forever eternally. A life created in both God's image and likeness and in hers. A bambino sent straight from the heart of God.

Christ logically appeals to man's responsibility.... The dignity and the vocation of women—as well as those of men—find their eternal source in the heart of God.[117]

Life itself is a calling to a deeper life lived with God. Our dignity and vocation as women and men can only be found in the heart of God. For that is where our very existence has sprung forth from. The call to be responsible before God as mothers and fathers of our own children comes from the heart of God, who is both a mother and a father to His children (Is 49:15, Dt 32:6). Both women and men can succeed in fulfilling their high calling but only with God's grace and our effort. This is what we were born to do.

Yet all women and men are subjected to trials and temptations, which aim to lure them into the deadly trap of sin, which causes so much harm to the human person and all of their relationships. This painful division can be found in families, society, and even the Church. Whenever sin happens it causes a negative ripple effect of division and hatred that is passed down from generation to generation. Only in Christ is it overcome.

A woman's heart has been made for unity with a longing that comes to her as a gift from the heart of God. This gift from the heart of God helps her to be open to receiving and giving love. Yet loving another can be very hard in a world that has been broken by sin. She might reason to herself, "If I just take contraception, it will be all right," or "If this relationship does not work, I will move on to another man," or If I get pregnant, I can just have an abortion," all for the sake of some kind of unity…to maintain the relationship and to avoid shame. She just wants to keep the relationship. These all might seem like reasonable answers for the problems women face in relationships or potential motherhood, but relationships based on this reasoning will never satisfy the deepest longing of her heart.

Lust is the strong desire that leads us to use someone as an object and then throw them away. Whether it is in a sexual relationship or some other type of human relationship, lust can lead you to take something that does not belong to you. What we do with our bodies matters, because it is through our bodies that we communicate as a person the intentions of our soul. We are made to love as God loves. We will either love as God loves, or we will lust. So pay attention to your actions and those of others because you cannot love someone and use them at the same time.

St. Augustine speaks about it this way, "Even a thief does not want to be stolen from."[118] This means that even if you are a thief and steal from or use others, you still do not want anyone to steal from or use you. This is because our dignity as human persons is deeply ingrained in us. It is also why we were made to love our neighbor as ourselves.

Life itself is a gift from God and at the same time a calling to a higher life. For God has entrusted us to each other, the man to the woman, the woman to the man, and the child to its parents. Every one of us has our own mother and father who have given us life within the Providence of God's plan. The woman, as well as the man, is entrusted always and everywhere, in every circumstance, to be a daughter or son, sister or brother, wife or husband, friend, and companion. We belong to each other. This is what it means to be human.

Women on a Mission (Guardians of the Gospel)

Did you ever notice that Jesus does not worry about what people think about Him? Jesus only cares about what is good and true: "They marveled that he was talking to a woman" (Jn 4:27). If Jesus did worry about what the disciples thought, He might not have many women followers. Jesus empowered and called women, from the very young to the very old, to love and follow Him. We have the opportunity to learn about and emulate Mary Magdalene, St. Maria Goretti, St. Joan of Arc, St. Catherine of Siena, Mother Teresa, and many more courageous women who heard God's call and said "yes."

> **They feel *"liberated" by this truth*, restored to themselves: they feel loved with "eternal love," with a love which finds direct expression in Christ himself. In Christ's sphere of action their position is transformed.**[119]

The Samaritan woman is sent off to evangelize a town. The woman with the stoop is healed of her stoop, but the bigger healing is her discovery of her true identity as a daughter of Abraham. Even the woman caught in the act of adultery becomes a gospel example, since Jesus convinces those who wished to kill her that they too have sinned and have fallen short. In the end, women who encounter the true person of Jesus Christ come to a deeper sense of themselves as persons. Like the Samaritan woman, they too will be able to take

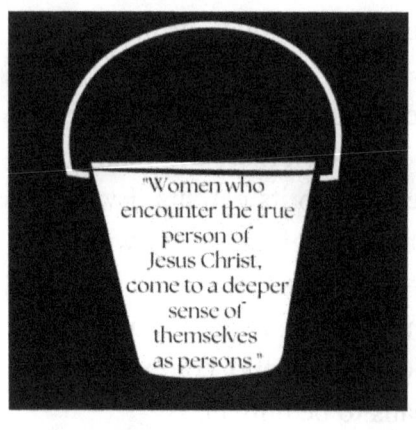

"Women who encounter the true person of Jesus Christ, come to a deeper sense of themselves as persons."

greater responsibility for their own lives and those entrusted to them.

***Jesus*—who knows that [the Samaritan woman at the well] is a sinner and speaks to her about this—*discusses the most profound mysteries of God with her.* He speaks to her of God's infinite gift of love, which is like a "spring of water welling up to eternal life" (Jn 4:14). He speaks to her about God who is Spirit, and about the true adoration which the Father has a right to receive in spirit and truth (cf. Jn 4:24). Finally he reveals to her that he is the Messiah promised to Israel (cf. Jn 4:26).**[120]

The Samaritan woman goes from being an outcast to a woman on a mission. Like many others, she had heard about a coming Messiah, but little did she know that this day she would actually meet the Messiah personally. Her personal encounter with Jesus Christ transformed her bitter, empty life. She goes out with her message of hope: "Come, see a man who told me all that I ever did. Can this be the Christ?" (Jn 4:29).

We must ask, what really happened at that well, between her and Jesus? Whatever happened, it really impacted her, it was a big deal, and she would make it hers, "He must be the Christ, for He knows all about me." Bottom line, Jesus convinced her that despite it all she was known and cherished by God. This awareness of faith gave her hope against hope that God was for her. She belonged. *When God is for you, nothing can stop you.* To believe means to belong; to belong means to gain access to your true identity and purpose in your Creator. With the forgiveness and freedom she found that day at the well in her encounter with Christ the Messiah, the Samaritan woman was ready to fly.

This is an event without precedent: that a *woman*, and what

is more a "sinful woman," becomes a "disciple" of Christ. Indeed, once taught, she proclaims Christ to the inhabitants of Samaria, so that they too receive him with faith (cf. Jn 4:39-42). This is an unprecedented event, if one remembers the usual way women were treated by those who were teachers in Israel; whereas in Jesus of Nazareth's way of acting such an event becomes normal.[121]

Jesus does something that has not ever been done for a woman, let alone a sinful woman. Jesus speaks with her about the deepest mysteries of God. In doing so, Jesus affirms her as a person who is capable of much more than the life she is living. Right away after her encounter with the Son of God, she begins to tell others about her encounter with the Messiah and all that has happened to her. She, the outcast, now becomes a "witness to hope" of the new beginning that only the Christ can bring. That is why Jesus as talking to her at the well. That is why Jesus is talking to you today.

Christ speaks to women about the things of God, and they understand them; there is a true resonance of mind and heart, a response of faith. Jesus expresses appreciation and admiration for this distinctly "feminine" response, as in the case of the Canaanite woman (cf. Mt 15:28).[122]

A woman's response of faith might look much different than a man's response. It's important that women are aware of their distinct ability to recognize and accept God's divine revelation of love. Jesus knows what is in the heart of each and every woman as seen in his encounter with the Canaanite woman whose daughter suffered from a demon. Remember this story? This mother's persistent plea for Jesus to help her daughter is grounded in an admirable persistence of both mind and heart as she firmly stands her ground, saying, "Yes, Lord, yet even the dogs eat the crumbs that fall from their master's table." While the disciples are annoyed with her cries, Jesus, who can see her heart, responds to her unshakable faith with warmth and affirmation,

"Oh woman, great is your faith! Let it be done for you as you desire." Instantly her daughter is healed (Mt 15:22-28). This Mama Bear teaches us that we too must be persistent in the midst of difficulty or opposition. If God does not answer our prayers right away, it may be that He wants to squeeze a little more faith out of us. We must always persevere, putting our faith in Him.

Jesus has a human heart that is divine and holy. It is not afflicted with the brokenness caused by original sin, hardness of heart, sinful desires, or preconceived notions about the rank and place of a woman. Women from all walks of life, like Mary, Martha, and the Canaanite woman, were drawn to His divine love. Women who were great sinners, such as the Samaritan woman and Mary Magdalene, were attracted to the force of that forgiveness and restoration that could only be found in the kind and gentle words of Jesus the Messiah. They were not forgotten, and neither are women today. Will we too recognize Christ speaking to us?

Jesus proved the great love of God by freely laying down His life. His darkest hour became our bright new morning. The Gospels make us aware that many women remained faithful to Christ at the foot of the Cross. The response of faith given by the Mother of God as well as the other women followers was much different than that of the Apostles. This response teaches women who they are and what they are capable of. For Mary and the women to stand with Christ under the Cross reveals the strength and love a woman is capable of with grace. This feminine response of faith is both heroic and necessary for the task that the Church faces today, to evangelize and build a Civilization of Love.

> ...*women were in the forefront at the foot of the Cross*, at the decisive moment in Jesus of Nazareth's whole messianic mission. John was the only Apostle who remained faithful, but there were many faithful women. Not only the Mother of Christ and "his mother's sister, Mary the wife of Clopas and Mary Magdalene" (Jn 19:25) were present, but "there were also many women there, looking on from afar, who

> had followed Jesus from Galilee, ministering to him" (Mt 27:55). As we see, in this most arduous test of faith and fidelity the women proved stronger than the Apostles. In this moment of danger, those who love much succeed in overcoming their fear.[123]

Those who love much succeed in overcoming their fears. At great cost, Jesus came into this world to love us and to conquer what we could not. The decisive moment in Jesus of Nazareth's messianic mission was the suffering that He courageously embraced for you and me. Jesus was able to overcome His fear because of His great love for the Father and His great love for us. This does not mean that it was easy for Him. Especially hurtful to Jesus were the wounds caused by those who betrayed and abandoned Him. The women who followed Jesus were able to remain with Him under the Cross because of their great faith and fidelity.

By that Cross of His, Jesus conquered all of the problems of the whole world. He came into this world as the Son of God, searching for human hearts that were open to God's mercy and love. In great love and anguish, Jesus died for us. Then they laid Him in a tomb.

Who Will Move the Stone? (First Witnesses of the Resurrection)

Mary Magdalene and the other Mary are the first to arrive at the tomb of Christ that Easter morning. They come with spices, intending to finish Jesus's burial rite. They are worried about who will move the heavy stone at the tomb, yet their concerns and anxieties do not stop them from trying to give Jesus the best they can. *It is their love, their devotion to Christ, that compels them to keep going.* The courageous women are rewarded for their faithfulness. When they arrive at the tomb, they are greeted by an angel and an earthquake. It is an angel who pushes the rock to the side, revealing the empty tomb and announcing to the women that the Lord Jesus has risen from the dead. The women are then *sent* to go to the Apostles to announce the good news. He has risen! (Mt 28:1-20)

The women *are the first at the tomb*. They are the first to find it empty. They are the first to hear: "He is not here. *He has risen,* as he said" (Mt 28:6).[124]

Remember, these are the same women who remained with Christ at the time of His greatest anguish, the crucifixion (Mt 27: 55-56), and witnessed His burial (Mt 27: 61). As they make their way to the Apostles to report what the angel told them, they are rewarded with an encounter with the risen Jesus Christ. Holy smokes!

Jesus tells them, "Do not be afraid; but go and tell my brethren to go to Galilee, and there they will see me" (Mt 28:9). If Jesus's incarnation and death proved God's love, His Resurrection proves He is God. He is full of all authority and power. For no one has ever risen gloriously from the dead but Jesus Christ. Nor does anyone ever follow a dead man. Why? He is dead. The Resurrection of Jesus Christ from the dead gives proof that Jesus is truly who He says He is, the Son of God. For only God can rise from the dead. Satan's power that held humanity in bondage since the fall, death itself, is now overcome.

On a recent trip to the Holy Land, I visited the Holy Sepulcher, the tomb of Jesus Christ. We saw images of the shroud or burial garment of Christ, which has an imprint of Christ's body on it, revealing the power of the Resurrection. Our guide taught us many interesting facts about the shroud. One noteworthy point was that Christ's Resurrection was not like one of us waking up in the morning and getting out of bed. It was a strong, powerful experience of the light and life of the thrice Holy God, that Jesus literally sprang forth from death as the fountain of life for all who thirst! (Jn 7:37-39)

It is also significant to point out that Mary Magdalene is the "apostle to the Apostles," the first to announce the good news of the Resurrection to the Apostles.[125] Why does Jesus send her, a woman, to the Apostles if not to show, from the earliest beginnings of Christianity, the important place that Christ gives to the women disciples? Entrusting the good news of His Resurrection to Mary Magdalene, Christ saw it best to send her out as if to say, "See what the love of God has done, conquering all sin and division." Thus, the relationships between God and humanity, and between women and men, characterized by sin and division since the fall, are now restored in Christ. Blessed be God.

> **Hence she came to be called "the apostle of the Apostles." Mary Magdalene was the first eyewitness of the Risen Christ, and for this reason she was also *the first to bear witness to him before the Apostles.* This event, in a sense, crowns all that has been said previously about Christ entrusting divine truths to women as well as men. One can say that this fulfilled the words of the Prophet: *"I will pour out my spirit on all flesh; your sons and your daughters shall prophesy."*[126]**

What does it mean to prophesy? It means that by living out our purpose—our calling—with grace, personally and collectively, we bear witness to the Gospel. Jesus Christ, before his ascension into heaven, commissioned the Apostles to go to all nations and make disciples, saying, "All authority in heaven and on earth has been given unto me. Go therefore and make disciples of all nations, baptizing them in the name of the Father and of the Son and of the Holy Spirit, teaching them to observe all that I have commanded you; and behold, I am with you always to the close of the age" (Mt 28:18-20).

Christ's promise to remain with His Church was fulfilled through the gift of the Holy Spirit Who was poured out upon the Blessed Mother, the Apostles, and the women who were gathered together in that upper room. Side by side, they gathered and waited for the descent of the Holy Spirit. The cost of the Holy Spirit was the death and resurrection of Christ. All present received the gift of the Holy Spirit. Both men and women were empowered to do "the mighty works of God." This great mystery of humanity's reconciliation with God and with each other has already happened. We are forgiven.

"To prophesy" means to express by one's words and one's

> life *"the mighty works of God"* (Acts 2:11) ... Gospel "equality," the "equality" of women and men in regard to the "mighty works of God"—manifested so clearly in the words and deeds of Jesus of Nazareth—constitutes the most obvious basis for the dignity and vocation of women in the Church and in the world. Every *vocation has* a profoundly *personal and prophetic meaning.*[127]

The forgiveness Christ brings to humanity is celebrated at every Holy Mass where the Spirit of Christ is given, grace upon grace, to all the faithful. When celebrated with faith and conversion, mighty acts are sure to follow. I remember a teenage girl saying to me, "I would like very much to be a priest, but who would ever want to be a nun?" I want to say to her and all young women, "You do not know what you do not know!"

The "something bigger, bigger" that God has planned for your life is to live your life in union with Him. This life will be exciting and definitely challenging because it is a life lived with God in the Holy Spirit. God wants your life to bear witness to His great love for the world. That means you are called to love who God loves—people. This is the challenging part since people can be very difficult. Yet God calls you, like Mary and all the other women disciples, to trust in Him. If you do, He will then equip you to do incredible things that will glorify Him. It is also important to remember, if you put your trust in the Lord, God has promised to give you, "the desires of your heart" (Ps 37:4). Each woman's "yes," to her own unique vocation not only corresponds to the desires of her heart but contributes to the "mighty works of God."

> In "vocation" understood in this way, what is personally feminine reaches a new dimension: the dimension of the "mighty works of God," of which the woman becomes the living subject and an irreplaceable witness.[128]

As a woman, I was attracted to the faith and wanted to study and develop my gifts to evangelize and teach. I studied, earning an undergraduate degree and a master's degree in Catholic theology. I began working in the field of youth ministry and was frequently invited to give talks or parish reflections. On one particular occasion, I was asked to help give a night of reflection at a parish. I was excited to have the opportunity. I was praying in the chapel when the pastor came in and said he had changed his mind, he would give the talk, and at the end, I could share a small reflection for a few minutes. Internally I was crushed. But what could I do? He went up and talked for quite a while. I heard nothing that he said, as I was trying to hold myself together and figure out what I was going to say within a "few minutes."

I remember asking the Holy Spirit, "Help, help, help!" Then, I was given the cue to go up and begin. When I did, I opened my mouth, and the Holy Spirit took over. All the prayer and study paid off. I was finally doing what God had called me to do.

After a few minutes, I stopped. I started to go back to my chair when I looked up and saw at the back of the church, the same pastor, his hand motioning me to keep going. So, I did my whole talk! The parish was very responsive to the message and *affirmed my gifts*. Later, the pastor *affirmed* me and told me that I was gifted at speaking and teaching. I was meant to keep on doing what God had so clearly given me as a gift. All the gifts that God has given to a woman are necessary to help build up and strengthen humanity. At this particular time in history, Jesus is calling each woman to take her place. Jesus is calling you to take your spot, to become who you were created to be, and to do so for the sake of humanity, which is faltering.

You can be a woman who, with grace, impacts the world for good. God who loves you has brought you into existence at this particular time in history, and God says to you today, *"This is Jesus Christ, and I am talking to you!"*

Questions for Reflection
Chapter 5
Jesus Christ Is Talking to You

1. What are one or two takeaways from this chapter?

2. What does the reality of the Redemption mean for the dignity and vocation of women? In Jesus Christ every loss that women's dignity has suffered is found and restored. What makes it difficult to believe that Jesus can restore your life? What losses has your dignity suffered?

3. The inheritance of sin is expressed in a habitual discrimination against women in favor of men; this inheritance is also in women themselves. Reflecting on this, can you see changes that you need to make in your attitude toward and interactions with women? Who are the women in your life that you would like to uphold and appreciate more?

4. Jesus challenges us to rise each day and to carry our cross so as to take our place, our spot in His messianic mission. Where is Jesus calling you to work in His mission? What gifts or skills would you be willing to work on in order to value your dignity and also fulfill your calling?

5. Do you struggle to believe that Jesus knows you and loves you? Do you believe you are forgiven when you go to confession?

6. Many people miss out on what God is doing in their lives, like the Pharisees who were at the temple the day the woman with the stoop was healed. What could you be missing out on? Is Jesus Christ talking to you?

Notes

The Holy Spirit in You (Motherhood-Virginity)

"The Holy Spirit will come upon you"—your motherhood will not be the consequence of matrimonial "knowledge," but will be the work of the Holy Spirit; the "power of the Most High" will "overshadow" the mystery of the Son's conception and birth; as the Son of the Most High, he is given to you exclusively by God, in a manner known to God.[129]

Another Little One for Heaven (Two Dimensions of Women's Vocation)

August 22, 1990, was the day that my first son was born. My husband and I left early in the morning to drive to the hospital. It was still dark out with the sun just beginning to rise. As he drove, he held my hand, and I, in labor, did my best to breathe and stay calm.... This was it, I was going to become a mother soon. Was I going to be able to do this? Then my husband quietly said, "I sure hope it's a boy." I asked, "Why do you say that?" He said, "I don't know, maybe I would be a better father for the first one if it was a boy." I said, "Well, it's too late to worry about that now. I am sure you will be fine either way."

After Michael was born and I was alone with him, I held him up and gave him a good look over and then his first mother's talk. I explained to him that I had never been a mother before and that I would do my absolute best. He would have to be patient with me. He stared back at me with one eye open, like a little pirate, as if to say,

"OK, I guess we are in this together." I then tucked him in at my side and fell asleep. Soon after falling asleep, I had two dreams about motherhood. In the first one, I dreamt that I was still pregnant. I remember thinking, "Oh no! I need to go through that again." Then in my dream, my younger sister came in and started dancing and singing, "There is another one, there is another one, there's another little one for heaven." I remember, after waking up, thinking, "I never thought about it that way."

I did not realize that in becoming a mother, I would cooperate with God in bringing my babies to their future destiny, heaven. This is called spiritual motherhood. This child's life's purpose, unknown yet at this point, has a promised eternal value and future, for he is heaven-bound! With this new awareness of faith came the realization of the importance of my own role as a mother. "The Holy Spirit will come upon you" (Lk 1:35): in the Holy Spirit, motherhood (and fatherhood) with all its responsibility takes on a new spiritual dimension, an eternal calling to bring the child to life in its physical body, as well as to life in the Holy Spirit. This awareness of faith in God and supernatural life begins on earth and is fully realized in the joy of heaven.

The teachings of St. John Paul II focus on two dimensions of a women's vocation: virginity and motherhood. The first time I read his teachings, I did not understand the point he was trying to make. I thought, "Isn't there more to a woman than her sexuality and potential for motherhood?" After further study, I came to believe that St. John Paul II is simply pointing us to the core of who we are created to be as women, "just as God wanted her to be, a person for her own sake, who discovers herself 'by means of a sincere gift of self.' "[130]

Every woman has a vocation, a personal calling by God to become who she is. You are to become the real you! This real you is so much more than you could ever imagine yourself to be. Your human relationships, career, possessions, or status are all worthy human endeavors, but they do not define all your possibilities as a woman. Only by living your life in the Holy Spirit will you hope to be able to discover your life's work and all that God wants for you, to the honor of the Holy Trinity. That's right, a life well lived is the best way to give God glory for all He has done for us. Blessed Mary is a good example of what I am trying to say. She was only able to live out her full potential as a woman by being open to God's call and living her life in the Holy Spirit. We can do the same if we set our minds and our hearts to it.

Think about it. Mary, a young Jewish woman, had already made plans for her life which included a personal vow of her virginity, the gift of self to God. This is important because Mary teaches us as women that we are to value our own dignity and the gift of being a woman. It is within that understanding that we are "to give the gift of self." Mary, who is full of grace, loves God so much that she has vowed to give her life completely to God. This gift meant she would remain a virgin.

So, when the angel surprises her by showing up and asking her to become the Mother of God, she immediately responds, "How can this be, since I do not know man?" (Lk 1:31, 34) Under normal circumstances the question, "How can this be?" would not make any sense since she is betrothed to Joseph. Being betrothed meant she was already married to Joseph. According to Jewish betrothal customs, even though they were married they would live separately for six months, then Mary would move into Joseph's home. Normally this would mean being intimate with him after moving into his home. The question does make sense, however, if she had made a personal vow to God and meant to keep it.

Mary, firm in her resolve to preserve her virginity, puts this question to the divine messenger, and obtains from him the explanation: *"The Holy Spirit will come upon you"*— **your motherhood will not be the consequence of matrimonial "knowledge," but will be the work of the Holy Spirit; the "power of the Most High" will "overshadow" the mystery of the Son's conception and birth; as the Son of the**

Most High, he is given to you exclusively by God, in a manner known to God.[131]

Being a mother was not a part of Mary's plans, but it was a part of God's plan for Mary. Because Mary was open to God, she was able to receive the gift that God offered to her. The Son of God was given to Mary exclusively and in a way known only to God through the power of the Holy Spirit. To each one of us, Jesus also comes exclusively and in a manner known to God, so that we might discover who we are by receiving our calling in God. This is the authentic life God wants to give you, your true life in the Holy Spirit!

When talking with different women about this theme, many could relate more to Eve than to Mary. I know sometimes Mary seems so beyond us, yet we must remember that Mary is not God. She is also not some perfect statue, but, in fact, is a real woman, a human being who, transformed by the fullness of grace, has so much love and goodness to give. It was her great love that united her so closely to God, which is why she wanted to remain a virgin, giving the "gift of herself" only to God. This capacity for a relationship with God is revealed to us in Jesus Christ. Jesus Christ is the great mystery for us as human beings to understand. For it is only with God's help that we can have a life of grace—that is, a life in the Holy Spirit. To experience the divine love that God wants to lavish upon us is the greatest joy of human life.

Yet so often, like Eve, by our own disbelief and lack of trust, we limit God, choosing instead to live a mediocre existence that fails to satisfy us (1 Cor 12:31). Like Mary, we are made for greatness within our own realm and calling. The question is, will we, through grace, respond as Mary did to God's invitation: "Behold, I am the handmaid of the Lord; let it be to me according to your word" (Lk 1:38)?

God created everything for man, but man in turn was created to serve and love God and to offer all creation back to him. [132]

Woman must consciously choose to fight to live a life of purpose that God has called her to, forsaking a mediocre life. By fulfilling her vocation to love and serve God, she will attain eternal happiness. Mary is woman's exemplar, for her "yes" was the complete fulfillment of her vocation. She continued to say "yes" to God throughout her life, most heroically at the foot of the Cross. Mary, who is full of grace, is deeply aware of "God's gift, of his generosity" to her as a woman, a creature, and a human being.[133] She is able to respond with a sincere gift of self, which allows her to discover her true identity as a beloved daughter and Mother of God. It is this discovery that causes her to sing with joy and bless God for His generous gifts of graces and salvation: "My soul magnifies the Lord, and my spirit rejoices in God my savior" (Lk 1:46). In becoming the Mother of God, she also becomes our spiritual mother; she becomes the New Eve whose motherhood is united to her Son's mission, the welfare and salvation of the human race.

Mary's life of grace sheds light on all women's lives. For in her, we see this impossible hope played out: a woman remains a virgin yet becomes a mother, the Mother of God. In Mary both the natural and the supernatural co-exist. *This same hope is available to us in a life of grace;* that is, in our lives the natural and supernatural can exist when the Holy Trinity comes to dwell in our souls. This is the mission of the Holy Spirit: to bring "another little one for heaven." We are born into this world to become a temple of the Holy Spirit. Every human person that has ever been created or will be created is created for God. Each woman is willed and wanted by God. Everyone is called, whether single, married, consecrated, or religious, to find her identity in the Most High as a beloved daughter, like Mary, with her life full of grace.

Indeed, the person of the Mother of God helps everyone—especially women—to see how these two dimensions [motherhood and virginity], these two paths in the vocation of women as persons, explain and complete each other.[134]

The first dimension of a woman's vocation (and analogously, a man's too) involves a free choice to give the gift of self, including virginity, to another in marriage. It is this gift of self that makes motherhood a real possibility. She is also free to remain an unmarried woman (to remain a virgin), which is the second dimension. An unmarried woman might also make vows to God giving the gift of self through consecrated or religious life.

All women therefore are invited by God to gift themselves totally to God. The essence of a woman's very being calls her to love God and cherish all those God places in her path. It is important to understand that every woman, by virtue of her identity in Christ, as a daughter of God, is a spiritual mother.

The first time I shared this insight at a conference, an older woman came up to me in tears; she had never heard of this concept of spiritual motherhood. She had never been married and had not ever heard a call to religious life. She felt like she was a misfit (remember Rudolph the Red-Nosed Reindeer and the island of misfit toys?). No, I reassured her that she was called by Christ to take her place in His messianic mission. She was, in fact, a daughter of God and had been given a mission by God on the day of her Baptism. She had become, "'a new creature'" who was also "a 'partaker of the divine nature,' member of Christ, and coheir with him, and a temple of the Holy Spirit."[135]

It was because of her close relationship with God through prayer that Mary was able to live her life in the Holy Spirit. This is key if we are going to live our lives in the Holy Spirit. Think about it. Mary experienced many difficulties in her life, yet she was never alone in anything she faced, from the possibility of Joseph divorcing her, to the birth of Christ in the stable of Bethlehem, to the massacre of the innocents, the flight into Egypt, and then finally the Cross of her Son. She also experienced daily life with the boy Jesus and Joseph, where they talked, laughed, worked, and prayed together much like our family life today. Step by step, she was able to succeed in the mission God gave her, to be Jesus's Mother as well as our spiritual mother. Mary was enough with grace. What about you and me?

What is it that the Holy Spirit would like to do in our lives? Whatever it is we must pray or, simply put, talk to Jesus, if we are to grow in the attitude of faith that helps us to live life in the Holy Spirit. Despite our fallen nature (Eve attitudes), we are to live in the simple truth that we are loved and that our lives on earth are meant to be lived closely with God in the power of the Holy Spirit. Just as the gentle rain refreshes the earth on a summer day, so does the light and warmth of the Holy Spirit bring strength, purpose, and refreshment to our lives if we are open. You do not want to miss this.... Your life in the Holy Spirit.

"You do not want to miss this... Your life in the Holy Spirit."

When I was little, I was asked what I would like to be when I grew up: a nurse, teacher, or fireman. I chose fireman—I liked their hats, the sirens, and the big red fire trucks. As I grew older, I was often asked what I thought I would do with my life. I cannot ever remember being asked, "How is God calling you to love and serve Him?"

I thought I wanted to marry someday and have children, but in the meanwhile, I needed to make a living. So I became career focused. Wake-up call; a career is not necessarily a vocation. From God's point of view, our ultimate fulfillment is going to be found in our relationship with Him. This means we should not base our lives solely on meeting our own needs or on our personal accomplishments. From God's point of view, it's all about love, so our lives must be based on how much we become a gift to others. In other words, how much do we love?

Our different gifts and talents are meant to serve our calling to love God and neighbor, as ourselves. Without a proper understanding of who we are and why God has created us, many of us forge on in a sea of darkness, doing what comes next with little or no thought of what God's plans for our life might be. As one woman stated, "I decided to be married by age twenty-six. It is what I thought should happen, and sure enough, it did." Later she wished that she had made

God a part of her life and plans at that time. She might have chosen differently.

Being a human person means that I have free will to choose to live my life in the capacity that I think is best for me. As a follower of Christ, I know that I can depend on the guidance and direction of God the Holy Spirit to make my life happen in the best possible way.

It's All About Love (Motherhood)

One afternoon I received a phone call from a distraught woman whom I had not previously met. She said that she had gotten my name from a friend and wondered if I could meet with her. We agreed to meet at my house the next day. When the doorbell rang, I saw a beautiful woman with dark hair and big brown eyes. I invited her in and poured her a cup of coffee. She began to tell me all about her life. When she came to the part that pertained to her current situation, she said that she had married because she felt it was what was supposed to come next, followed by, "Now, after several years of marriage, I have spit out three children and I want to know, *is this all there is to my life?*" I looked at her and said, "No. There is so, so much more to your life. It is time for you to seek the truth and meaning of your life." Yes, it is time for us to seek a deeper understanding of the truth about the human person.

> **In order to share in this "vision," we must once again *seek a deeper understanding of the truth about the human person*...The human being—both male and female—is the only being in the world which God willed for its own sake. The human being is a person, a subject who decides for himself. At the same time, man "cannot fully find himself except through a sincere gift of self."**[136]

There is so much more. The wife and mother sitting at my kitchen table did not realize the value of her own life, let alone her husband's and children's lives. Her purpose, her calling to love and be loved, can only be properly understood in the light of faith. Without this knowledge of God's love and purpose in creating us with the potential of the indwelling power of the Holy Spirit, everything in human life can seem empty and unfulfilling.

As we talked about her life and her relationship with God, it was clear that her role as a wife and mother was a big concern for her. I assured her that God wanted more for her life and that it is often our negative outlook that makes it seem as if our days are filled with drudgery—nothing but dishes, diapers, and food preparation. Her life had incredible meaning from God's point of view: her husband and their children are a gift given to her, and she is a gift given to them. All the small acts of selfless love done daily with gratitude make a big difference, for then the drudgery has meaning…love.

…the value of the gift of self, the gift of the person.[137]

Without the knowledge of our own worth, we cannot value the gift of our own lives, much less anyone else's. The consequence of not valuing the gift of self or the other person is that many women simply do not want to commit to being married, or if they do marry, often they do not want to be mothers. Without God's grace, our vision of marriage, children, or the meaning of our families can become somewhat distorted, meaning it is pulled or twisted out of shape. Spouses and children can seem like objects that get in the way of our pleasures or personal goals. Instead, in fact, our families are given to us as a gift from the heavenly Father (Eph 3:15). God gives us our families and our lives as a gift, a gratuitous gift, so that we might discover the gift of our own "self" by being a gift to the other persons with whom we do life.

Ultimately, we belong to God and to each other. In this belonging to each other, we are often called by God to love even when it hurts. It is this suffering that challenges us the most. It is also how we can grow in our capacity to love. We need God's grace if we are to be faithful to the people that we are to love and serve.

So when a young mother asks, "Is this all there is?" we can wholeheartedly assure her, "Oh there is so much more!" Why?

Because of all the mothers (and fathers) who have gone before us, sacrificing so much to love each other and their bambinos. Is it worth it? Yes, you bet it is; love is worth it.

> **Motherhood is the fruit of the marriage union of a man and a woman, of that biblical "knowledge" [sexual intimacy] which corresponds to the "union of the two in one flesh" (cf. Gen 2:24). This brings about—on the woman's part—a special "gift of self," as an expression of that spousal love whereby the two are united to each other so closely that they become "one flesh."**[138]

If we are going to talk about motherhood, we are also going to talk about fatherhood. Marriage in Christ means that a man and a woman give themselves freely as a "gift of self" exclusively to each other for life. The gift or fruit of this union is the new life of the child.

It may seem sometimes that it is impossible to be married to one person for life. Jesus's disciples thought so too. When Jesus is questioned about divorce, He teaches that Moses allowed divorce because of their hard hearts, "but from the beginning it was not so" (Mt 19:8). God, from the very beginning of creation, created man and woman and called them to an exclusive relationship that would be lived out in a covenant of marriage.

When I heard that a young unmarried couple had decided to move in together, I was troubled. Why? Because the young man had been raised in the faith and was very involved with his church. I wanted the best for him and for her, as God wants for all of us. It can be difficult to make the decision to get married. Yet if he loved her, why was he settling on living together instead of preparing for and committing to God's vocation, the calling for his life, their life together in Christ?

> **Biblical "knowledge" [sexual intimacy] is achieved in accordance with the truth of the person only when the mutual self-giving is not distorted either by the desire of the**

man to become the "master" of his wife ("he shall rule over you") or by the woman remaining closed within her own instincts ("your desire shall be for your husband": Gen 3:16).[139]

It is so important to recognize that, in our fallen nature, we can be intimate with people for many reasons, good and bad. Couples may choose to live together for reasons that seem to make sense; this does not mean it is good for the relationship. It might be that the couple want to save up money for the big day, or make sure this is the right one, or just enjoy the satisfaction of having someone to share life with, without the responsibility or commitment of being in a marriage. Whatever the reason, sexual "knowledge" can only be achieved if we love each other God's way.

Loving people God's way makes sense since God is the Creator of the human person you are with. God, as the author of people, has the divine plan for human love. In order to love we must have self-control and always do what is best for the other. That is love. We are also happier when we are loving others as God created us to do. We are created by Love, for love, to love. We need God's grace to be able to mutually give the gift of ourselves for the sake of the other person really loving them as God loves them. This love in marriage can open the gift of a new life, a new little bambino, who is a person in the likeness of his parents.

> **This *mutual gift of the person in marriage* opens to the gift of a new life, *a new human being*, who is also a person in the likeness of his parents. Motherhood implies from the beginning a special openness to the new person…The gift of interior readiness to accept the child and bring it into the world is linked to the marriage union, which…should constitute a special moment in the mutual self-giving both by the woman and the man.**[140]

I decided to give this young couple a call. After a happy

"hello," I asked if I could talk to them about their decision to live together. "Yes, we guess so," was good enough. I said, "I know that you have been together for some time now and have many good reasons for being together. It makes sense to you, plus weddings are expensive." "Yes," they said, "That is all true." I went on, "It is also wonderful to be close to one person and to be able to rest in each other's arms." "Yes! Yes!" they replied.

I continued, "But then again, how do you feel in the morning when you wake up?" The phone became quiet. I continued, "I would think that you might feel that something is off in your relationship." Yes, they both quietly acknowledged the truth that something might be off. I went on to explain the power of the dignity of the human person and how the conscience in particular plays a big part in helping us to live out that dignity.

> **It is precisely the *conscience* in particular which determines this dignity. For the conscience is "the *most secret core and sanctuary* of a man, where he is alone with God, whose voice echoes in his depths." It "can…speak to his heart more specifically: do this, shun that." This capacity to command what is good and to forbid evil, placed in man by the Creator, *is the main characteristic of the personal* [human] *subject.***[141]

I continued to teach the couple, "Your conscience might be speaking to you because you have closed the door to God in your relationship by not allowing God to join your souls in marriage. Your love is good and beautiful, yet it is lacking in the stability, grace, and true commitment that you are created for." It is when two people love each other fully and without conditions that they often want to commit their lives to each other before family and friends in a celebration of a sacrament of love, holy marriage. People want good marriages yet often fail at putting in the groundwork to make them happen. It's important to understand why, as people of faith, we would want to prepare and choose to marry in Christ.

When a man and a woman stand together and profess their vows before God, they do so because they want to invite God into their relationship. God is able to strengthen your relationship with His grace; meaning God is able to help you to see and love this person as God sees and loves them. Marriage in Christ elevates your union to a sacrament. This means that each of you puts your relationship with God first in your life before your marriage. Then with your marriage vows, your "I do, I do," you are asking God to join your hearts and souls together, till death do us part.

Only God can join two souls together! Think of it this way: If two people were standing in a gymnasium and they ran at each other at a hundred miles an hour, body parts would fly but they could not join their souls! "Therefore, a man leaves his father and his mother and clings to his wife, and they become one flesh" (Gen 2:24). I continued, "When you as a couple say your vows to each other, it means something. You are saying, 'This is the one that God has asked me to love, forsaking all others.' The grace of God is then given to help you to be faithful to God and to your marriage.

"After all, you are responsible for each other. God has so much more for you both if you will just turn things around and do it His way. God wants you to love and cherish each other for His sake. Then God will help you to love and cherish each other for life."

Keep your heart with all vigilance; for from it flows the springs of life. (Prv 4:23)

The word "vigilance" means to keep careful watch for danger or difficulties. From the Latin word *vigilare,* it means "keep awake." The Holy Spirit wants to help us in all the difficult moments of life to love God and each other well. God does not want us to use each other.

God wants us to love each other and to always do what is best for the other person. You can become a gift to each other with real love that comes to you in the Holy Spirit. Grace makes us one with God and one with each other. In God's love, lifelong marriages can become strong. With your marriage strong, if God gives the gift of a child, your children—your bambinos—will be in God's image and yours. As parents, you will give them a secure home in which to live and grow. After I explained this teaching, the couple began to laugh with joy.

> **"I have brought a man into being with the help of the Lord" (Gen 4:1). This exclamation of Eve, the "mother of all the living" is repeated every time a new human being comes into the world. It expresses the woman's joy and awareness that she is sharing in the great mystery of eternal generation. The spouses share in the creative power of God!**[142]

Becoming a mother. Wow. It is so intense. I remember when I felt the life of my baby for the first time. It was like I was a jar, and I had a butterfly inside me. It is so incredible to experience your baby growing, a human person growing inside you. So weird! Yet this is how we all got started. I remember going out for Mexican food and an intense high-speed movie when I was about eight months along with one of my baby boys. Between the spicy food and the movie, he just tossed and turned inside me, with his little feet poking around. I kept saying, "Sorry, little baby," while I enjoyed the show. The love that grows in your heart for your child is very profound.

> **The mother is filled with wonder at this mystery of life, and "understands" with unique intuition what is happening inside her. In the light of the "beginning," the mother accepts and loves as a person the child she is carrying in her womb.**[143]

I remember talking to my doctor about all the challenges and hardships that are a part of being a mother. I told her that men could never fully appreciate how vulnerable and difficult it is for a woman to bring this new little person into the world. There is nausea for the first few months and weight gain; you get very clumsy, awkward, and emotional with all the hormones doing their job. With my third baby, at eight months along, I fell and fractured my leg while bowling. The male nurses at the hospital told me how pathetic that was. I laughingly agreed with them. All of this leads up to labor and delivery with a broken leg. My doctor replied to me, "Yes, it's true the men will never understand all that the women have been through, but they will also never know the depth of love and affection that you have for your child, that comes with all the troubles to bring them into the world."

It is the woman who "pays" directly for this shared generation, which literally absorbs the energies of her body and soul. It is therefore necessary that *the man* be fully aware that in their shared parenthood he owes *a special debt to the woman*. No program of "equal rights" between women and men is valid unless it takes this fact fully into account.[144]

St. John Paul II wants to bring up something that is absolutely true and often not talked about or recognized: that the woman's gift of giving life to the child is, in fact, very heroic and something to be praised and esteemed. As one mother of seven told me, "My children are my treasures!" Our children are worth it. Every child comes into existence with an immortal soul created by God with the cooperation of his or her parents. Therefore, we are forever linked to our mothers and fathers both now and eternally. The child's conception initiates a relationship with his or her parents that begins on earth but ultimately reaches its fulfillment as perfect friendship in heaven. This brings such hope and joy to anyone who has ever lost a loved one.

That is why the answer to a difficult pregnancy is never to take the life of a child, even if the mother and father are not able to raise the child. We all must recognize that our very lives depended on our mothers. Instead of being pressured or manipulated to end the life of the child, the mother should be given proper care and compassion. This is the debt owed to all the mothers of the world.

Programs and societies must defend and consider the rights of all: the mother's right to non-judgmental care and support, the father's right to support and defend the life of both the mother and the child, the child's right to life, and the Creator's right to govern us with the commands "Do good, not evil" (Ps 34:14, 1 Pt 3:11) and "Thou shall not kill." (Ex 20:13)

Either way, God does not ever forget the child: "Can a woman forget her sucking child, that she should have no compassion on the son of her womb? Even these may forget, yet I will not forget you" (Is 49:15). Women and men are entrusted by God with the gift of life and are responsible to care for and protect life.

The child's upbringing, taken as a whole, should include the contribution of both parents: the maternal and paternal contribution. In any event, the mother's contribution is decisive in laying the foundation for a new human personality.[145]

The mother's contribution is very decisive since her decisions will result in the life or death of her child. Many mothers and fathers listen to the father of lies, who deceives them by saying it is impossible for them to have this child. I remember taking a group of teens to pray at an abortion clinic. The teens wanted to go and pray, to be a sign of hope in the darkness. I was quietly standing by the corner of the clinic watching and praying while the kids sang the Divine Mercy Chaplet right in front of the clinic. Then I witnessed something I will never forget. The clinic escorts started to bring a couple from their car into the clinic for their abortion. It was so dramatic—the kids singing, the couple crying, and the stoic escort accompanying them into the clinic where the child would have to die. I dropped to my knees, still praying. As I looked right into the couple's eyes, I saw them as Adam and Eve long ago. They had found their resolve. They would do it their way. I silently asked, "Why God? Why are we here?" As I knelt and continued to pray, I became aware that we were witnessing to God's love so that for all of eternity this couple would know that God's mercy was present.

Life itself is a calling; it is a fight to do the right thing. As children of God, we must always say "yes" to life and to love. God is so misunderstood. God is love and God loves us all. God always has a plan, an answer to our deepest concerns and to every problem. We were never meant to do life without Him.

Mama Bear (Motherhood in Relation to the Covenant)

I will put enmity between you and the woman and between your seed and her seed; he shall bruise your head and you shall bruise his heel. (Gen 3:15)

One night before bed I was looking at some online videos when I found myself watching a film in which a baby bear was rolling around happily in a field of grass and dirt. The scene suddenly switched to a cougar who was eyeing the baby bear with hungry eyes. The cougar began to chase after the baby bear, who made a heroic effort to escape. After a few minutes, I began to think, "Why am I watching a video of a baby bear who is about to be eaten by a cougar?" "Keep watching," I thought. The cougar trapped the baby bear and began to attack it. Suddenly I heard a roar and the camera turned to capture a giant mama bear who immediately defended her cub. The cougar was no match for the fierce mama bear. The cougar took off. The mama bear reminded me of Mother Mary; the baby bear of you and me; and the cougar of God's enemy, the devil. Mary is the Woman of Genesis 3:15, and her great enemy, the devil, makes war with her offspring, her children, who bear witness to her Son, Jesus Christ (Rev 12:17).

Mother Mary wages battle with the devil who is ultimately already defeated in Jesus Christ. Jesus and Mary want to teach us how to fight against the evil that threatens us and our families. They want us to realize that, with the grace God offers us in the Holy Spirit, we too can be victorious, but not without a fight.

God has and always will have our backs, as promised in the New Covenant that began with Mary. Jesus, the offspring of the woman, delivers us all from evil and death. Mary is the mama bear that He chose to get things started (Gen 3:15)!

> **We see that through Mary—through her maternal "fiat," ("Let it be done to me")—God *begins a New Covenant with humanity*. This is the eternal and definitive Covenant in Christ, in his body and blood, in his Cross and Resurrection. Precisely because this Covenant is to be fulfilled "in flesh and blood" its beginning is in the Mother.**[146]

Remember that Mary as the Mother of Jesus is the *exceptional link* between God and all human beings of the world. Redemption, the New Covenant with humanity, began with her, a Mother who freely said "yes" to God's invitation. Mary participates in the mission of her Son and also witnesses the sword piercing her Son's heart, causing His precious blood (representing the Eucharist) and water (representing Baptism) to flow out (Jn 19:34). His divine love, proven in His suffering and death, seals the New Covenant with humanity—a Covenant made in His blood, poured out for each and every human person. Jesus loved us to the end with a human heart, but a divine love.

> **[The New Covenant's] beginning is in the Mother. Thanks solely to her and to her virginal and maternal "fiat," the "Son of the Most High" can say to the Father: "A body you have prepared for me. Lo, I have come to do your will, O God" (cf. Heb 10:5, 7).**[147]

Lord, why this way? Why did God choose to save humanity by becoming a human baby and dying on that Cross? We know that Mary is the Mother of Jesus. Together Mary and Jesus undo the harmful consequences caused by the sin of Adam and Eve.

On that Cross, Jesus suffered in His body for all of the ways our bodies harm others, for our sin, for all of it. His head was crowned with thorns for all the ways our thoughts cause us to say and do things that harm another person: gossiping, ruining someone's reputation, or tearing them apart verbally. For all the ways we sin with our bodies through lust, sexual abuse, adultery, and pornography, Jesus was stripped, beaten, and scourged. For our heavy burdens—guilt and addictions that are too much for us to carry; regrets, tragedies, and failures; and poverty, sickness, and illness—Jesus carried His heavy Cross. For our ultimate suffering, death itself, Jesus died a most painful and awful death.

Jesus, Who is God, humbled Himself to the point of death, death on a Cross, to enter into the messiness of our sinful lives so that we could have a new beginning. It was the magnitude of His love for you and me that kept Jesus on that Cross. In His own flesh and blood, he made up for our sins "so that by his stripes [wounds] we might be healed" (1 Pt 2:24). Thus, the New Covenant is fulfilled in the flesh and blood of Jesus Christ. For those who say "yes" to God, Jesus re-establishes the connection that was lost between God and humanity, so that God's divine life, God's grace, can dwell in us once again. We are forgiven.

For it is always in thy power to show great strength... (Wis 11:21)

God's great power comes to strengthen every woman, every mother who suffers because of her child or a child that is entrusted to her. The Blessed Mother was strengthened by God's grace. In giving birth to Jesus Christ, she cooperated with God in making the possibility of the Incarnation a reality. The incredible dignity of a human person is revealed in this truth: God became man. God became man to teach us the value of human life as well as the value of women, upon whom every new human person mainly depends. Mary's motherhood gives credence to all women as to the meaning and value of motherhood. No Mary, no Jesus.

> **...motherhood *in its personal-ethical sense* [what an individual becomes through their choices] expresses a very important creativity on the part of the woman, upon whom the very humanity of the new human being mainly depends.**[148]

St. John Paul II is reminding us that even Jesus was dependent on His Mother for human life. Mary becomes the biblical exemplar for all women, because an exemplar fulfills all the possibilities of her role in a most excellent way. Mary is faithful to God, fulfilling her calling as a wife, mother, and spouse of the Holy Spirit. Mary inspires women to value faithfulness to God, love for their families, and most of all the gift of motherhood.

By the power of the Holy Spirit Mary becomes a mother, the Mother of God. This powerful gift of the Holy Spirit reveals the truth about motherhood. In the Holy Spirit we discover that every child is wanted and loved by God. Mothers, in fact, have the highest privilege in being called to guard and defend human life. *That is why we call mothers "mama bears."* While it is true that not all women are called to be mothers, all women are called to be spiritual mothers. Likewise, all men are called to spiritual fatherhood. For both women and men are to fight against any evil—physical or spiritual—that would threaten human life. Humanity is worth the fight. *We are worth the fight.*

As human persons we are made up of a body and an immortal soul, which means we will live forever. The body clothes and shelters the soul, which is the powerhouse of the body. God created us to live and grow in physical bodies as well as to grow spiritually in our souls with grace. Like the baby bear playing in the field, sometimes we are caught off guard by the evil in life. It can be hard at times just to live life, let alone handle natural disasters, illnesses, or death. In order to continue to grow and mature physically as well as spiritually, we need to know how to live Mary's "yes," "Let it be done to me" (Lk 1:38). The call from God to love and defend human life is what motherhood and spiritual motherhood are all about.

At the same time, these questions must be addressed to men: What is the value of the woman who has the potential for being a mother? What is the value of the man with his own potential for fatherhood, his "yes" to God?

> **In this sense too the woman's motherhood presents a special call and a special challenge to the man and to his fatherhood.**[149]

A young man came to talk to me about his girlfriend's pregnancy. He had not thought at all about what would happen if she got pregnant. He was not aware of his own special calling and challenge of being a man and the potential for fatherhood. In fact, he told me that it really was all about the excitement and pleasure of having a girlfriend. Now, reality was setting in; he was very young, and he was the father of a child. Even worse, his girlfriend had made the decision, with her parents, to have an abortion, and there was nothing he could do to change her mind. As the father of his child, he felt profound remorse that he had acted in such a way as to place the life of his own child in danger. Sadly, the baby was aborted and the father had no say.

Another father shared the experience of his call to fatherhood and what it felt like at the birth of his firstborn daughter. He stated, "I was immediately smitten with her! She tried to follow my voice with her little heavy eyes as though she might recognize who I might be. It was not until six or seven months later that I felt that I was beginning to bond with her when something I said or did would make her smile or laugh!"

> **Each and every time that *motherhood* [and fatherhood] is repeated in human history, it is always *related to the Covenant* which God established with the human race through the motherhood of the Mother of God.**[150]

Mary took her place in the plan of salvation; her "yes" meant that Jesus would come into the world, born in a body, as the Savior of the human race. The Covenant that God established with the human race was established through the motherhood of Mary. This teaches us the value and dignity of every human person who comes into the world born of a human mother. Even Jesus needed His mother.

Mary's motherhood also teaches us that, in light of the Gospel, motherhood (and fatherhood) takes on a profoundly deeper spiritual meaning. Every little child who comes into the world via a human mother is an immortal being capable of receiving an inheritance, which is God Himself. God wants each child who comes into the world to live, otherwise the child would not be. For the new and irrevocable Covenant of God teaches us the truth that every child is "another little one for heaven!"

For it is precisely those born of earthly mothers, the sons and daughters of the human race, who receive from the Son of God the power to become "children of God" (Jn 1:12).[151]

When children are baptized in the name of the Father, Son, and Holy Spirit with water poured out upon them, they are filled with the grace of divine life (Mt 28:19). The spoken word of God and the action of the minister are efficacious. "Efficacious" means, "It works!" We understand the power of the spoken word and actions accordingly in the physical world. We see it every day. For example, you go to a Chick-fil-A to order deliciousness. You drive up and speak the words describing what you want, you go to the next window, you pay, and then you receive your food. Your words and actions are effective, meaning they produce the results of obtaining the food that you desired. In a similar way, spiritually in Christ, when the words of baptism are spoken and the water is poured out, the Holy Spirit is given by God to the people being baptized. They really receive the Spirit of Christ! The words and the actions are effective; they produce the result in the people receiving baptism. They are new creations in Christ. This is God's gratuitous, free gift of sanctifying grace, which puts the people receiving the sacrament into a right relationship with

God, who is Lord.

> **One Lord, one faith, one baptism; one God and Father of all, who is over all and through all and in all. (Eph 4:4-6)**

This is a big deal. Jesus continually taught us how to walk in the Holy Spirit. For example, when Jesus's Mother was praised, "Blessed is the womb that bore you," Jesus answered back by saying, "Blessed rather are those who hear the word of God and keep it" (Lk 11:27-28). By saying this, Jesus is pointing to the deeper meaning of life in the Holy Spirit. Remember earlier that St. John Paul II said that a woman's motherhood points to a deeper meaning: "it is a sign of the Covenant with God."[152] Every woman's "yes" to God's plan for her life is related to that Covenant that God made that began with Mary. It is as if the Covenant is renewed again and again, every time a child is born. For each child is created to receive God as his or her heavenly Father in the gift of baptism into Jesus Christ.

After my second son was born, we went to visit my husband's parents and extended family. Everyone was sitting around enjoying lunch and the beautiful new little baby, who really was not that little, born weighing ten pounds. I mentioned that his birth darn near did me in, and my husband's mother said, "But now that he is here, you do not think about that anymore." I promptly replied, with all sincerity, "No, when I think about it, I still cry." This was followed by much family laughter. As the family laughter filled the room it also filled my heart with joy, for my son was born safely into the world and into our family, and we were all together.

> **The history of every human being passes through the threshold of a woman's motherhood; crossing it conditions "the revelation of the children of God" (cf. Rom 8:19). *"When a woman is in travail* [labor] *she has sorrow,* because her hour has come; but when she is delivered of the child, *she no longer remembers the anguish,* for joy that a child is born into the world" (Jn 16:21).**[153]

Just as women suffer to bring their children into the world, Mary with the whole Church labors to bring the children of God to new birth in Christ. Mary, the Mother of Christ, is also our spiritual mother, given to us by Christ while he was dying on the Cross: "Behold, your mother" (Jn 19:27). As Simeon foretold at the Presentation, Mary's heart would be pierced: "Behold, this child is set for the fall and rising of many in Israel, and for a sign that is spoken against and a sword will pierce through your own soul also, that the thoughts of many hearts may be revealed" (Lk 2:35). Mary, perhaps more than any other human being, understood the pain and suffering of her salvation and ours, for it cost her dearly, her very own beloved Son.

...the Mother who through faith shares in the amazing mystery of her Son's "self-emptying": "This is perhaps the deepest 'kenosis' [self-emptying] of faith in human history."[154]

When we think about Mary's suffering under the Cross, we also must think about all *women who suffer throughout the world.* I remember a woman I met while visiting the city of Bethlehem on our pilgrimage to the Holy Land. At the time, many Christians who lived in Bethlehem were not allowed to leave. As tourists, we were allowed in to visit the holy sites and buy goods. Our pilgrimage included an afternoon to visit with individual Catholic families in Bethlehem, to bring encouragement and gifts. We shared a meal together in one of the homes, where the mother of the family showed us the bullets that had been shot into her house and told us how they were not allowed to leave Bethlehem because of war and the persecution of Christians. With dark circles under her eyes, she spoke of her husband's store, still allowed to be open, but for how long? She had such overwhelming trials, yet she spoke of the hope of the One who protected them and of her great longing for the return of Christ the King. I had no idea this kind of suffering was going on in Bethlehem.

> As we contemplate this Mother, whose heart "a sword has pierced" (cf. Lk 2:35), our thoughts go to *all the suffering women in the world,* suffering either physically or morally. In this suffering a woman's sensitivity plays a role, even though she often succeeds in resisting suffering better than a man.[155]

One of my sons was in a terrible bike accident. The front wheel of his bike came off while he was riding at a high speed down a big hill. The ground met with his face and body. As I approached his room at the hospital, he must have heard me coming, for he said, "Mom, it's not as bad as it looks!" To be honest, he looked like one of those pictures of Jesus, with the crown of thorns and blood dripping—really awful.

This suffering of women comes in many forms: a woman in a war-torn country trying to care for her children, a widow who longs for her husband, a single mother struggling to provide, or a mother of a child who is very ill or struggling with depression. Many children and teens today are threatened by suicidal thoughts or despair.

I also think of the mothers I have worked with throughout the years in my job as a youth minister. Many have suffered greatly when their children are bullied or fail morally, having been caught up in drugs, alcohol, or bad relationships that threaten their young lives and futures.

Finally, there is within every woman's heart the capacity to suffer from her own faults and failures, with guilt or remorse arising from personal regrets and mistakes. These wounds do not heal easily and must be brought to the foot of the Cross.

> "So, you have sorrow now [Jesus said these words the day before His Passion and death]; but I will see you again and your hearts will rejoice, and no one will take your joy from you" (Jn 16:22-23).[156]

While in the Holy Land, I also visited the site where Jesus died on the Cross. It is moving to stand at the very spot where Jesus laid down his life. We were allowed to pray and venerate the site of the crucifixion of our Lord, by placing our hand where the Cross is believed to have stood. The foot of the Cross is where we must bring all of our guilt, remorse, and pain, as well as that of the whole world. On the Cross, Jesus has already paid a high price to set every one of us free.

In suffering, it is often a woman's sensitivity and ability to empathize with the other that allows her to succeed in bearing the load. It is true that, at the time of the crucifixion, it was Mary and the women followers who stood under the Cross with Jesus (Jn 19:25). The apostle John also stood, but the other Apostles, terrified by what was happening to Jesus, ran and hid.

The women were greatly rewarded, for it was to Mary Magdalene that Christ first appeared after His Resurrection (Jn 20:11). It was she who became the apostle to the Apostles, announcing the Resurrection of our Lord, His great victory over death itself.

Radical Love (Virginity for the Sake of the Kingdom)

> **From the moment of Christ's coming, the expectation of the People of God has to be directed to the eschatological [Heavenly] Kingdom which is coming and to which he must lead "the new Israel." A new awareness of faith is essential for such a turn-about and change of values.**[157]

A group of Dominican sisters was walking through a major US airport one morning. As they walked through the airport every eye turned toward them; with their long white habits, veils, and quick smiles, they brought light and hope to the weary travelers. As one older gentleman stated, "Aw, the good sisters, who turn our hearts and minds back to God!" This "awareness of faith" is made new and ever-present on earth, in an airport, by real women who have chosen virginity in order to give themselves completely to the Lord, as well as to humanity.

These women radically proclaim the Gospel, the good news, with their very lives.

It is, then, a voluntary celibacy, chosen for the sake of the Kingdom of heaven, in view of man's eschatological [life after death] vocation to union with God.[158]

These courageous women leave everything to follow after Christ, freely choosing virginity for the sake of the heavenly Kingdom and their divine Bridegroom. Since Christ, the Lord of love, is the final destiny of all of humanity, our calling as human persons has an eschatological meaning. *Eschatological refers to death, judgment, and the final destiny of the soul and humankind.* Big meaning for a big word. Jesus Christ, the divine Bridegroom, is the divine spouse of our souls. The sisters live out this spousal relationship already in their earthly lives, pointing to the reality of God and our supreme calling in Christ. Our human heart longs for God from the time we are young, whether we realize it or not. What the consecrated religious as well as those in the ordained ministerial priesthood live out on earth is a spousal relationship with Jesus Christ. As women we are all called to do the same within our specific vocation.

My youngest daughter, at around age three, asked her dad one day if she could marry him. My husband gently said, "No, I am married to your mother." A little sad, she turned to her older brother and asked him, "Well, will you marry me?" He said, "I am sorry, I cannot marry you. I am your brother." Then she turned to her other brother, "Will you marry me?" He also said, "I am sorry, I am your brother too, so I cannot marry you." She looked at us all and said, "Well then who am I going to marry?"

My daughter, in asking the big question: "Who am I going to marry?" was also asking the bigger question, "Who am I going to love?" Every human person is created by God with a vocation or a calling to love. This calling begins in this life and leads to a future lived with God beyond the veil, in the next life. The vocation to love is lived out on earth in the married life, the single life, or the consecrated life of virginity. All vocations involve loving other human persons for the sake of God. Loving others is a way of putting into action our love for God. Our vocations also point to our supreme calling, to live and love in that Kingdom of God which is to come.

In heaven there will be no more marrying: "For at the Resurrection of the dead there will be no more marrying or those given in marriage, but all will be like the angels" (Mt 22:30). This indicates that in heaven our relationships with God and each other will be on a different level, a better level, that is clearer and spiritually higher. Thus, the capacity for happiness in heaven will be much greater than here on earth.

This longing to love and be loved is a desire of each person. For all are created by God with this longing and are called to a spousal relationship with God the Creator. The question for each person is then "Who am I going to love?" On earth, this desire to love and be loved is often manifested in the pursuit of human love.

I have someone better for you. is the thought that a young woman had while praying to Jesus. She was struggling to discern if her boyfriend in college was the one for her. That relationship ended some time later. While she was praying one afternoon about another young man she was seeing in college, she sensed a similar response: *He can't love you the way you need to be loved!* When they later broke up, this boyfriend told her sorry, but he was not feeling it for her. She said, "I felt free to discern my vocation, for I was not feeling it either."

Women, called from the very "beginning" to be loved and to love, in a vocation to virginity *find Christ* first of all as the Redeemer who "loved until the end" through his total gift of self; *and they respond to this gift with a "sincere gift"* of their whole lives.[159]

Then the same young woman, while at Mass, asked the Lord, "What have you made me for?" She said that during the consecration, the priest disappeared and she saw only Jesus, the Divine Bridegroom present. Jesus said to her, "I am going to give myself totally to you! Body, blood, soul, and divinity." She knew her only appropriate response back to the Lord was, "I am going to give myself totally to you!" She later said, "Total gift...I needed that!" When asked if she has ever regretted her decision, she said without hesitation, "No, not ever!"

He who is able to receive this, let him receive it. (Mt 19:13)

These are the words Christ taught his disciples with the view that some women and men would freely choose to be celibate for the Kingdom of Heaven and would be given special graces to live this life. As one young priest said, "I was aware that God was calling me to be a priest. I had not put much into my studies in high school. I would much rather be outside hunting and fishing than in a classroom with books. After graduation at eighteen years of age, the calling to the priesthood grew stronger. I went into the seminary and all my attention became focused on my studies. There was so much to learn about the faith. All my grades went up to As, for I loved what I studied, and Who I studied, God. Little by little, He drew me to Himself. Finally, I was strong enough to say to God, 'If you want me to be Your priest, I will be Your priest.'"

> *One cannot correctly understand virginity*—**a woman's consecration in virginity**—*without referring to spousal love. It is through this kind of love that a person becomes a gift for the other. Moreover, a man's consecration in priestly celibacy or in the religious state is to be understood analogously* **[comparable in certain aspects]**.[160]

Another consecrated woman shared, "Jesus began to call me to Himself several times over a period of several years. At first, I was somewhat overwhelmed by His call, even hiding from it, not feeling worthy, and also not sure what this call would mean. One day while on retreat, I saw an image of myself running, followed by an image of myself sitting under a tree. That is when Jesus reached out His hands to me. I knew He was calling me to total surrender. Several months later I discerned in prayer God seeming to challenge me: *How much do you need your life? How much do others need your life?* It seemed at this moment that Jesus was asking me to give my entire life for others. Then again at another time while I was praying in Eucharistic adoration, the image came to my mind of a big mahogany desk which symbolized a successful career, followed by an image of Jesus Christ crucified. These were the images of the two paths my life could take. It became so clear that God was calling me to dedicate myself completely to Jesus in a vocation to the Consecrated Apostolic Life."

> **By freely choosing virginity, women confirm themselves as persons, as beings whom the Creator from the beginning has willed for their own sake. At the same time they realize the personal value of their own femininity by becoming "a sincere gift" for God…a gift for Christ, the Redeemer of humanity and the Spouse of souls.**[161]

The "new awareness of faith"[162] is lived out in those persons who, for the sake of their love for Christ, lay down their lives as he did, not marrying but instead living totally vertically; their angle on life is straight up! For the sake of the Heavenly Kingdom, they become a living sign that points to the truth that we are not alone! As God told Moses, "I Am who I Am!" (Ex 3:14) We live our lives on the threshold of eternity. The lives of the consecrated religious and priests say to the rest of us, "God alone is enough for you in whatever vocation he wants you." Thus, the consecrated sisters and priests bring about "a new awareness of faith," showing us that we are all called by God to live out our faith on earth. By their very lives, they also remind everyone—their families, friends, the Church, and all they meet—*that God is real and has created us for Himself.*

"Well, what if I want to become a nun?" one feisty young lady boldly asked her father when he began to question the wisdom and expense of attending a Catholic University to study theology. This young lady also brought about "a new awareness of faith" in her father, who was so shocked that his own daughter was even thinking

about becoming a sister. He had no idea!

> **In virginity…the so-called *radicalism of the Gospel* finds expression: "Leave everything and follow Christ" (cf. Mt 19:27). This cannot be compared to remaining simply unmarried or single, because virginity is not restricted to a mere "no," but contains a profound "yes" in the spousal order: the gift of self for love in a total and undivided manner.**[163]

"This is what you are supposed to do, so you do it." This is the response given by a young woman who, as a freshman in college, was praying before Jesus in adoration of the Blessed Sacrament. "I want you to be a sister," is what she understood Him to say to her. "Yes," she thought. "This is what I am supposed to do, so I will just do it." She is indeed a happy little nun today! She'd had some exposure to religious life from two of her great aunts who were sisters. She'd also spent time as a child visiting a local convent where her mother worked. However, she had not thought a lot about the life of a religious. After her decision to become a sister, she began to prepare by learning about what that life might entail as she finished her college studies. With help from some different sisters, she was able to discern a community that fit perfectly with her personality and desire to work in the field of communications. Eight and a half years later, making her final vows as a Franciscan sister, she could joyfully say, "This is a beautiful life; I want this!"

Heaven Bound (Motherhood According to the Spirit)

As I was walking home from class one afternoon, I passed by a big old Catholic church in the neighborhood. I noticed a young woman happily skipping out of the church. I could hear her singing and wondered what she was so happy about. As I made my way, I realized the young woman was my older sister, so I called out her name. She turned back and gave me a cheerful greeting. I asked her what she was up to. She smiled and told me that during her prayer that day, she sensed that Jesus had asked her to be His. I said to her, "How did you respond to that?" She replied, "I realized it would mean that I would never have children of my own." She continued, "I deeply sensed that Jesus already knew this and that it would be alright."

> **Virginity according to the Gospel means** *renouncing marriage and thus physical motherhood....a renunciation that can involve great sacrifice for a woman, makes possible a different kind of motherhood: motherhood "according to the Spirit" (cf. Rom 8:4).*[164]

Motherhood "according to the Spirit" involves loving Christ the Spouse as well as each person who comes across a woman's path for the sake of her Spouse. When I questioned a consecrated woman about the difficulties encountered or sacrifices asked of her in the consecrated life, she truthfully shared, "*I learned all about this in the school of hard knocks.* The Cross was something that I could not convince myself of; it was totally our Lord's idea. I could not understand or immediately accept the sacrifice that would be asked of me. I ran from it. I learned over time that the Cross of Jesus is to be accepted and embraced. I was not to run away from the Cross. The Cross surprised me!"

> **...virginity as a woman's vocation is always the vocation of a person—of a unique, individual person. Therefore the spiritual motherhood which makes itself felt in this vocation is also profoundly personal.**[165]

This same consecrated woman went on to share, "The example of spiritual motherhood can be seen best in our Blessed Mother, who walked with our Lord in faith alongside her Son. She is the best example to me of spiritual motherhood, the total gift of self. Does not every mother suffer in such a way with her children, especially in times of distress? I was also surprised and very happy when people came back to me later in my life and said, 'I owe you everything,' or 'I am who I am because of you!'" In her vocation to consecrated life, this woman's spiritual motherhood bore fruit by helping others. She began to see how the difficulties and challenges of her cross, endured as an expression of love for Christ her Spouse, also brought blessings and even joy to her spiritual children.

> ***In this way a consecrated woman finds her Spouse,*** **different and the same in each and every person, according to his very words: "As you did it to one of the least of these my brethren, you did it to me" (Mt 25:40).**[166]

Spiritual motherhood takes on many forms since each woman is a unique, unrepeatable person created in the image of God, with different spiritual charisms and gifts, called to different vocations by the same Lord. We share in this mystery: that we are able to love the God we do not see by loving His children for His sake. Each woman is, in fact, showing her love to Christ her Spouse by loving those who are entrusted to her. Mother Teresa referenced this Scripture often: "As you did it to the least of these, you did it to me" (Mt 25:40). When working with the poor in the slums of Calcutta, she once stated, "In the Mass…we have Jesus in the appearance of bread, while in the slums I see Christ in the distressing disguise of the poor. The Eucharist and the poor are but one love for me."[167] This is also true for every Christian; we love and serve Christ in every person we care for and serve in His name.

Another Franciscan Sister talked about her time spent caring for the elderly. She enjoyed caring for them, making sure to bring them a quick joke or smile when the occasion warranted it. She saw and loved Christ in each elderly person she worked with.

A member of another consecrated order spoke of the universality of her spiritual motherhood. She explained that while she was confined to her room for two weeks of quarantine for an illness, her union with Christ, together with an offering up of her life in all of its circumstances, could mean that a little child in China would be helped by God: "I will not fully know until heaven the spiritual fruit that my life, given to Jesus my Spouse, will bear. It could be that He will use it to bless someone that I do not even know!"

Spousal love always involves a special readiness to be poured out for the sake of those who come within one's range of activity.[168]

Jesus, by his own words and example, called women to be His disciples, therefore each woman's vocation must be nurtured and formed if she is to find fulfillment in her life. We can miss our calling if we are not open to God. In speaking to religious sisters and consecrated women, I have experienced strong women of grace. Their confidence and love for God and people definitely contribute to "the mighty works of God." I mentioned before, a teenage girl who said to me, "I would like very much to be a priest, but who would ever want to be a nun?" I think this teenage girl, as well as many women today, have no idea how great an honor it is to be called by the Lord to consecrate oneself to Him. Sure, there is a cross when we follow the King of Kings. Love can transform everything, every day, making life lived with Christ a joy. Love is worth everything, and in the end, it is all that matters.

Life on earth has not always been easy for women. Jesus Christ came so that we could have a new beginning. The hope of St. John Paul II is that all women would encounter Christ, personally experiencing His love and calling. Women who do will never experience their lives as women and mothers the same again.

Spiritual motherhood also takes on many forms for a woman whose vocation is marriage. As a wife and mother, she is primarily entrusted with the well-being of her husband and their children. Together both spouses are entrusted with the physical and spiritual needs of their children. They are entrusted to care for their little bodies by providing clothing, food, and education. Because they have immortal souls, parents must also teach their children from the time they are little about the love of God.

In marriage this readiness, even though open to all, consists

mainly in the love that parents give to their children. ... And does not physical motherhood also have to be a spiritual motherhood, in order to respond to the whole truth about the human being who is a unity of body and spirit?[169]

Mothers (and fathers too!) are called by God to teach the love and faithfulness of God, so that the good of both the spouses and their children may come to be. It is not enough just to clothe and feed our children; we have to form them in the ways of love and a truly human life.

Another Little One for Heaven (My Little Children with Whom I Am Again in Travail [Labor])

As stated at the beginning of this chapter, I had two dreams that morning in the hospital after my baby was born. I had fallen back asleep when I immediately had the second dream, in which my brother was talking to me about some of his life's sorrows. As he was finishing speaking the same sister came back into the dream and started singing and dancing, saying again, "There is another one, another one, another little one for heaven." I woke up again, startled at the connection between the two dreams. Each of us is heaven bound.

Yes, my brother had been going through a rough time in his life recently with some significant disappointments. He had set aside the practice of his faith. Without his faith, life had not gotten easier for him. In fact, things had only gotten worse. One night, several months after I'd had this dream about him, he asked me if I had time to talk. It happened as in the dream.

He began to tell me about a "perfect storm" in his life that had uprooted everything that he had thought made him happy. One morning, when he was at his lowest, he knew he was at a crossroads in his life and had to choose between numbing the pain with even more of the same and asking God for help. He took one of the many rosaries that our mother had sent him and knelt in front of his kitchen stove. You see, above the stove hung the crucifix from Grandma Milton's coffin that our mother had given to him. He began to stumble his way through the rosary that he still remembered from our family rosaries growing up. The morning sun rays streaming through the window reflected off the gold crucifix and made his white stove look like an altar at Church. The anointing had begun.

A few weeks later, he found himself in line for confession at a first Saturday devotion he was attending with our parents. While he was waiting in line to go to confession, the anointing returned. It was just like the story of the prodigal son, when the father comes out to greet him and the son experiences the healing peace of Christ that is beyond all understanding.

Sometimes we leave God only to find out that life without God is much worse than life with God. Like my fish, Goldie, who jumped out of the aquarium, we discover then that it's very difficult to live without water.

People may set aside or leave their faith in God and organized religion for various reasons. In our times, some have left due to some serious fault or teaching that has upset them. Sometimes it's because of a really bad scandal or the sin of a clergyman or pastor. What they do not realize is that God is perfect. God promised He would never leave us. That is why God sent the very best, Jesus. We needed a perfect, infinite love to be our rock, the anchor and foundation for our lives. The sin of others is finite; it must be fought with the infinite love of God. Sinners must be loved and converted, then taught the faith. This is where the fight comes in. The temptation is to give up on God and our faith in love, walking away because it seems so impossible. The truth is, even if we walk away, we are still loved. We still belong to God.

I was struggling terribly with some great imperfections of others and my own faults. I was not winning this fight. The Holy Spirit began to challenge me (whack, whack) to forgive and accept that being imperfect and dealing with the faults and sins of others is a part of this life. I would not need God if life were easy and people were perfect.

I began to pray; I gave all of it to God. As I prayed quietly to the Father, I began to thank Him for all my blessings, my life, my career, my friends, and most importantly my family and my husband. Then we dealt with the painful memories together. I dealt; God listened. When I finally finished, I said, "Father in heaven, I give all of this now to You and to Your Son Jesus and that Cross of His." A deep peace began to fill me; I was very aware that all had been heard. Then in the quiet of my heart I sensed the still small voice that seemed to say, "And I give you My Son!" echoing the Scripture, "For God so loved the world that he gave his only-begotten Son" (Jn 3:16). As tears welled up, I thought, "Well, that is a pretty good exchange!"

Jesus started the Church. He founded it upon the Apostles with Mother Mary and all the other disciples who followed Him at that time. None of them was perfect—only Jesus and His Mother. Jesus promised to remain with His Church through the power of the Holy Spirit and see us through to the end (Mt 28:19-20). I like to remind people that Jesus told us that the gates of hell would not prevail. If hell is fighting against us, it is going to get hot—meaning there is going to be a battle. We must understand that this is a real fight for our very lives. Jesus thought we were worth fighting for. We too must believe that we are worth the fight. Love is a battle, and the fight takes place in the human heart.

At the end of our lives, we will be asked to give an account of our life on earth. How well did we love? How well did we fight the good fight of faith, in the effort to love? The Catholic faith is more than a religion to keep us on our toes; it is the vehicle that God uses to help us to discover the great mystery of life: who we are and Who God is. The Catholic faith will not make any sense unless we are able to open our hearts to the possibility of God's love and divine truths given through the Church. Even though the Church is made up of sinners, Christ remains and will never walk away from us. We must pray! It was by prayer that my brother was able to make a spiritual connection with God and, from there, figure out what he was called to do next. Many people historically have made a similar spiritual connection with God through prayer and have found that the narrow path does indeed lead to life.

> **The Gospel helps every woman and every man to live it and thus attain fulfillment. There exists a total equality with respect to the gifts of the Holy Spirit, with respect to the "mighty works of God" (Acts 2:11).**[170]

You are a mighty work of God! God created you and brought you into your human existence so that you could learn about life, yourself, and others. It's all about love here on planet Earth. There are many, many gifts of the Holy Spirit. As human beings, we have free will to make choices and to live our lives with grace. Grace helps us to figure out what the truth is, and even if we make mistakes, we can learn from those mistakes and grow in wisdom.

God takes this all into account when creating us and redeeming us. Ultimately, we all get to choose if we are going to accept the Gospel and learn how to live our lives in the Holy Spirit. Our real life is in God. For it is only by living our lives in the Holy Spirit that we are able to find fulfillment. In the example of my brother, who was stuck in the sin and failures of his own life, it was only when he returned to his faith in Christ that he was able to begin his real life again—the life that God wanted him to have.

It began by letting go of the past through forgiveness. This freed him up to receive the vocation, the calling to marriage that God had for him. So many people are afraid to love and commit themselves to another because, on their own, they know they are not strong enough. Christ's spousal love for all married couples is available for them here and now on earth. Many do not realize that God, who is love, is the source of the love and strength they need. The courage needed to attempt to live a life of love begins in a relationship with Jesus Christ, who is the Bridegroom of each person's soul. With His help, my brother was able to forgive hurts from the past and begin anew, growing strong in love.

Sure enough, with grace, he was able to man up, meaning spiritually heal and mature, which allowed him to marry and adopt three little boys who needed a dad and a place to call home. In returning to his faith, he actually found the vehicle to return to his true self and was able to find fulfillment. Despite the many temptations, trials, and setbacks of this life, God is faithful and calls each of us to Undivided Love that is only possible with grace and a good fight!

"For by [the Church's] preaching and by baptism she brings forth to a new and immortal life children who are conceived by the Holy Spirit and born of God." This is motherhood [and fatherhood] "according to the Spirit" with regard to the sons and daughters of the human race.[171]

What if my brother had not said "yes" to the Lord? What would that have meant for his wife and children? Sometimes it takes a while for us to understand and accept the ways of God. It has taken me many years to be able to trust in God and believe God loves me. God the Father is willing to forgive all of our sins, *all of them*. We only need to repent of our sins and accept His loving forgiveness.

In Jesus, God has provided everything that we need to have life. Our part is to receive the gift of His only Son by faith. Like Mary, we have free will. It was her open heart and love that helped her to trust God and accept the grace that God wanted to bless her life with! (Lk 1:46) *Acceptance is grace.* God comes to each and every person and asks, "Will you give me your little life now, in exchange for the *real life* I want to give you?" This life of grace is offered to you in Jesus Christ the Bridegroom.

Questions for Reflection
Chapter 6
The Holy Spirit in You

1. What are one or two takeaways from this chapter?

2. Pursuing human relationships, career, possessions, or status are all worthy human endeavors, but they do not encompass all your potentialities as a woman. How do you describe your life? What defines your worth as a human person? Where does the struggle come in between your identity as beloved of God and your own fallen nature?

3. Step by step, the Virgin Mary was able to succeed in the mission God gave her, to be Jesus's Mother as well as our spiritual mother. Mary was enough with grace. What about you and me? Are we enough with grace? Where do we need to grow in trust?

4. The word "vigilance" means to keep careful watch for danger or difficulties. The Latin word *vigilare* means "keep awake." Where do you need the Holy Spirit to help you to keep awake in order to love well?

5. At the Cross, Jesus paid a high price to set every one of us free. Where do you need to be set free in your life right now?

6. Prayer is our relationship with God; it is the prayer of the heart that changes us, giving us confidence and self-control. Are you having a hard time overcoming any sinful or addiction-like behaviors? How can you remember to call on the Holy Spirit to help you overcome your faults and to gain freedom?

Notes

Will You Be Mine?
(The Church the Bride of Christ)

> "Husbands, love your wives, as Christ loved the Church and gave himself up for her, that he might sanctify her, having cleansed her by the washing of water with the word, that he might present the Church to himself in splendor, without spot or wrinkle or any such thing, that she might be holy and without blemish. Even so husbands should love their wives as their own bodies. He who loves his wife loves himself. For no man ever hates his own flesh, but nourishes and cherishes it, as Christ does the Church, because we are members of his body. 'For this reason a man shall leave his father and mother and be joined to his wife, and the two shall become one flesh'. *This mystery is a profound one,* and I am saying that *it refers to Christ and the Church*" ([Eph] 5:25-32).[172]

Take Your Place (The Great Mystery)

The great mystery of God's love for humanity is revealed fully in Jesus Christ the Bridegroom, Who gives Himself up for the Church, the Bride, that she might be "without spot or wrinkle." The greatest loss human beings suffer from is the immense absence of a relationship with our heavenly Father. The Father's response to our suffering and misery is the sending of His only begotten Son, Jesus Christ, the Word made flesh, Who died sacrificially for each human person, revealing the immense mercy and love of God. Christ continues to come as a self-gift in the Holy Eucharist to nourish and

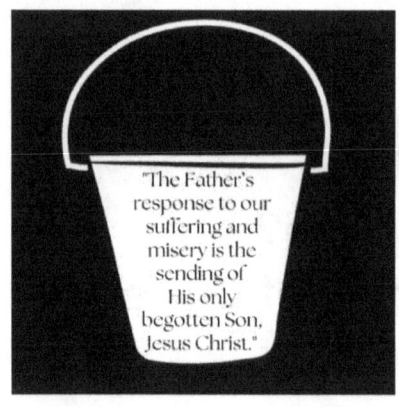

"The Father's response to our suffering and misery is the sending of His only begotten Son, Jesus Christ."

strengthen His Bride, the Church. If, by faith, we can come to believe in and belong to Christ, we too can hope to take our place in the great mystery of God's love.

The challenge for women is to seek out a higher love that can only be found in Christ. Too often, as women, we choose to look for love in all the wrong places. Christ wants us to be women who, guided by the Holy Spirit, are willing to learn and develop the necessary skills and attitude of faith that is very much needed today. Only in this way can we equip ourselves to share our gifts and talents effectively, letting our light shine brightly in a dark world.

A young woman told me that she was dating a man she really cared for, who was fun to be with—at least in the beginning. Her father had said that he did not approve of her boyfriend, that someone with his type of character might harm her. He wanted her to choose wisely the man she would date. She began to justify her decision to continue seeing him. She knew her father was good and had only the best intentions for her; she just did not believe he understood her. After all, this was her choice, her relationship. One evening as she was setting out to go on a date with him, her father called her back into the house. He wanted to talk to her again. He carefully went over her boyfriend's character and the red flags that left him deeply concerned for her safety.

Despite the warnings, she continued to see him. She was lonely and thought she could change him. Sometime later they were out on a date when he took her for a ride in the country. After parking the car on a dark road in a corn field, he began to pressure her to be more intimate with him. She had been clear with him from the beginning that she did not want that right now in her life; that was for later, for marriage and her forever man. It did not matter what she wanted or thought; he became angry when she refused him. Then he told her to get out of the car and drove away, leaving her terrified. She sat alone in the dark, not really knowing where she was or how to get home. She began to cry out into the night for her dad. After awhile, she started feeling a little foolish. Here she was practically all grown up, sitting in a dark cornfield, crying out for her daddy. How did her life get so messed up? Then it slowly occurred to her that it was God, her heavenly Father, Whom she was calling out to for help. As her awareness of God's presence grew in the cornfield, she began to pray, really hard. She asked God for forgiveness and for help to know what to do next. She said, "Then a quiet peace took hold of me, and I knew that I was not alone. God, my heavenly Father, was with me!" Eventually, the man she was dating came back and drove her home. However, the relationship was over.

God created us as men and women in His image and likeness, with the intention that we would experience a beautiful spousal relationship. The love between spouses is a foreshadowing of the faithful, steadfast love that God has for each of us human persons. Our relationship with God is so important because it is the Father's love that orders all relationships, especially the spousal love of man and woman.

Created in the image and likeness of God as a "unity of the two," both have been called to a spousal love.[173]

Spousal love is the heart of the home. The man and the woman are called to a profound spousal love that imitates the divine union, the oneness of the Holy Trinity. In Christianity, charity includes *agape* love which is usually defined as unconditional, selfless, sacrificial love. Charity does not hesitate to sacrifice for the spiritual good of others. Charity is the highest form of love. It transcends and guides *philia* (brotherly love), *storge* (family love), and *eros* (passionate love). Charity is a supernatural virtue that is God-given and calls each of us to respond to God's love by giving God love in return: "If you love Me, you will keep My Commandments" (Jn 14:15).

God, who is like the father in this story, wants us to choose wisely the highest form of love that is revealed in the sending of Jesus Christ the Bridegroom, who comes to us especially in the Holy Eucharist. It is the love of Christ that gives us the grace and strength to respond to the gracious love of God. Christ the Bridegroom gives the sacrificial gift of self to His Bride the Church. By nourishing her with His Body and Blood, Christ empowers and restores our relationship with God the Father, lost long ago in that garden. Grace frees us up to love again, to make a gift of our lives to God, Who loves each of us and longs to give us life. When we choose to make God our first love, all of the other loves in our lives can be ordered as a response to His love. The question is, Is God our first love?

> **...the expression of God's love is *"human,"* but the *love* itself is *divine*. Since it is God's love, its spousal character is properly divine, even though it is expressed by the analogy of a man's love for a woman.**[174]

God created us to be in relationships with one another that are good, holy, and ordered to the divine love with which He has created us. This allows us to receive and give in mutual life-giving relationships. The purpose of dating is to see if you are called by God to a spousal relationship, lived within the covenant of marriage (Gen 2:18-25). It is also to see whom you should choose to marry if you are called to get married. Even with God's grace, it is still difficult, because we have been weakened by sin and must fight the good fight to keep ourselves under control. Only with grace, charity, and determination are we able to give selfless love to one another, especially when the difficulties and temptations of life shake things up a bit.

Without God, relationships can go bad—really bad. Like a man and woman who are dating; at first, everything is good as they both enjoy discovering the other person and spending time together. As they spend more time together, things begin to get difficult. Without realizing it, they begin to experience the opposite of God's love. They both fall into sin and lust. They, in fact, experience evil, which is the absence of God. Like the father's concern for his daughter's well-being, God is concerned for us as men and women. God wants us to be happy. *Remember, it's good to be good!* The loving concern that God has for us calls us to act with love and care in all of our human relationships, especially in our dating and spousal relationships. In the story of the couple in the cornfield, we see how far we have strayed from God's plan. For a man and woman are called to a spousal relationship that reflects Christ's love for the Church.

For the mountains may depart and the hills be removed, but my steadfast love shall not depart from you, and my covenant of peace shall not be removed, says the Lord, who has compassion on you. (Is 54:10)

As for the young woman in the cornfield, as well as for all the rest of us, God was with her, guiding her, if only she would listen. God was also speaking to the young man through her, "This is not the way you are supposed to love her." Jesus came to give Himself in love to the human race. Jesus is the true Bridegroom. We can be the Bride; Jesus came to deliver us from bad relationships by restoring our relationship with God. If only we would listen. If only we would say "yes" to the Bridegroom.

Christ is the Bridegroom of the Church—the Church is the Bride of Christ.[175]

The experience of falling in love is beautiful and comes from the heart of God. Adam, "the man manifests for the first time joy and even exultation, for which he had no reason before..."[176] Adam is filled with God's own love for Eve, for "They see and know each other with all the peace of the interior gaze, which creates precisely the fullness of the intimacy of persons."[177] God created us as male and female to be in relationship as a "unity of the two." It explains why those who are single enjoy meeting a new person with the possibility of dating and romance. It is the joy of discovering a person who likes you, whom you might even fall in love with and choose to marry.

My parents were married for sixty years. As I talked with them about their marriage, my dad said, "We just took it all as it came and everything worked out great. We both came from good families, we had a good spiritual background, and she liked me!" "She liked me" was said with great joy and a big smile. My mother's love revealed a personal truth to my dad that he was likable. Even more, if she liked him, then God could like him too. Do we ever think about God that way? God likes us—a lot. In fact, God is love. You and I are loved with an infinite love that overcomes finite sin and brokenness (1 Jn 4:15-16). If I abide in God, God abides in me, giving me a share in His own divine love. It is this divine love that empowers me as a woman to love my spouse with the highest form of love, charity. I can only strive for that highest form of love because Christ abides in me and my spouse, enabling us to love one another as He has loved us.

> **Although not directly, the very description of the "beginning" (cf. Gen 1:27; 2:24) shows that the whole "ethos" [characteristic spirit] of mutual relations between men and women has to correspond to the personal truth of their being.**[178]

Duane and I met on a retreat for young adults called "Relationships Really Matter." Duane asked me out on a date at the end of the retreat and we hit it off. He would often jokingly say to me, "I like Jesus with skin on!" Isn't this true for all of us? We are called to love God with all our hearts. Yet it's difficult for us as human persons to love a God that we cannot see. God asks us to love those we can see, especially when it comes to dating and spousal love. In this way we give love and honor to the God we cannot see.

The experience of loving and being loved by a human spouse

with God's grace, exclusively and forever, "until death do us part," corresponds to the personal truth of my being, the truth that I am created to be loved and to love. This personal truth is fundamental to my existence and comes from my Creator and heavenly Father.

> **...as a "unity of the two," both have been called to a spousal love. Following the description of creation in the book of Genesis (2:18-25), one can also say that this fundamental call appears in the creation of woman, and is inscribed by the Creator in the institution of marriage, which, according to Genesis 2:24, has the character of a union of persons** *("communio personarum")* **from the very beginning.**[179]

The "unity of the two," beginning with the fall of Adam and Eve, to the present time, has experienced much division and suffering as the direct result of the personal refusal to accept the love of God and to love the "other" for their own sake. Only with grace is this type of love possible. Yet this is how God loves and accepts us. It is also how God wants us to live our lives on earth. St. Francis once walked through the streets of Assisi proclaiming, "Love is not loved!" When a couple closes the doors to God, the divine source of human love, both people risk losing the love they have for the other, the love God intended for them as a "unity of the two."

This is why Christ came as the faithful Bridegroom. He came with a human heart like us, but a divine love that could heal, bringing men's and women's hearts back together in a union that reflects God's love. Adam and Eve abused their freedom, turning away from doing what God wanted and thereby choosing to live their lives without God. Today many people follow that path. Even if they are miserable from living this way, they keep making excuses: "I can't help it, this is just the way I am." Instead of turning back to God, they continue on this path, stubbornly saying, "I did it my way." Yet the truth is, the refusal to love and live life with God is selfish and prideful. It will never lead to happiness or fulfillment. It is also why there is so much pain and suffering in the world today. *Yet God never gives up on us.*

> **On the part of God the Covenant is a lasting "commitment"; he remains faithful to his spousal love even if the bride often shows herself to be unfaithful.**[180]

Human suffering and death are not what God wanted for us. I recently heard a woman speak of her anger over the crazy sufferings she had endured, which included a worldwide pandemic and two hurricanes that did much damage to her home state, while she was pregnant and giving birth to her child. She grew so angry that, in the midst of it all, she found herself shouting at God, "I hate all of this!" After she had finished, she sensed God's own frustration. She realized that he hated it too. God allows suffering; that does not mean God likes it or even wants it. It came along with God's decision to create creatures who have free will. Unlike the moon and the stars, people can choose to do their own thing, which, if it opposes God's will, creates a lot of messes.

> **This dramatic situation of "the whole world [which] is in the power of the evil one" makes man's life a battle:**
>> **The whole of man's history has been the story of dour combat with the powers of evil, stretching, so our Lord tells us, from the very dawn of history until the last day. Finding himself in the midst of the battlefield man has to struggle to do what is right, and it is at great cost to himself, and aided by God's grace, that he succeeds in achieving his own inner integrity.**[181]

No wonder we have such a hard time being the people God intended. This is why the Father sent Jesus, to get us out of the cornfield of rebellion and disobedience. Christ, through faithful love and obedience, submitted Himself to the Father's will, taking all of our rebellion and sin to that Cross. This is the fullest expression of the truth of Christ the Redeemer's love. The holy Bridegroom's invitation to you and to me is: "Will you be Mine?" Jesus the Bridegroom fully expresses the love that God has for us by freely laying down his life so that we could become holy. This means our hearts can be healed and we can, with grace, learn to live and love again.

> **But the fullest expression of the truth about Christ the Redeemer's love, according to the analogy of spousal love in marriage, is found in the Letter to the Ephesians:** *"Christ loved the Church and gave himself up for her"* **(5:25), thereby fully confirming the fact that the Church is the bride of Christ: "The Holy One of Israel is your Redeemer" (Is 54:5).**[182]

What is the love of Christ like? Well, it is simply the purest, most excellent, perfect love you will ever know. The Bridegroom is the Holy One of Israel who relentlessly pursues the Bride—that is, you and me. This means all that has threatened or harmed us—our sin, the sin of others, even death itself—is taken care of by His supreme act of sacrificial love offered once and for all at Calvary. At the same time, the love of Christ calls us to renew and order our lives, including our relationships. The love of Christ makes it possible for man and woman to love each other in a spousal relationship. The question is, will you accept Christ, making a gift of your whole life to Him in return? For it is Christ in you that your future spouse will need, more than you will ever know.

Later, when Duane asked me to marry him, I said, "Yes, I will!" With this "yes," I freely gave consent to enter into a spousal relationship, with Duane as my husband, in the sacrament of marriage, a holy covenant of love. This call for Duane and me to love as a "unity of the two" originates from and sheds light on the "great sacrament" of the union of Christ with the Church. In this covenant, both of our lives were changed forever. Our married love has helped us to mature in charity and in our knowledge of each other. As long as the three of us are living out this sacrament of love—God, Duane, and I—we will be able to continue to grow in our love for God and each other. This can only happen with grace and a continual effort to generously love the other for his or her own sake.

> **The covenant proper to spouses "explains" the spousal character of the union of Christ with the Church, and in its turn this union, as a "great sacrament," determines the sacramentality of marriage as a holy covenant between two spouses, man and woman.**[183]

The call to sacramental marriage in Christ has brought many blessings to us as a couple, especially the gift of our children, our families, and our friends. But most especially, the tremendous growth in our ability to love each other, in good times and in bad, as husband and wife, and as parents to each of our children. We both agree that we have willed to love each other even when it hurts and especially when life is hard. How is this possible? Simply said, with grace we have learned that we are enough. This grace flows from our commitment to follow Jesus, through prayer, the sacraments—especially the Eucharist—and the frequent reading of the Word of God. Our spiritual life in Christ is the center and rock of our marriage. This mutual love for Christ has fostered our ability to forgive each other and to communicate well and has brought about a steady growth in our love for one another. Christ is the reason we have thrived in our marriage union, despite many obstacles and challenges.

> **For the grace of matrimony to be fully effective, we need to have a disposition of a disciple: faith and obedience to the word of God. Both the husband and the wife need to live in a state of grace and to understand and follow the Lord's teaching about family life contained in Scripture and taught by the Church.**[184]

Willed by God, the sacrament of holy marriage, which finds its source in the heart of God, strengthens couples to enter into a lifelong holy covenant of marriage, lived out as spouses. God instituted this sacrament, which shines a spotlight on the great mystery of Christ's love for the Church. God is the great mystery, the divine being we are all moving toward every day of our earthly existence. How we choose to love our spouse matters. Jesus Christ came to restore unity and friendship between God and all of God's children, especially in marriage. It is the greatest love story. You don't want to miss out on the best thing your "little life" was offered! Jesus is the reset button for your life; He is also the reset button for spousal love. For Jesus promises "to make all things new" (Rev 21:5).

Game Changer (The Gospel "Innovation")

Ephesians 5:21-33 has long been misunderstood, often causing women especially to cringe as the words are read: "Wives be subject to your husbands, as to the Lord." St. John Paul II sheds light on how we are to understand the oneness in marriage that can only come about for spouses who are in Christ.

Christian marriage is a game changer and a cause to rejoice! St. Paul is actually conveying a new and proper understanding of how the relationship between husbands and wives, and ultimately all relationships between men and women, have been dramatically renewed in Christ who gives us a new commandment: "Love one another. As I have loved you, so must you love one another" (Jn 13:34). Yes, in real, everyday life.

> **[Paul's Letter to the Ephesians 5:25-32] is addressed to the spouses as real women and men.**[185]

In the command "husbands, love your wives," we see St. Paul calling the husband to be a Christ figure for his wife. In imitation of Christ, the husband is called say "yes" to being a servant, which means laying down his life for his bride. He is called to be a man who is able to acknowledge her as equal to him in dignity, who will cherish and protect her as his own, as Christ does. "I have given you a model to follow, so that as I have done for you, you should also do" (Jn 13:15).

Women, it is important to understand what St. Paul is asking of the men. If they will say "yes" to loving you as Christ does, that is the game changer, the new innovation that is necessary if we as spouses are to love one another as Christ has loved us. The question is, will we as women allow ourselves to be loved? First, will you allow Christ to love you? Then, will you allow yourself to be loved by your husband? For it is Christ Who calls you to a lifelong spousal relationship with your husband. If you are called to marriage, it is Christ who will call you and join you with a man of grace who will love and cherish you as his wife. If you trust Christ, you will be able to trust your husband, and he will be able to trust you.

Many women go chasing after a man that they think is attractive and then try to change him or get him to love and commit. As the young woman in the cornfield found out, it is not going to happen. Only doing it God's way will bring about a joyful spousal union. Spousal love in Christ requires the personal integrity of both the man and woman, which brings about mutual honesty and trust. Only with grace can you both experience oneness and the love you both desire to give and receive.

The woman who says "yes" to the gift of her husband's love allows herself to be loved by her husband. She responds with the gift of her life, her own "yes" to his love. In this way, the oneness in the Christian marriage relationship is brought about by the Holy Spirit who joins their souls in the sacrament of marriage. St. John Paul II expands on the true oneness between spouses in marriage. Peter Williamson, a scholar of John Paul II's work, puts it this way:

> **According to John Paul II, the "essence of the love of a husband is to lay down his life for his bride." This kind of "love" excludes every kind of submission by which the wife would become a servant or slave of the husband, an object of one-sided submission. Love makes** *the husband simultaneously subject* **to the wife, and** *subject* **in this** *to the Lord himself,* **as the wife is to the husband."**[186]

"Be subordinate to one another out of reverence for Christ" (Eph 5:21). St. John Paul II is not doing away with St. Paul's metaphor of the husband being the "head." Love makes the husband simultaneously subject to his wife and through this, to the Lord, which in no way takes away from his role as the "head" of his family. The husband and father's role as "head" means he is called to be the defender, the watchdog of his family. St. Joseph is a great example of this, for it was he who was asked by the angel to defend Mary and baby Jesus from King Herod by fleeing to Egypt, which he did without hesitation. This is a subjection in which he served his wife and son out of love.

The mutual subjection of the spouses brings about consent and collaboration between them based on their mutual love for Christ which calls them "to love one another as I have loved you." Subjection requires us to be other-centered. It saves us from the sea of narcissism. This means the wife subjects herself freely to her husband's love, while he also freely subjects himself to her. This is required because of the equality they share based on their dignity as persons: "In the divine image He created them" (Gen 1:27). Husbands and wives receive particular graces to accomplish their unique and different roles as husbands and wives. Their shared spousal love becomes the heart of their home. Motherhood is femininity's greatest gift, and fatherhood is masculinity's greatest gift. Motherhood and fatherhood are the fulfillment of spousal love.

My parents loved each other well in the sacrament of marriage during their sixty-four years of married life. They wanted to have a big family and raised eight children. (Mom always wanted sixteen kids!) Dad was a loving husband and a rock-solid father, who supported the family through his medical practice. His number one trait was definitely the way he lived his moral principles, faithful to his wife, children, and patients. He spoke emphatically about their marriage, "If you both have your faith in God, so many of life's problems are solved."

As a family doctor and pediatrician, Dad saw firsthand the harmful effects that pornography, birth control, and abortion had on the family and on humanity. Unwilling to risk harm to his wife or any other woman, he refused to use pornography, and he wouldn't prescribe the birth control pill even though that decision resulted in decreased income and the loss of some of his patients. In this way, he acted as a watchdog by defending the dignity of not only his wife, but all of his patients. Dad stepped up in the 1960s, promoting Natural Family Planning (NFP) in its early years of development and speaking out against the legalization of abortion in 1973 with the Roe v. Wade decision by the US Supreme Court. Dad was also willing to make house calls or go the extra mile to help one of his patients out, for example, if someone was unable to pay a bill, "I would have them bring eggs from their farm or do some jobs, and then I would write off their bill."

> **Accordingly, since all are obligated to do the good that they can, men who realize the harm done by the sexual objectification of women are obligated to defend women from that objectification. ... This means not only fighting against pornography and other forms of objectification, but also against the demand that women reject the fertility of their bodies, and use contraceptives, or have abortions, to keep their jobs and to participate in culture. ... Only together can man and woman make human history a story of consideration and kindness.**[187]

Dad and Mom faithfully practiced their faith, going to Mass on Sundays and confession monthly, and praying together as well as with us kids, especially the rosary. I remember once asking Mom why there was a rosary in my dad's truck. Her quick reply was, "If you had seven daughters, you would pray the rosary every day too!" These are just some of the ways my father defended his family, leading us through some pretty difficult times by staying close to the Church and putting his faith into practice.

Mom was first of all a wife to a busy doctor and mother to us eight children. A teacher by profession, she gave much of her extra time to teaching the children at our parish church about their faith. Mom also worked with Dad to defend human life by setting up booths at fairs and at our parish to give out information to educate people about life issues, particularly abortion. Her love for babies drove her to do all that she could to defend their lives and help their mothers. Her number one traits were definitely her kindness and willingness to forgive as a mother. When you have eight children, you have to be very forgiving. If there were an Olympic gold medal for acts of forgiveness, she would have won it. Mom was also a very gifted singer and sang whenever the opportunity presented itself, whether in the church choir or around the piano at home. She loved to sing!

My parents also both loved to dance. It is especially important in marriage to dance together. Enjoying each other's company, having fun together, praying, forgiving, and, of course, working together, side by side, throughout their life, they continually made a sincere gift of their lives to one another and to us children. I can honestly never remember a time when my dad did not honor my mother. If she wanted to go somewhere or had a project to do around the house, she always had his support. He appreciated her and wanted the best for her always. If ever one of us kids was disrespectful to her, no matter where he was in the house, somehow, he heard. Then immediately he was there defending her, for she was first "his bride" and then our mother. This means that, as his wife, she helped him fulfill his vocation. In return, he helped her live out her vocation as well.

> **This is precisely the way Christ acts as the bridegroom of the Church; he desires that she be "in splendor, without spot or wrinkle" (Eph 5:27). One can say that this fully captures the whole "style" of Christ in dealing with women. Husbands should make their own the elements of this style in regard to their wives; analogously, all men should do the same in regard to women in every situation. In this way both men and women bring about "the sincere gift of self."[188]**

Christ's way of thinking and acting challenges both men and women to live holier lives, creating holier spousal unions. I think everyone would agree it is challenging to say "yes" to God. Yet this is what brings honor to God. It honors God when, as women and men, we choose to act as God created us to act, with kindness and charity toward the other spouse, willing the best for one another.

Dad enjoyed being the "head" of our family, often saying, "I am the captain, and this is my ship; when I say jump, you say how high!" He only said that to us kids of course and never to his wife. He would also add, "And when your mother says jump, you say how high." The sincere "gift of self" was found in the way Dad loved Mom but also in her mutual entrustment of herself to him. She trusted him and had no problem asking for his advice or help with anything. They rarely disagreed on anything in front of us kids. They frequently spent time talking together—just the two of them—on Saturday mornings. The only way we got in there on Saturday mornings was to bring them breakfast in bed. Then we were out. Mom was also very quick to back up Dad. If ever we would talk negatively about or disagree with him, she would almost always defend him.

This is the way spouses are to act toward one another, with kindness, trust, and affection, helping each other out. Especially as they aged, Dad went out of his way to be at Mom's side and care for her.

Not all people come from good families, and even good families struggle. If you are one of those people, all hope is not lost. Find a family that you want to be a part of and spend time with them, learning from them the necessary skills and knowledge. Then go build your own family with God and someone who wants this dream too!

This Gospel innovation that St. Paul is teaching on is actually bringing about "the something new," the game changer for Christian marriage and love, for it is a reversal of how things were done according to the customs of ancient times. Traditionally, men in ancient times could leave or divorce their wives for any reason (Mt 18:8-9). Women basically had no rights and were not treated as equals in the relationship.

> **[St. Paul] knows that this way of speaking, so profoundly rooted in the customs and religious tradition of the time, is to be understood and carried out in a new way: as a *"mutual subjection out of reverence for Christ"* (cf. Eph 5:21). This is especially true because the husband is called the "head" of the wife *as* Christ is the head of the Church; he is so in order to give "himself up for her" (Eph 5:25), and giving himself up for her means giving up even his own life.**[189]

This is the new innovation—the game changer—that the man of grace gains a greater awareness of his wife's dignity, her worth as God's daughter. She is given to him by God as a gift. The husband's role of being the "head," following Christ's example, is the game changer. Christ came to reestablish the "oneness" of the marital union of husband and wife. So, it is not a one-sided subjection of the wife. In a particular way, the husband is called to be the Christ figure in the home, serving his wife and family with kindness and strength, laying down his life as Christ did.

One of the husband's first priorities is his family's spiritual growth, praying and sacrificing for them. Second, he will work to defend his wife's dignity as an equal to him, as established in Genesis 1:27. Finally, he will work with his wife to develop and ensure, within their marriage relationship, a mutual oneness and unity that comes from a mutual subjection. Mutual subjection means that the couple defers to the husband as needed, such as in the example of St. Joseph packing up and moving his family to Egypt at the angel's request, yet also defers to the wife as needed, for example, when Mary says "yes" to becoming the Mother of God without Joseph's knowledge. In this way, Christ becomes the true source of their unity as Christ is the true source of the Church's unity.

> **However, whereas in the relationship between Christ and the Church the subjection is only on the part of the**

> Church, in the relationship between husband and wife the "subjection" is not one-sided but mutual.[190]

St. John Paul II is urging a spousal love and oneness in Christ that is beautiful and inspiring. Married couples who love each other with devotion and sacrificial love will inspire courage and bring hope to a world desperate for meaning and purpose. In Christ there will be no more, "… he will lord it over you" (Gen 3:16). For in Christ the old order is passing away and the new order of love has already come. Many couples who are married in Christ live out spousal love with much joy, as I witnessed with my parents and so many others. Christian marriage powerfully witnesses to the love and grace that Christ brings to the lives of those who choose to marry in Him.

The challenge for us as women is to seek out and let ourselves receive a higher love that can only be found in Christ. Too often we instead settle for a lukewarm commitment that disguises itself as real love. You, as a woman, will have a greater opportunity for self-discovery and fulfillment in your marriage if you choose wisely whom you marry. Think about it. A man who has discovered his own self-worth and life's purpose is someone you can trust. A man who is able to orient his whole existence and purpose in God knows that he is called to serve and defend his wife and family. Wow! This is something new and wonderful for you, as a woman, but also for the man, who can unite himself with his wife, thereby giving himself totally to her as a self-gift. When his total self-gift is met by her sincere gift of self to him, they truly become one. This is a deep spiritual reality as well as a physical one, for in the one-flesh union they are both affirmed in their true personal worth. This is especially so for the woman.

> **"Husbands, love your wives,"** love them because of that special and unique bond whereby in marriage a man and a woman become "one flesh" (Gen 2:24; Eph 5:31). In this love there is a fundamental *affirmation of the woman* as a person. This affirmation makes it possible for the female

personality to develop fully and be enriched.[191]

I have noticed that often when my husband is making a tasty sandwich to nourish himself, he will put a little more love into it, adding extra cheese and mayo and grilling it until it is delightful wonderfulness. So one day when he asked me, "Would you like a sandwich?" I said, "Yes and I want you to make me a sandwich like you are going to make *you* a sandwich!" The husband is to love his wife as he loves his own body (Eph 5:28). The love the husband has for himself should be the same love he has for his wife, cherishing her and delighting in her, even dying if necessary—or perhaps just making her a delicious sandwich.

My husband, Duane, takes seriously St. Paul's exhortation to put on the new man (Rom 6:6). Often, he will say, "Don't let the old man drive," meaning do not let the sin or brokenness of our past determine our new path. If we can keep our eyes on Christ and keep moving forward, no matter what, in the manner that each member of our family is called to by God, we will all be okay. Duane has believed in me and our kids, encouraging us to be faithful and to trust. He has given us the strength and confidence—truly the freedom—to become the family we are called to be.

Undivided Love. The love we share together as spouses and with our children reflects and mirrors the love and unity within the Most Holy Trinity. Side by side, the marriage union of a man and woman is strong, as it is willed to be. Yet there are still those who would prefer to have the one-sided subjection. I do not understand, for how can a one-sided subjection bring about a proper "unity of the two"?

> **However, the awareness that in marriage there is a mutual "subjection of the spouses out of reverence for Christ," and not just that of the wife to the husband, must gradually establish itself in hearts, consciences, behavior and customs.**[192]

Christ is bringing about a new order, a new way of doing

things, and it will take time and grace for this "new innovation" of marriage to be lived out. Recently, I was at a seminar in which the teachings of St. John Paul II on "mutual 'subjection of the spouses out of reverence for Christ'" were being presented by a professor at a local Catholic university. Colleagues had flown in from other universities to present different papers written on this same Apostolic Letter, *Mulieris Dignitatem*. Several of the professors were against the teaching on "mutual subjection of the spouses," declaring adamantly that the Scripture from Ephesians makes it clear that it is a one-sided subjection of the wife to her husband. One of the professors even said, "Well, it's just the Pope who taught this," to which I raised my hand and when called upon said, "Well, I am just glad that he did!" I was happy that St. John Paul II argued for "mutual subjection of the spouses" based on the equal dignity they shared from the beginning, as taught in Genesis 1:27: "So God created man in his own image, in the image of God he created him; male and female he created them." Peter Williamson states:

> **Pope John Paul's extensive treatment of Eph 5:21-33 emphasizes the equal dignity of women, the mutual subordination of husband and wife, and the responsibility of husbands to love their wives sacrificially and to relate to them with respect. The pope clearly sees that traditional patterns need to be reformed, and he emphasizes this side of the issue. However, the pope insists on the irreducible differences between male and female. Rather than reject the metaphor of husband as head or the instruction that wives should be subordinate to their husbands, he interprets each in a way that prioritizes mutual submission, love, and oneness in marriage.**[193]

As women, we might not be aware of our supreme calling to love as Christ loves us, within the order of love. It is Christ who summons some women to the mission of life and love within the family. It is Christ who provides grace, strengthening marriages to endure and thrive. The marriage itself becomes a great sign of God's divine love and mercy for "with grace" the couple becomes a witness to God's very real love, kindness, and fidelity.

Sacramental love flows from the heart of God. The more we understand marriage as a sacrament, given by Christ to give grace, the more we will ask Christ for the grace to love our spouse. It was a whole new way of thinking for the women and men of Ephesus. It is, however, what God wanted for the man and woman created as a "unity of the two" from the beginning! A oneness and unity that point to the great mystery of how Christ loves the Church and gives Himself up for her.

God's Love (The Symbolic Dimension of the Great Mystery)

A woman shared an experience she had during her prayer while on retreat in which she became aware of Jesus the Bridegroom: "Surprisingly Jesus came to me dressed in a tuxedo. I was in a long white gown. Jesus wanted to dance with me, so we started to dance; as we were dancing, he looked into my eyes with his own piercing eyes that gave me chills." She continued, saying that she had never felt more loved and cherished in her life. After her time in the chapel, she went back to her room and wept. As she was telling me about her experience she emphatically stated, "You cannot make this stuff up!"

The analogy of a Bridegroom's love is the symbolic dimension of the great mystery of God's love. It is a symbol that can help us to understand who God is and who we are, Bridegroom and bride. Yet even though we are like God, we are not God. I liked to tell the audiences that I have worked with over the years that *"there is a God and it's not you!"* So, even though we are like God, we are not God. If we are not God, then in some ways we are also not like God.

> **For the analogy implies a likeness, while at the same time leaving ample room for non-likeness.**[194]

Adam and Eve were created in the image and likeness of God. When they chose to sin, they became unlike God in many ways.

Firstly, they used their power to turn away from God and do their own thing. It caused their life to get messy real fast. What if God did that? What if God woke up one day and decided to pull the plug on humanity? We would be done for. God, however, remains faithful to who God is, meaning God cannot sin, since sin would be a contradiction of what it means to be God. God Who is love, can only love (1 Jn 4:16). The suffering from our brokenness and sin results in violence, wars, and death for people. God hates sin and the consequences of sin which affects us all: women, men, children, and families, as well as our societies and the Church. God, faithful to us, sent Christ to redeem all from sin without exception, to give us an extraordinary new beginning.

> **"Christ has loved the Church" (Eph 5:25) precisely as a community, as the People of God. At the same time… he has loved every individual person. For Christ has redeemed all without exception, every man and woman.**[195]

The love that Jesus has for us is like that of the bridegroom for his bride yet, naturally, it is not the same! God's love is divine; it is a supernatural love that is not limited like human love, with its communication limits and passions. God's supernatural ability to love is incomprehensible; we truly cannot begin to fathom it. God's powerful love is able to love a whole community of believers while at the same time loving each of us as if we were the only one. I like to think about it like the ocean. A whole lot of people could jump into the ocean and experience the waves at the same time, yet each one has their own experience of the ocean in a unique, personal way. Jesus Christ the Bridegroom gives to each and every person, from the greatest to the least, access to the ocean of God's merciful love.

> **Christ has entered [human] history and remains in it as the Bridegroom who "has given himself." "To give" means "to become a sincere gift" in the most complete and radical way: "Greater love has no man than this" (Jn 15:13).**[196]

When a man and a woman love in this way, it is one of the most beautiful of loves known to human beings, a love that is willing to lay down its life. With the loss of grace came the failure of women and men to love selflessly. God, not willing to give up on love, pursues humanity with great love. Also, like a father or mother who gives their son or daughter in marriage, God the Father gives us His only beloved Son, Jesus Christ, as the Bridegroom of the Church.

This woman's prayer meditation shows how much God wants you and me to know that we are deeply loved and cared for, like this woman who experienced Jesus coming to her in a tuxedo, dancing with her, and gazing into her eyes with the "interior gaze" that revealed to her the personal love of God for her: **"For your Maker is your husband…the God of the whole earth He is called"** (Is 54:5). This is the symbolic dimension of the great mystery. The prophet Isaiah compares God's love to the love shared between a bridegroom and the bride. Jesus proves His love for His bride by sacrificially loving her to the end (Jn 3:16). In the gift of His own life, Jesus makes the way for "the bride" who is every human being, male or female, who accepts the gift of the Son. As Bridegroom, Jesus gives Himself and makes us anew. For it was by God's gratuitous gift in Jesus that the new order of love, a new beginning, is made possible for every human being.

> **At the moment of the incarnation … God reached out to humanity and love; and, Mary responded with the totality of her being. … Mary exemplifies that the vocation of every human being (man or woman) is to respond fully to God's love. God loves first, humans reciprocate. This is what John Paul II calls the "order of love" (citations omitted).**[197]

> **In the Church every human being—male and female—is the "Bride," in that he or she accepts the gift of the love of Christ the Redeemer, and seeks to respond to it with the gift of his or her own person.**[198]

Throughout the New Testament, we see Christ restoring the dignity and vocation of women as the "daughters of Israel" (Lk 13:16, Mk 5:34, Lk 23:28). This divine love of Christ, shown toward His Bride, is given not only to heal and restore the dignity of each woman; It is also given to each man, to heal and affirm the goodness of masculinity and to restore the dignity of men, the "sons of Israel." So it is because of Christ the Bridegroom that women and men will take their place, their spot within the heart of Christ, in the halls of the heavenly kingdom as "daughters and sons" on equal footing.

> **Meditating on what the Gospels say about Christ's attitude towards women, we can conclude that *as a man,* a son of Israel, he *revealed* the dignity of the "daughters of Abraham" (cf. Lk 13:16), *the dignity belonging to women from the very "beginning" on an equal footing with men.*** [199]

Christ loved everyone—especially you—to the end, that is, to the end of His life lived on earth. And now, as the risen Lord, He still loves you. Christ wants you to love Him in return with your whole heart, mind, and soul. Who wants to marry someone who does not love them in return? It is up to you to examine your heart to see if you have accepted the gift of His grace that is being offered. Does this matter? Yes, very much.

Yet, so often, we are afraid to love, afraid of what it might cost us. When I was serving the Church as a youth director, I remember going through a hard time, carrying a heavy cross. I thought about quitting and looking for other work. I said to Jesus one night as I prayed in adoration, "I will keep working for you if you promise me that this will never happen again." *Then you want nothing to do with Me,* is what the Holy Spirit seemed to say, reminding me of Jesus's words: "If any man would come after me, let him deny himself and take up his cross and follow me" (Mt 16:24). Although the words shook me up a bit, I realized that, as the bride of Christ, I must, like Him, take up my cross and give love to God and neighbor "to the end"

(Jn 13:1).

We know that God will love us in good times and bad, in sickness and in health, until death. But will we choose to love Him? The love that Christ offers takes nothing away from our lives—in fact, it only enriches us. God's grace grants us the freedom to live now with confidence in the great mystery of God's love. God's plan will be fully revealed in His perfect timing, "a plan for the fullness of time, to unite all things in Him, things in heaven and things on earth" (Eph 1:10). Truly, the best is yet to come! As Pope Benedict once said,

> **Do not be afraid of Christ! He takes nothing away, and he gives you everything. When we give ourselves to him, we receive a hundredfold in return. Yes, open, open wide the doors to Christ—and you will find true life.**[200]

The true life that Christ wants us to experience in our marriages can be an encounter with the great mystery of the love of God. I say "can be" since many marriages fail, causing much stress and anxiety to our families and communities. The failure of families to thrive has caused many people to fear commitment and marriage. People must return to Christ. Only in this way will we find the grace to forgive those who have harmed us, closing the door to evil, while opening a door to a new life. With Christ at the center of the couple's relationship, the family itself is called to its own mission, a mission to share life and love with all they encounter.

> **Willed by God in the very act of creation, marriage and the family are interiorly ordained to fulfillment in Christ and have need of his graces in order to be healed from the wounds of sin and restored to their "beginning," that is, to the full understanding and the full realization of God's plan.**[201]

In particular, the love Jesus reveals and communicates to women allows us to discover our identity, our self-worth, and our purpose as persons created for our *own sake*. Is it any wonder when society, especially the family, is so disrupted, that we forget how to love and care for each other? When we do not feel loved and respected as human beings, we cannot appreciate the gift of our own life, let alone the life of another. *Remember you can never earn your worth or your dignity because God has already given it to you!*

Every woman has her inheritance as a "daughter of Abraham." We truly are daughters of God. This means that, no matter how badly we have been treated, no one has the power to take away our worth or dignity. It also means that when we experience a true, faithful love we can come to better know our own dignity and worth. This is why God wants us to come to a deep understanding of how we are loved in Him, in the new order of love. God wants us to come to understand the mystery of His great love in our relationships, particularly the spousal relationship.

Your maker, the God of all of creation, is your husband. The hallmarks of a spouse's love are power and tenderness. I was at an evening reflection for married couples when I heard this moving quote from King Baudouin, king of the Belgians from 1951-1993, written in his journal as a prayer to the Blessed Mother for his wife, Her Excellency, Dona Fabiola Fernanda Marie:

> **Mary, show me what I should do so as to not miss an opportunity of loving, of denying myself for your sake, as if it were my last, and of loving darling Fabiola infinitely more. Yes, Mother teach me to love her with tenderness, gentleness, thoughtfulness, respect, and teach me to have faith in her.**[202]

This King's tender prayer to the Blessed Mother and for his wife, the Queen of the Belgians, is a beautiful example of how we are to love God and each other during our reign on earth—for to serve is to reign.

Heaven on Earth (The Eucharist)

> **We find ourselves at the very heart of the Paschal Mystery [the sacrifice of the Cross], which completely reveals the spousal love of God. Christ is the Bridegroom because "he has given himself": his body has been "given," his blood has been "poured out" (cf. Lk 22:19-20). In this way "he loved them to the end" (Jn 13:1).**[203]

Each of us is called to take our place in our response to the Great Mystery of God's love revealed in Jesus, Who in a certain sense, said His wedding vows to His Bride at the Last Supper: "And he took bread, gave thanks, and broke it, and gave it to them saying, 'This is my body given up for you; do this in remembrance of me.' Then in the same way, he took the cup, saying, 'This cup is the new covenant in my blood, which is poured out for you'" (Lk 22:19-20). Jesus died out of love for you and me on that Cross, laying down His life for His Bride: "Greater love has no man than this, that a man lay down his life for his friends" (Jn 15:13).

While I was in college studying for a degree in theology, I decided to apply to work in the national parks as a summer student missionary. I was accepted and assigned to Yellowstone National Park. My duties included helping out with a Christian prayer service in the park on the weekends. As a Catholic, I consider Mass essential, so I planned on attending Mass Saturday evenings in the park. If some of our missionary activities were planned at the same time, I would simply join in after Mass. Because I was the only Catholic on our team, it became an opportunity for me to discover more about my faith and the Real Presence of Christ in the Eucharist.

One typical Saturday night I joined the team after Mass for prayer and fellowship. As I was heading back to my sleeping quarters, one of my team leaders, who was the preacher—and also happened to be a very handsome, six-foot man from Buford, Georgia—approached me and asked if he could talk to me for a minute. After I agreed, he fired away, asking in a slow southern drawl, "Do you really believe that the bread and the wine become the Body and Blood of Our Lord

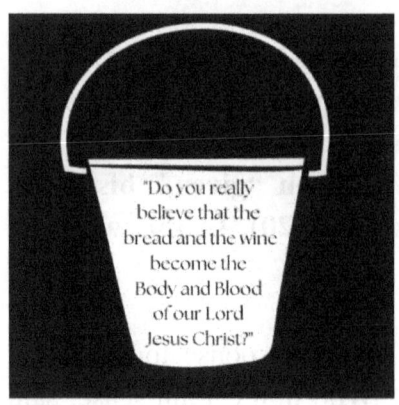

Jesus Christ?" I just stared back into his questioning face. It was as though he was saying, "Do you really believe in Santa Claus?" After thinking for a moment, I looked into those eyes and made an act of faith, saying, "Yes! Yes, I do!" He shook his head, and as he walked away he said, "Well, I guess you will just have to keep going then."

It was difficult for him to understand why I insisted on going to Mass every Saturday night when our ministry team hosted several Christian services in the park every Sunday. "Wasn't that enough?"

This conversation with the Southern Baptist preacher was a turning point for me and my Catholic faith. No one had ever asked me the question: "Do you really believe that the bread and the wine change into the Body, Blood, Soul, and Divinity of our Lord Jesus Christ?" Transubstantiation? It challenged me to really think and pray about the teaching of Christ on Holy Communion. As I began to look into the teachings on the Eucharist, I saw that Jesus and the Church seemed pretty clear about belief in the Real Presence of Christ. *But did I believe it?*

> **This is the bread which comes down from heaven, that a man may eat of it and not die. I am the living bread which comes down from heaven; if anyone eats of this bread, he will live forever; and the bread which I shall give for the life of the world is my flesh. (Jn 6:50-51)**

As the Son of God, Jesus had full authority to act and to establish the Eucharist in the manner that He saw best as the sacrament of His love and self-gift on that Cross (Mt 28:18-20). When we receive Holy Communion, we receive the risen and glorified Lord Jesus Christ, *"fire and Spirit."*

He who eats it with faith eats Fire and Spirit... thus by the gift of his body and blood Christ increases within us the gift of his Spirit, already poured out in Baptism, and bestowed as a "seal" in the sacrament of Confirmation.[204]

In the Gospel of John, chapter 6, we see Jesus teaching the bread of life discourse which many of His followers are unable to grasp. They begin to murmur and complain, "These teachings are too hard to accept" (Jn 6:60). We do this, too. We get upset and say things like, "This is just too much," or "How could anyone ever believe this?"

Truly, truly, I say to you unless you eat the flesh of the Son of Man and drink his blood, you have no life within you. (Jn 6:53)

Jesus is testing the faith of His disciples, for with God nothing is impossible, right? If God can become a baby, God can become the "Bread of Life." Jesus turns to the twelve Apostles and asks, *"Will you too turn away?"* to which Simon Peter answers, "Lord to whom shall we go? You have the words of eternal life; And we have believed and have come to know, that you are the Holy One of God" (Jn 6:66-69). It is by faith and through their relationships with Jesus that the twelve Apostles come to know that Jesus Christ is the Messiah. It is not enough to know about Jesus; like Mary, they need to put their faith in Him. They need to belong to Him.

In order to be a disciple of Jesus, we have to be humble; that means we need to be teachable. Simon Peter asked the right question, "Lord to whom shall we go?" This is followed by a declaration of faith, "You have the words of eternal life." Jesus did many miracles, giving evidence that He is the Son of God. Rising from the dead was the greatest sign of His divinity, for no one has ever risen from the dead by their own power. When we receive Jesus in Holy Communion with faith, we receive that same power and divinity.

We simply do not understand everything about God. Simon

Peter did not get everything Jesus was saying and doing, but because he was humble, he was teachable. Jesus responded to those who murmured and complained by asking, "What if you were to see the Son of Man ascending where He was before?" (Jn 6:62) Jesus is like, "Hello, what if you were to see Me go up, up and away into the heavenlies? Do you think that I came into the world only to show you what you think you know? *No, I came to show you what you could not know.* This is so that you might have life. Yes, abundant life in Me! You often see Me as being like you, which **I am**, *but I also am not like you*. I come from heaven. **I Am God**."

> **It is the Spirit that gives life, the flesh is of no avail; the words that I have spoken to you are Spirit and life. But there are some of you that do not believe. (Jn 6:63-64)**

Many of Jesus's followers left Him that day. They took offense at Jesus's teaching. Many Catholics leave Jesus too or, even worse, they never give Him a chance. I gave an enthusiastic teaching on the Holy Eucharist to a bunch of teenagers who were in confirmation prep. After the talk, the priest of the parish came up to me and said, "I wonder if that was a little too strong. It may have turned a few of them off." I replied in all sincerity, "I do not know Father. It may have been too strong. I am, however, more afraid that we will never turn them on!" to which he replied, "Good point!"

Jesus came down from heaven to turn us on to the truth that God loves us and wants to give us a grace-filled, abundant life. God invites everyone, from the greatest to the least, to the heavenly wedding banquet: "Come to me all you who labor and are heavily burdened and I will give you rest" (Mt 11:28) —rest from all the worries and burdens of daily life. We as people need to rest in God's love and strength in order to have peace in our hearts, our homes, and our world. This is what God wants for all people. If we ask for more faith, Jesus will give us more faith. "Lord, I believe, help my unbelief" (Mk 9:24), is a favorite prayer for many who struggle to believe. It is by faith that we can grow in hope and love. When the sum of love is greater in the world than the sum of hate, humanity will be taking a step in the right direction. *Jesus made that step for us.* Now He offers us all that great love at every Mass, which is the portal to Calvary where Christ reconciled the world to the Father and unified heaven and earth through His love. So going to Mass is not just going to church, it is also going to Calvary. By receiving the Eucharist, we receive Christ Himself. The One Who became incarnate, died on the Cross, rose from the dead, and unifies us to Himself with all of heaven offers a oneness that is unknown to humanity. This love is so wonderful that once it is experienced, sharing it becomes irresistible. By sharing God's love, we can increase the sum of love in the world, one heart at a time.

After a summer working in Yellowstone, I returned to school that fall, where I continued to pray and study theology. I began attending daily Mass, thinking very hard about the meaning of it all, our Catholic faith, and the relationship that I really wanted with God. I remember praying one night that I did not want to die and find out that it was all true and that I had missed out. How many Catholics have missed out on the opportunity to experience the love that God offers to us each day, especially in that "little host" (Jn 6:35)? What a sweet, loving God, Who so carefully laid the foundations of the earth, planning and creating all that was necessary so that we could exist and have life. But then to go so far as to become God in a Bod™, giving Himself on that Cross. And on top of that, He comes to us in the Eucharist so that we can partake of His divine love. Yes, we are created by love, for love, to love. The Holy Mass is the fountain of life and love that flows freely, grace upon grace, into every human heart that is open, for

"I did not want to die and find out that it was all true, and that I had missed out."

> **the Eucharist is "the source and summit of the Christian life."... For in the blessed Eucharist is contained the whole spiritual good of the Church, namely Christ himself, our**

Pasch.[205]

One evening during final exams week at college, I attended a Mass held in the dorms for all the stressed-out students. I remember feeling a little overwhelmed with finals, plus more coffee was not the answer. I needed peace. As I approached the altar to receive Holy Communion, I was not praying for faith in and understanding of the Real Presence of Christ; I was simply praying for help! As soon as I received the Host, a deep supernatural peace filled my entire being. I was so surprised and simultaneously filled with joy. Jesus really was here, present in the little consecrated Host; the peace I felt was indescribable. All those years I had been receiving Him in faith; now God filled me with the grace of a deeper awareness of Jesus, present in that little Host, coming to me personally to "give me rest." Many times, after going to Mass, I have had a deeper sense of peace and clarity. It is, however, not as strong as that special day when God answered my prayers. The Scriptures say, "Seek and you will find; knock and the door will be open" (Mt 7:7). It's really true. As St. John Paul II is known to have said,

…in that little Host is the solution to all the problems of the world.

As I continued to study theology for my undergraduate work, I was approached by some other students on campus who were curious as to why I was studying theology. "Do you want to be a priest?" they asked. If we are going to begin to understand and believe in the Eucharist, we are also going to have to understand and believe in the ministerial priesthood. For just as the Baptist preacher did not understand why I wanted to attend Mass to receive the Eucharist, many people do not accept or believe that Christ calls ordinary men to the ordained ministerial priesthood. Many people, also, simply do not understand why a woman would not be called by Christ to be a ministerial priest.

So, who is the ministerial priest? The ministerial priest

becomes a sacrament of Christ so that Christ in the priest can make Christ in the Eucharist. Christ in the priest forgives the sins of the penitent. It is Christ who calls forth the Church, the Bride of Christ. This is not magic; it is grace. It is also the plan, straight from God, both in Creation and in the fullness of time, "to redeem all things in Christ!" (Col 1:20-22) This great mystery is so much "bigger bigger" than we are or could imagine. Christ came into the world as a man, as the Bridegroom. This is the reason God calls men to be priests. When acting as a priest, they are acting in the person of Christ.

> **Against the broad background of the "great mystery" expressed in the spousal relationship between Christ and the Church, it is possible to understand adequately the calling of the "Twelve."** *In calling only men as his Apostles,* **Christ acted** *in a completely free and sovereign manner.*[206]

The "something bigger" is the gift of the Holy Eucharist because it is in the Holy Eucharist that the Lord Jesus remains present on earth. "Take; this is my body" (Mk 14:22). Jesus instituted the Holy Eucharist as a sacrament of His love, the sign of the new beginning, the New Covenant.

To enable the Church to carry out the work of our redemption, Christ instituted the Sacrament of the Holy Eucharist along with Holy Orders. Both sacraments were instituted at the Last Supper. For only to the Twelve did Jesus say, "Do this in remembrance of me" (Lk 22:19). The twelve Apostles received their marching orders from Christ Himself, Who alone commissioned and empowered them to act on His behalf, *in persona Christi,* "in the person of Christ." The sacrament of penance was also instituted by Christ when, after He rose from the dead, He appeared only to the Twelve, saying, "Whose sins you forgive are forgiven them and whose sins you retain are retained" (Jn 20:23).

I have heard it said that more and more baptized Catholics do not believe in the Real Presence of Christ in the Holy Eucharist. In light of this, the decline in the number of people going to Holy Mass makes sense. Why would you go to Mass if you do not believe? We must come to the Eucharist with an attitude of faith and openness to conversion. This is the only way that the Mass will start to make sense. The mystery of the Holy Mass contains the greatest gift, for the redemptive act of Christ is made present, along with all of heaven. Every time we go to Holy Communion, we receive Jesus Christ in the Holy Eucharist. As the sovereign Lord, Jesus Christ set up the way in which he wanted the Mass, sacraments, and Church to be ordered.

Jesus, as the Son of God, was not limited in any way. He certainly would have gone against the customs of ancient times which systemically discriminated against women if this were only a cultural obstacle. So then, why? Why did Jesus only ordain men as His first priests?

> **It is *the Sacrament of the Bridegroom and of the Bride*. The Eucharist makes present and realizes anew in a sacramental manner the redemptive act of Christ, who "creates" the Church, his body. Christ is united with this "body" as the bridegroom with the bride.**[207]

Jesus ordained men because He came to the world as a man. He desired to express Himself in a sacramental manner through men who, by becoming ordained priests, would lay down their lives as He did, bringing the Person of Christ into the world. Thus, through the holy priesthood, Jesus Christ would continue to spiritually father and lead the Church, the Bride of Christ. Christ's tender, faithful, pure, and unfathomable love for His Bride would be revealed and continue through the holy priesthood "to the close of the age" (Mt 28:20). If we receive the Eucharist with an attitude of faith, Jesus will come to us personally, making it possible for us to access our *real life*. "For we are his workmanship, created in Christ Jesus for good works, which God prepared beforehand, that we should walk in them" (Eph 3:10). It's the highest calling and most urgent appeal from God, that in response to the gift of His Son, we would choose to make a *personal self-gift back to Christ the Bridegroom.*

Christ came into the world as a man born of a woman, thus affirming and redeeming the dignity and worth of both woman and man, while also re-establishing the "unity of the two" as it was planned by God from the beginning. Jesus came to redeem woman (femininity) and man (masculinity). This redemption includes the way men and women think, act, and relate to one another, especially in their marriages, but also in everyday relationships that happen in every aspect of human life: families, workplaces, and all of society. This is big for women, men, for everyone. What Christ came to accomplish, Christ will finish, redeeming all peoples and things in His Precious Blood.

> **Christ ... wished to express the relationship between man and woman, between what is "feminine" and what is "masculine." It is a relationship willed by God both in the mystery of creation and in the mystery of Redemption. It is *the Eucharist* above all that expresses *the redemptive act of Christ the Bridegroom towards the Church, the Bride.*** [208]

Only by seeking to sincerely understand one another and serve together, can we hope to achieve the unity and victory that is made possible in Christ. Through Christ, grace, and much human effort, women can get their lives under control. We can calm down, stop judging, stop competing, and work together with other women and men to accomplish what God calls us to do together as the Church, the Bride. This longing to be "one" comes straight from the heart of Christ, Who prayed with longing to the Father before His arrest, "May all be one; even as you, Father, are in me, and I in you" (Jn 17:21). The Eucharist is given so that you and I might enter into the love and unity of the Holy Trinity by remembrance ("Do this in memory of me.") of the great love and tenderness which Christ has shown us. His Body has been "given"; his Blood has been "poured out" (Lk 22:19-20). Jesus wanted us to remember Him with great love and affection.

I went to visit four teenagers to invite them to the youth program at the Catholic church where I was working. The mother of the crew just smiled and let me in. The kids were all playing a game. She introduced me and quickly left the room. The teens went back to their game without a word to me. Cold indifference.

I stood in the doorway for a few long minutes, wondering what to do. The mother finally came and showed me to the door. Later that day while attending Mass, I received the Eucharist. As I began to pray, I thought of poor Jesus and how often He is treated coldly by his people. How often are we like teenagers, preoccupied with life and ignoring the invitation in front of us? Many times receiving Holy Communion and forgetting to pray—or even worse, do not even think about Jesus at all?

The love of Jesus Christ the Bridegroom is given freely at every Holy Mass, for it is through the Eucharist that we receive Christ Who is our peace. The Eucharist is a living sign, a sacrament that supernaturally makes present in time the one great sacrifice of love offered by Christ over 2000 years ago at Calvary. Remember, heaven is very close to us, yet outside of human time and space. Christ remains present in time and space through the Eucharist, which is kept in all the tabernacles of the world until the end of time. That is why a candle remains burning by the tabernacle in a Catholic Church, to let you know Jesus Christ is always there waiting for you. It is also why we bend the knee to genuflect, a sign of love and devotion to Christ the King!

The Eucharist is the powerhouse of grace that seeks to unite us all in the divine love, bringing about a wonderful Undivided Love with Christ the Bridegroom, as well as with one another as the Bride.

I do! I do! (The Gift of the Bride)

"I do! I do!" This is the response given at baptism, where we profess our vows to Jesus. The celebrant asks, "Do you renounce Satan and all his empty promises?" Our response is, "I do!" "Do you reject the glamour of evil and refuse to be mastered by sin?" "I do!" "Do you believe in God, the Father Almighty?" "I do!" "In Jesus Christ, His only Son?" "I do!" They sound like the promises given at a wedding. That's because they are! In making our baptismal vows and being baptized, we take our place as members of the Bride of Christ. These vows are repeated also at first Holy Communion, at confirmation, and every year at the Easter Mass.

Yes, this blessing of Holy Baptism unites you with Jesus, marking your soul with an indelible seal that can never be destroyed. Just as God cannot be seen, neither can your soul, yet we know by faith and reason both exist. It is the gift of sanctifying grace that restores your inheritance as a child of God, calling you to mature in faith through a life of love and service. This personal calling is unique to you and given to you by God. This means you should not compare yourself to others. For you are a unique person with your own set of life circumstances, as well as your own particular gifts and talents, given to you for this time in history. God is still on the move today.

***All the baptized share in the one priesthood of Christ*, both men and women, inasmuch as they must "present their bodies as a living sacrifice, holy and acceptable to God (cf. Rom 12:1), give witness to Christ in every place, and give an explanation to anyone who asks the reason for the hope in eternal life that is in them (cf. 1 Pt 3:15)."**[209]

Grace opens the door, making the impossible, possible. It is grace that makes us holy and acceptable to God. If we are open to grace, it gives us light and power, allowing us to overcome the darkness in our lives. We see this with the Samaritan woman, a known sinner who encounters Jesus Christ at the well. After encountering Jesus, she *believes*; accepting grace, she *becomes* a prophet who goes on to give witness to Christ, to a whole town: "Come, see a man who told me all that I ever did" (Jn 4:29). The Samaritan woman had a choice and so do you.

My daughter was facing another difficult knee surgery. It was her second torn meniscus and ACL injury in a year. She shared: "I feel like I just climbed all the way up this gigantic hill with my sled, only to find myself being pushed down again." Isn't this the way life is at times? I did not blame her for being down; I was feeling overwhelmed and discouraged too. I needed encouragement and grace, so I decided to go to confession. After the priest absolved my sins, I was turning to leave when he said, *"You do have a choice on how you handle this."* I thought about how Christ fell while carrying His Cross; He kept going. I could too.

> **It expresses at the same time the "great mystery" described in the Letter to the Ephesians:** *the bride united to her Bridegroom...***united** *in such a manner as to respond* **with a "sincere gift"** of self *to the inexpressible gift of the love of the Bridegroom,* **the Redeemer of the world.**[210]

Despite the challenges and difficulties of life, we are not alone. We are free to choose in every circumstance. With God's grace, we will get through it, or He will show us how to go around the problem. Like my daughter's messed-up knee, this too will pass. It's what we learn in the process of life that matters. It's who we become that counts. This means choosing to be positive, calm, and grateful (versus tossing, turning, and grumbling). This means the tears, the surgery, and all the other difficulties of my "little life" not only give witness to my faith but become a "sincere gift" to His Majesty, Christ the King, as well as those people I am called to serve.

> **And holiness is measured according to the "great mystery" in which the Bride responds with the gift of love to the gift of the Bridegroom. She does this "in the Holy Spirit," since "God's love has been poured into our hearts through the Holy Spirit who has been given to us" (Rom 5:5).**[211]

Often, we do not have control over the things that happen in our lives. We do, however, always have a choice in how we respond. Handled with grace, the challenges and difficulties of our lives become a "sincere gift" to Christ and to those we serve. This is holiness; it is Christ in you and me. Holy women can have a great impact within their realm of influence in their homes, communities, and places of work. For what do we have in this life without our mothers, grandmothers, or other motherly figures? Where would Jesus or we be without Mother Mary?

> **...in the hierarchy of holiness, it is *precisely the "woman,"* Mary of Nazareth, who is the "figure" of the Church. She "precedes" everyone on the path to holiness; in her person "the Church has already reached that perfection whereby she exists without spot or wrinkle (cf. Eph 5:27)."[212]**

I do not think Mary will ever regret her choice to be Jesus's mother, her choice to belong to God. She did with her "little life" what God was asking of her, and, because she did, she became so much more than she could ever have dreamed of or imagined; she became the Mother of God. Mary is remembered and honored in every generation. I recently read about Mary in a National Geographic magazine article titled "The World's Most Powerful Woman." Talk about being a humble woman of great power and influence.

Being holy is likened to having a heart full of grace that allows you to love. This is where the "I do, I do" comes in. Christ already professed His "I do, I do" for you and me when He went to that Cross. Freely, the Holy Spirit is given to us, yet it cost Christ everything. Your life's purpose and calling is to be lived out in direct response to Christ's gift of love. You and I are called to simply learn how to love God and serve Him in this life and then to be with God forever in the next. This happens by becoming who you are in Christ. You do not want to waste your life; it is your most precious gift. Your life lived with grace will lead you home to God Himself, if you let it.

In the history of the Church, even from earliest times, there

were side-by-side with men *a number of women*, for whom the response of the Bride to the Bridegroom's redemptive love acquired full expressive force.[213]

Remember the young woman who said to me, "I would like very much to be a priest, but who would ever want to be a nun?" Why would a woman want to be a nun? Well, let's look to Mother Teresa. Why did she want to be a nun? "Jesus was my first love," wrote Agnes Gonxha Bojaxhiu, who already at the age of twelve, felt she might have a calling to the poor.[214] Agnes, whom we know today as Mother Teresa, became a nun at the age of eighteen with the Sisters of Loretto. The Sisters were stationed in Calcutta where Mother Teresa spent her first seventeen years teaching the Indian children of Calcutta.

Then on September 10th, 1946, while traveling on a train to her retreat, Mother Teresa received what she describes as her "calling within a call." She said it was on that day that Jesus revealed to her His pain at seeing the indifference and contempt for His poor. Jesus asked Teresa to be the face of His mercy; "Come be my light… I cannot go alone."[215] That day, Jesus made it known to her that He was asking her to leave the safety of the convent walls and go out into the streets of Calcutta to help the poorest of the poor. Jesus asked her to, "Carry Me into the holes of the poor… I want Indian nuns, Missionaries of Charity, who would be My fire of love among the poor, the sick, the dying and the little children."[216]

Mother Teresa started each day in communion with Jesus in the Eucharist and then went out, rosary in hand, to find and serve Him in the unwanted, the unloved, and the uncared for. In the streets of Calcutta, there was much social discrimination. Would Catholic nuns be accepted?

The new hospice—her Home for the Dying—raised the kind of faith issues that had nearly destroyed India. Hinduism divided society into castes, something like social classes only much more rigidly defined, and allowed only members of the lowest castes to deal with the dead, who

were considered spiritually unclean. The mere thought of Teresa's sisters, some of them highborn, tending the mortally ill in a facility right next to a sacred shrine infuriated some radical Hindus, who also accused Teresa of requiring deathbed conversions from her patients. As the story goes, an enraged mob entered the hospice and threatened to kill her. But when she replied calmly, "If you kill us, we would only hope to reach God sooner," they retreated.[217]

At times, especially at the beginning of her mission, her own life was threatened by some who did not understand her motives. She responded with unshakable confidence. It was her faith and determination that allowed her to take her place in the streets of Calcutta with no harm ever coming to her or to her sisters who joined her in the work of caring for the poor, the sick, and the dying people of Calcutta. So, who would ever want to be a nun? Maybe the better question to ask is: "Could God be asking *me* to be a nun?" Women, strengthened by their union with Christ, are able to live a life of freedom and service that has many blessings and great impact on serious social discrimination, as seen in Mother Teresa's work, as well as the work of many other women throughout the Church's history.

Even in the face of serious social discrimination, holy women have acted "freely," strengthened by their union with Christ. Such union and freedom rooted in God explain, for example, the great work of Saint Catherine of Siena in the life of the Church, and the work of Saint Teresa of Jesus in the monastic life. ... Holy women are an incarnation of the feminine ideal; they are also a model for all Christians, a model of the *"sequela Christi"* [the following of Christ], an example of how the Bride must respond with love to the love of the Bridegroom.[218]

"But the greatest of these is love" (1 Cor 13:13). The suffering of that Cross reveals God's deepest love and longing for fallen humanity, "for love is as strong as death". Christ sets you as a bride, as a seal upon His heart (Sg 8:6) —yes, His very heart, which is a human heart like yours and mine yet filled with divine love. This is why it is necessary to go to the inner room of your heart, to be with the God Who loves you. For Christ desires that we would love Him in return—yes, with our whole heart, soul, and strength (Dt 6:5). For the most important thing we will ever do with our lives is love our God and, in doing so, love one another.

This is a definite, "I do, I do," moment for all who allow themselves to be loved by Jesus Christ. For the supreme calling of each human person will one day be fully revealed when all will behold the Bride of Lamb (Rev 21).

> **"…Come, I will show you the Bride, the wife of the Lamb." And in the Spirit, he carried me to a great, high mountain, and showed me the holy city Jerusalem coming down out of heaven from God, having the glory of God, its radiance like a most rare jewel, like a jasper, clear as crystal. It had a great, high wall, with twelve gates, … on the gates the names of the twelve tribes of the sons of Israel … And the wall of the city had twelve foundations, and on them the twelve names of the twelve apostles of the Lamb … And I saw no temple in the city, for its temple is the Lord God the Almighty and the Lamb. (Rev 21:9-22)**

Questions for Reflection
Chapter 7
Will You Be Mine?

1. What are one or two takeaways from this chapter?

2. Will You Be Mine? Have you been able to say "yes" to belonging to Jesus? What is holding you back?

3. As He intervened in the life of the young woman in the cornfield, Jesus came to deliver us from bad relationships if only we would listen. What relationships do you need to set better boundaries in or end?

4. St. John Paul II is not doing away with St. Paul's metaphor of the husband being the "head." He is however expanding on it in order to shed light on the true "oneness" in marriage between the spouses. Why is this call for true spousal "oneness" important in Christian marriage?

5. The essence of the love of a husband is to lay down his life for his bride. Why does this kind of love exclude every kind of submission by which the wife would become a servant or a slave of the husband, or an object of one-sided submission?

6. What are the challenges to recognizing the equal dignity of women and men?

7. Many Catholics leave Jesus or, even worse, they never give Him a chance. What challenges do you face when it comes to the teachings about the Holy Eucharist in the Catholic Church? How can you choose to study the teachings in order to draw closer to Jesus in the Holy Eucharist?

Notes

"The Greatest of These Is Love"

"The Church believes that Christ, who died and was raised up for all, can through his Spirit offer man the light and the strength to respond to his supreme destiny." ... The particular reference to the dignity of women and their vocation, precisely in our time, can and must be received in the "light and power" which the Spirit grants to human beings, including the people of our own age, which is marked by so many different transformations.[219]

Light and Power (In the Face of Changes)

I was working in Yellowstone National Park at a summer job during college. In addition to a paycheck, I was looking for peace in the midst of the many changes I was undergoing, including graduating and finding a "real job." I was anxious about my future. I would go on runs every day in the beautiful park. As I was running, I would think and pray about everything I was hoping to accomplish in my future, going over things in my mind again and again. One day, while I was out on a run, an image came to me: a rabbit chasing after a carrot on a stick that kept going round and round. The rabbit could not catch the carrot. I realized that the carrot was the life that I was striving for; it seemed impossible for me to grasp. Who ultimately held that carrot? Who knew me and could help me figure it out?

I went back to my room, grabbed a little traveler's Bible I had brought from home, and headed back out to the park, to my favorite spot below the waterfalls at the Grand Canyon of Yellowstone. Here, I chose to pray and seek God's purpose for my life. I opened up the little Bible to the words, "My people, my people, what have I done to you…how have I burdened you?" (Mi 6:3) Then I read, "Else their eyes will see, their ears will hear, their hearts will understand, and they will turn and be healed" (Is 6:10). I immediately knew I had a choice to make. Did I believe? Faith in Jesus Christ is the key that opens the door to accessing the relationship with God that I was desperately seeking. Jesus Christ is the anchor, the focal point, and the goal of each human person.

> **The Church "holds that in her Lord and Master can be found the key, the focal point, and the goal" of man and "of all human history," and she "maintains *that beneath all changes there are many realities which do not change and which have their ultimate foundation in Christ,* who is the same yesterday and today, yes and forever."**[220]

The key, the focal point, and the goal for each woman's fulfillment lie in her ability to choose wisely the path for her own life, despite the many transitions and changes that present themselves to her. In believing and belonging to God, each woman can access the light and the power to find her real life in God, her Creator. No matter how many turns your life has taken or how messy it has become, your real life can begin again in Jesus Christ.

So that day in Yellowstone, the words of Micah and Isaiah cut me to the heart. I knew, with all the changes going on, I had been trying to figure out everything on my own. I felt God's compassion yet almost frustration in the words, "My people, my people, what have I done to you?" I wanted to believe in God. Yet my heart was sluggish, my ears dull, and my eyes closed to the truth about who God is and what that meant for my life. Why would God care about me?

"I wanted to believe in God"

Yet if I continued to search vainly on my own, I might miss out on the life God had for me, my spot, my place in the bigger plan of God.

That afternoon in front of the big waterfalls at Yellowstone National Park, I prayed to God with my whole heart. It was when I prayed with my whole heart that the door opened for me. I prayed to Jesus, "I am turning to you for help. I am asking you to heal me. Please heal me, help me, and let me see the meaning of my life. Heal my heart; I am so tired of doing this life alone. Show me my spot in you, my place in this world." As I prayed for this grace, a peace came over me, a deep peace that I had not experienced in a long time. God was real and He was listening.

> **We can face these changes correctly and adequately only *if we go back* to the foundations which are to be found in Christ, to those *"immutable"* [unchanging] *truths and values* of which he himself remains the "faithful witness" (cf. Rev 1:5) and Teacher.**[221]

So often our lives are like the life of the man my mom saved from drowning. The things we chase after, like the beach ball, cannot save us. Many people believe they can figure life out for themselves. An open, humble mindset and a willingness to be taught is necessary. Are you teachable? When we turn to Christ for true answers to our life's questions, like "Who am I?" and "What is my purpose?" we are able to discover the truths and values that Christ holds for us. These truths include the dignity, worth, and purpose that God had in mind for each one of us when creating us.

God places a calling in our hearts and waits for us to be open to that calling (Jer 29:13). The battlefield is within our hearts; we often must struggle to hear and to act as the voice of God directs us. The world, in so many ways, is like the beach ball, with its bright colors, tossing on the water, but when we grasp onto it, pop! For the created world, with all its good things, pleasures, and technology, will ultimately fail since loving God and loving people for God's sake are the ultimate reasons for our human existence.

What's Love Got to Do with It? (The Dignity of Women and the Order of Love)

> The passage from the Letter to the Ephesians [5:21-33] which we have been considering enables us to think of a special kind of "prophetism" that belongs to women in their femininity. The analogy of the Bridegroom and the Bride speaks of the love with which every human being—man and woman—is loved by God in Christ. [222]

In the passage from the Letter to the Ephesians, St. Paul is teaching a new innovation, a new beginning in the order of love for men and women, in the sacrament of holy marriage. This new beginning came through the self-emptying gift of Christ the Bridegroom. For Christ the Bridegroom loved first, in the order of love. The Bride of Christ is the Church; it is made up of each man and woman who allows himself or herself to be loved by Christ. This receiving of the love of Christ means we allow ourselves to be loved by God. The response we give back to God is the key to our happiness and fulfillment as women and men. It allows the love of God, by the power of grace, to fill us with love, so we might love God in return.

> **The Bridegroom is the one who loves. The Bride is loved:** *it is she who receives love, in order to love in return.*[223]

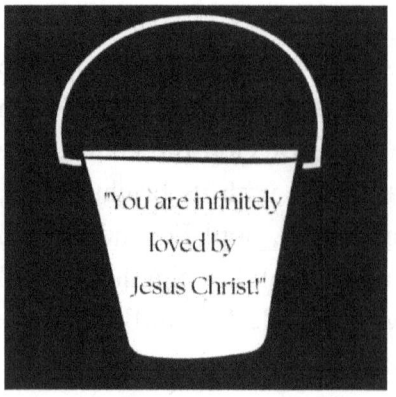

Our worth to God is much more than you or I could ever know or even begin to imagine. This is why it is necessary to entrust ourselves to Christ the Bridegroom of the Church. The bride is the one who responds to Jesus's love. You can be the bride. You are infinitely loved by Jesus Christ! In welcoming the infinite love of Jesus Christ, we receive the light and power to love God as well as each other, since sin and human brokenness are finite realities. Christ has truly overcome all of the sin and brokenness—and even death itself.

> ***Love, which is of God, communicates itself to creatures:* "God's love has been poured into our hearts through the Holy Spirit who has been given to us" (Rom 5:5).**[224]

In all human relationships, the commandment to love is preeminent, meaning it surpasses all others. Love is to be shown and received daily in all human relationships, but especially in spousal love and within the life of the family. From the very beginning, marriage is connected to the creation of man and woman in the image and likeness of God, making marriage between a man and woman a primordial sacrament that has existed from the beginning of time.[225] It is the woman in whom the order of love first takes root. Before Eve is created, Adam has no one like himself to love and give himself to as a gift. Adam is lonely. God creates Eve from the side of Adam so that he might love her as an equal. Side by side, they are to live together as husband and wife. Adam is called to love and serve his wife as Christ loved and served His wife, the Church, even dying if necessary for her good. The wife is loved by her husband and gives love back to him in return.

St. John Paul II wants us to know that God has a plan and purpose for the married love between man and woman, who were made in the image and likeness of God. This love of God extends and permeates every aspect of our human life with all its relationships. If we struggle to love each other as God has asked, we can ask for the graces! Through the sacrament of holy marriage, grace in abundance is given through Christ. A key to having a solid marriage is the ability to forgive and to be humble, which means freely saying to each other, "Please forgive me," and "I forgive you." These are important words in our human relationships. They are the words that Jesus said on the Cross as He was dying: "Father, forgive them; for they do not know what they do" (Lk 23:34). With grace and endurance, we can forgive those who trespass against us. We can learn to love again if we turn to

Christ for the answers we need to life's greatest problems. In receiving His love and grace, we are empowered to live and reflect the Undivided Love of God in our marriages, our societies, and the Church. We were born for this.

In my work with high school teens, I wanted to inspire the teens to be more open to God's love. I decided to experiment on my youngest sister who was still in high school at the time, so I asked her the question, "Can you remember a time that you knew you were deeply loved?" I was surprised and moved by her quick response. She said, "*Yes, I've always known that I was loved,* and I have never had a hard time believing that God loved me and that Jesus died for me. This is because, from the time I was little, I was told the story of how Mom could have died having me. She chose to have me, risking her own life. That is why I can honestly say that I never had a problem believing that I was loved or that Jesus died for me and that God loved me."

> **In God's eternal plan, woman is the one in whom the order of love in the created world of persons takes first root. The order of love belongs to the intimate life of God himself, the life of the Trinity. ... Through the Spirit, Uncreated Gift, love becomes a gift for created persons.** *Love, which is of God, communicates itself to creatures:* **"God's love has been poured into our hearts through the Holy Spirit who has been given to us" (Rom 5:5).**[226]

The woman is the one in whom the order of love and the created world of persons take first root. Woman is created by God for man so that he would be able to fulfill his calling to love another like himself (Gen 2:18). From the beginning, we see that love is the greatest gift and greatest calling for created persons. Love's challenges and truths remain the same, a reality that, despite everything, remains unchangeable. Love's ultimate foundation is in Jesus Christ, Who is the same yesterday, today, and forever (Heb 13:8). Grace is given by God, and it alone fulfills human love, making the "unity of the two" possible.

> **The calling of woman into existence at man's side as "a helper fit for him" (Gen 2:18) in the "unity of the two," provides the visible world of creatures with particular conditions so that "the love of God may be poured into the hearts" of the beings created in his image.**[227]

Who and what we choose to love in this short life really matters since this life is but a prelude to a future life that will be lived in union with the God of love. God's invitation to follow Him can be difficult and challenging since we do not always want to do things God's way. Those darn apples of temptation still call out to us today: "Did God really tell you not to…?" Often we want what we want, not thinking about the harm or consequences to ourselves or others.

Yet in the heat of the battle of life, we find a summoning in our hearts that calls us to a fair, pure, and selfless love, the priceless love of Jesus Christ, our Bridegroom. The love we are longing for awaits us and longs to give us rest. The battlefield is within our hearts; when we seek God with all our hearts, He will let us find Him (Jer 29:13).

It is the love of God poured into our hearts through the Holy Spirit that makes it possible for us to live a life of grace and wisdom. With grace, we are to do good and avoid evil. When we are tempted to do evil, it is the voice of our conscience, the Holy Spirit, who gives us a little "whack-whack" in order to help us recognize sin so that we can turn back to God. Without God's light and power, we as women and men are left defenseless and unprotected against the harsh realities of life, sin, and death that leave us empty, unfulfilled, and looking for love and comfort in all the wrong places.

The challenge for many women is to remain open and vulnerable to love. Many women do not think they are enough and often settle for unfulfilled lives. Like the Samaritan woman, they keep looking for love in all the wrong people because they are not aware that it is supposed to be so much more! As Christ's message brought healing and hope to the Samaritan woman, it can bring the same to today's woman if she is willing to sit at the well for a little while and talk to Jesus. Only with grace will we be able to love all people, even difficult people who will not love us in return and even when we are taken for granted, dismissed, ignored…not seen. The truth is, Jesus sees you.

Women are often seen as sources of temptation or obstacles instead of being seen as unique, gifted human persons whose contributions are necessary in order to love and rescue humanity that is in danger of falling. Yes, women can be weak, sinful, and prone to loving themselves more than they love God or others. We have all been there, so this is where the fight takes place—in your heart. For even with grace in Jesus Christ, the freedom to love does not come automatically. Yet with grace, prayer, formation, and encouragement, you can choose love. You are worth the fight!

> ***…the dignity of women is measured by the order of love, which is essentially the order of justice and charity.*** [228]

My mother entrusted herself to Jesus's love throughout her whole life, which is truly the right and just thing to do when you think about it. God became a man to teach us what love is. Then He died, proving that He really did love us: "There is no greater love than to lay down your life for a friend" (Jn 15:13). I was blessed to be with my mom in the final days before her passing. At one point, she asked for her picture of the Sacred Heart of Jesus to be brought to her. We placed it where she could easily see it. Later that afternoon she was resting, when she opened her eyes, pointed to the picture, and said, "Who is that?" I responded, "Mom, that's Jesus." She said, "He was always my first love." It's important to listen to people, especially when they are preparing to go to God. It gets real then; God might have something to say to us or to them if we are open. Right then, God was saying to me, "I was always your mother's first love, the driving force behind everything she lived her life for. Did her life matter? Yes, it mattered very much to Me." When Mom opened her eyes a little later, she  pointed to my dad, who was at her side, resting with his own grief and sorrow. She said, "I always loved him."

> **The person must be loved, since love alone corresponds to what the person is. This explains *the commandment of love*, known already in the Old Testament (cf. Deut 6:5; Lev 19:18) and placed by Christ at the very center of the Gospel *"ethos"* (cf. Mt 22:36-40; Mk 12:28-34). This also explains the *primacy of love* expressed by Saint Paul in the First Letter to the Corinthians: "the greatest of these is love" (cf. 13:13).**[229]

Just as Mother Mary received the love of God into her heart—into her very being—and gave Him back to the world, so all women have the capacity to receive the love of God through the power of the Holy Spirit. This is the prophetic gift that the Creator has given to the character of women, a gift that defines the true dignity and vocation of women, the gift to love, given to women in the order of love. This gift of love and grace is poured into the woman's heart at baptism. If she is taught and formed to walk in love according to the Spirit, she will grow strong in loving and defending the human person for its own sake. She will become a mama bear.

> **This *"prophetic" character of women in their femininity* finds its highest expression in the Virgin Mother of God.**

> **She emphasizes, in the fullest and most direct way, the intimate linking of the order of love—which enters the world of human persons through a Woman—with the Holy Spirit. At the Annunciation Mary hears the words: "The Holy Spirit will come upon you" (Lk 1:35).**[230]

Mama Mary first gave witness and modeled for the feminine genius the woman's prophetic role in being an intimate link in the order of love. Mary's "yes" witnessed to and modeled for all women a vocation that focuses on the dignity of the human person. The calling to love God and to bring that love to the human person is very much needed today. Does a person-centered vocation matter? It matters very much to God, for God chose Mary to be the Mother of His Son. The mystery of Mary's innermost reality, her heart filled with grace, is recognized in the response she gives to the angel in faith, obedience, and perfect charity. The response of Mary is to be the response of all women who, with hearts filled with grace and faith, give loving obedience to God their Father. What's love got to do with it? Everything.

We see Mary's joy in receiving the gift of faith when she proclaims to Elizabeth: "My soul proclaims the greatness of the Lord, my spirit rejoices in God my savior, for He has looked upon his handmaid's lowliness..." (Lk 1:14-48). It is a prophetic voice that not only exclaims her own joy and recognition of the greatness of the Lord but also foreshadows all those to come who will share in that same prophetic joy and recognition of faith. Therefore, Mama Mary, the spiritual mother and model for all, teaches women that their own "yes" to the God of love matters. Every woman is called by God to be a prophet of light, hope, and love to each human person.

A civilization of love cannot be built without women of grace. Women must be responsible for their lives and learn how to choose wisely by saying "yes to the yes," their supreme calling in God. Men must recognize the dignity and value of women and their ability to contribute to the great mission of Christ. For just as Jesus chose twelve men to be His Apostles, He also chose His mother Mary, Mary

Magdalene, Mary the mother of James and Joseph, the unnamed mother of James and John, Joanna, Susanna, and many other women to be His followers in order to fulfill His mission of love on earth and in heaven. Women's role is not secondary; it is a primary role since "the greatest of these is love" (1 Cor 13:13).

Grace Is the New Strong (Awareness of Mission)

After my son went to college, he came home one night to visit and he shared, "Mom, so many kids I know have nothing to live for." I replied, "What do you mean?" He said, "They have no meaning. They have no meaning in their life; they have nothing to live for." He continued, "The greatest thing that could ever happen is if we won the Super Bowl and that's as good as life gets." I responded, "Now you are beginning to see."

We must become aware of the truth that St. John Paul II taught, that while humanity is undergoing a deep transformation, the truth remains that many realities do not change. These unchanging realities, the truths Christ taught us and died to give us, remain the foundation, the cornerstone of all of human history. We are loved with infinite love. So many people have lost their faith, their belief in God. They have no meaning; they have nothing to live for. This crisis of faith that so many are experiencing can only be resolved with a turning back to Christ.

Christ fully reveals the truth of the great dignity of men and women, who share equally in the "supreme calling" to life. Christ offers you the "supreme calling" to life without which you can have no ultimate meaning or purpose, since you are a finite creature. You possess an infinite longing to live, love, and belong to something greater than yourself, and Christ is the answer to that longing. Christ freely offers this grace, yet it does not come without a fight. You must fight for your real life

"Christ fully reveals the truth of the great dignity of men and women, who share equally in the 'supreme calling' to life."

in Christ. Is it worth it? You bet!

Mother Mary received the love of God into her heart, into her very being, and gave Him back to the world, so all women have the capacity to receive the love of God and bring that love of Christ to the world. This capacity to receive grace affects everything and all our relationships, for Christ is the driving force in how we relate to one another as man and woman, brother and sister, husband and wife—and in all of our human relationships. Before the fall, our relationships with each other were compared to the inner life of God, within the Holy Trinity: Undivided Love.

This love we are called to can only come about if we are willing to give ourselves as a sincere gift. We are willed by God for our own sake and can only find meaning and purpose through a sincere gift of self. Grace restores our capacity to become a sincere gift of self—a gift first of all for God and then for others. It is also what we as human persons are made for and is the greatest power. The power of love, to love and be loved, is what it means to be human, made in the image and likeness of God.

> **"Man, who is the only creature on earth that God willed for its own sake, cannot fully find himself except through a sincere gift of self." This applies to every human being, as a person created in God's image, whether man or woman. This ontological [the reality of being/existence] affirmation also indicates the ethical dimension of a person's vocation. *Woman can only find herself by giving love to others.*** [231]

What does this mean for women? God has already given you dignity and worth. You cannot earn it because it has already been given to you in Jesus Christ. As a beloved daughter, God has placed in your heart the desire for something greater than the world can offer. God is the "bigger, bigger" that our lives are looking for, and God has a job that only you can do during your life on earth. Your calling can only be fulfilled by you. It will give your life meaning and purpose. It is what you were born to do. You can find examples of great women of faith whose lives witnessed to their essential calling: to believe, belong, and become that woman, full of dignity and purpose, who, through grace, is able to do so much to aid humanity in not falling. We see these women in the Old Testament: Judith, Esther, and Susanna; and at the time of Jesus: Mother Mary, Elizabeth, Mary Magdalene, and the Samaritan woman; and after Jesus's time: St. Catherine of Siena, Edith Stein (St. Teresa Benedicta), Mother Teresa, St. Therese of Lisieux, and Sister Mary of the Holy Trinity. All of these women, with the help of God's grace, became aware of their missions, forsaking their own paths for His.

> **Is not the Bible trying to tell us that it is precisely in the "woman"—Eve-Mary—that history witnesses a dramatic struggle for every human being, the struggle for his or her fundamental "yes" or "no" to God and God's eternal plan for humanity?**[232]

Grace brings about a new awareness of mission, a new beginning. With all of the dramatic struggles and challenges of life, it's not ever going to work to just go with the flow and see how things turn out. Still, so many do this. God's generous love and gift in Christ requires a personal response of self-gift, our "yes." Grace is the "new strong," given to each woman in Christ, that brings about her awareness of her mission. This awareness of mission makes her strong in love and strong in purpose, for the human person is entrusted to her by God.

> ***A woman is strong because of her awareness of this entrusting,*** **strong because of the fact that God "entrusts the human being to her," always and in every way, even in the situations of social discrimination in which she may find herself.**[233]

"*I believe in you.*" Jesus wants you to know that He knows who you are and the purpose He has created you for. Despite everything that has happened in your life and in the world, everything will be all right if you can keep believing in Jesus. If you are a follower of Jesus, many times in your life you will simply need to have faith in Him. Jesus also wants you to find a special place in your heart for the woman, Mama Mary. Mary teaches you how to believe so that you too might belong to Christ and find a new beginning as a woman of grace in the order of love. God created each of you for Himself. For you are called to an Undivided Love with God and each other, as a woman or man of grace. You Are Worth the Fight!

> **"If you knew the gift of God" (Jn 4:10) ... for all women as they have come forth from the heart of God in all the beauty and richness of their femininity; as they have been embraced by his eternal love; as, together with men, they are pilgrims on this earth, which is the temporal "homeland" of all people and is transformed sometimes into a "valley of tears"; as they assume, together with men,** *a common responsibility for the destiny of humanity* **according to daily necessities and according to that definitive destiny which the human family has in God himself, in the bosom of the ineffable Trinity.**[234]

Questions for Reflection
Chapter 8
"The Greatest of These Is Love"

1. What are one or two takeaways from this chapter?

2. How can Jesus help you to find "your real life"? What do you need to do to strengthen your ability to choose wisely the path for this season in your life?

3. How will you better take care of your physical and spiritual life in order to serve God and the personal mission he has entrusted to you for this season of your life? What will happen if you choose to take these steps? What will happen if you do not choose to take these steps? How will others be affected if you do not fulfill your mission?

4. The calling to love God and to bring that love to the human person is very much needed in today's world. Women in general are person-centered. What does your person-centered vocation bring to the people in your life?

5. How has God revealed the love of Jesus the Bridegroom to you? Why is love the greatest gift that we can receive? How is God calling you to be a self-gift of love, laying down your life for the people you serve?

Notes

About the Author

Gina is a dynamic and entertaining author, speaker, teacher, and trainer with years of experience serving dioceses, parishes, families, youth, young adults, and men's and women's groups. She captivates and engages her audience with lively stories and humor. She is able to convey Catholic teachings in a compassionate, down-to-earth style that reaches the hearts of listeners. Her vocation as a wife and mother of four personally connects her to audiences on a very real and  practical level, drawing them into the beautiful love story of the Catholic Church. She inspires and moves people, equipping them with practical tools to live holy lives in today's culture, drawing in particular on her expertise on the dignity of the human person.

Gina received her undergraduate degree from the University of St. Thomas in St. Paul, Minnesota, and her master's in Theological Studies from the University of Dallas Institute for Religious and Pastoral Studies.

Gina has been a youth minister for many years, successfully pioneering youth programs in parishes throughout Minnesota. She developed and administered vibrant programs, providing opportunities for young people to participate in annual pilgrimages to the Steubenville Youth Conference, yearly retreats, weekly Eucharistic adoration, and frequent participation in the sacraments.

Gina has extensive experience training and mentoring religious leaders, lay leaders, and Catholic educators throughout the country. She was invited to the LifeTeen program's founding parish to train youth ministers from around the country. Gina has been a teacher and speaker for St. Paul Seminary in Minnesota, NET Ministries in the Twin Cities, and the St. John Bosco Conference for catechists and religious educators in Steubenville, Ohio. She has traveled the country serving as a retreat master and trainer for youth and adult groups alike at the Ave Maria Catholic Youth Conference in Florida, diocesan events, individual parish programs, and private retreats.

When she is not working, Gina enjoys spending time with family and friends, especially her husband, Duane, and cooking, hiking, and visiting Red Lodge, Montana.

Endnotes

[1] John Paul II, Apostolic Letter *Mulieris Dignitatem: On the Dignity and Vocation of Women*. 15 August 1988 (Hereafter cited as *MD*), Section 1. Quoting the Second Vatican Council's Message to Women (8 December 1965); *AAS* 58 (1966), 13-14.
[2] *Ibid*, 28.
[3] *Ibid.*, 1.
[4] *Ibid.*, 2.
[5] *The Didache Bible: With Commentaries Based on the Catechism of the Catholic Church, Ignatius Bible Edition*. (San Francisco, CA: Ignatius Press, 2014). This edition will be used when Scripture is quoted or referenced.
[6] *MD*, Section 1. Quoting the Second Vatican Council's Message to Women (8 December 1965), 13-14.
[7] *Ibid.*
[8] *Ibid.*, 2.
[9] *Ibid.*
[10] John Paul II, Apostolic Letter *Familiaris Consortio: The Role of the Christian Family in the Modern World*. 22 November 1981 (Hereafter cited as *FC*), 21.
[11] *MD*, 1. Quoting Paul VI, Address to participants at the National Meeting of the Centro Italiano Femminile (6 December 1976): *Insegnamenti di Paolo VI*, XIV (1976), 1017.
[12] Pére Jean du Coeur de Jésus D'Elbée, *I Believe in Love*, trans. Marilyn Teichart and Madeleine Stebbins (Petersham, MA: St. Bede's Publications, 1974), 3.
[13] *MD*, Section 7.
[14] *Ibid.*, 2.
[15] *Ibid.*
[16] *Ibid.*, 3.
[17] Xavier Léon-Dufor, *Dictionary of Biblical Theology* (Frederick, ML: The Word Among Us Press, 1988), 218.
[18] Catholic Church, *Catechism of the Catholic Church*, 2nd ed. (Liberia Editrice Vaticana: Vatican City, 1997), (Hereafter cited as *CCC*), 1996.
[19] *MD*, Section 3.
[20] *Ibid.*
[21] Rev. Reginald Garrigou-Lagrange, O.P., *The Three Ages of the Interior Life: Prelude of Eternal Life*, trans. Sr. M. Timothea Doyle, O.P., vol. 1 (Rockford, IL: Tan Books and Publishers, Inc., 1947), 29.
[22] *MD*, Section 3.
[23] *Ibid.*
[24] *Ibid.*
[25] *Ibid.*
[26] *Ibid.*
[27] *Ibid.*, 11.
[28] *Ibid.*, 4.
[29] *Ibid.*
[30] *Ibid.*
[31] *Ibid.*

[32] Benedict XVI, General Audience of 16 November 2005: Psalm 136[135] – To the God of Heaven give thanks, (16 November 2005), 4.
[33] *MD*, Section 5.
[34] *Ibid.*
[35] *Ibid.* Quoting the Second Vatican Ecumenical Council, Dogmatic Constitution on the Church *Lumen Gentium*, 36.
[36] *Ibid.*
[37] *CCC*, Paragraph 2515.
[38] *MD*, Section 5.
[39] *Ibid.*, 6.
[40] *Ibid.*, 7.
[41] John Paul II, *The Theology of the Body: Human Love in the Divine Plan* (Boston, MA: Pauline Books and Media, 1997), (Hereafter cited as *TOB*), 38.
[42] *MD*, Section 6.
[43] *Ibid.*, 9.
[44] *CCC*, Paragraphs 375-376.
[45] *CCC*, Paragraph 306.
[46] *MD*, Section 6.
[47] Catherine of Siena, *The Dialogue*, trans. Suzanne Noffke, O.P. (Mahwah, NJ: Paulist Press, Inc., 1980), 38.
[48] *TOB*, 38.
[49] *Ibid.*, 41.
[50] *CCC*, Paragraph 1008. Quoting *Gaudium et Spes*, 18.
[51] *MD*, Section 6.
[52] *Ibid.*
[53] *TOB*, 45.
[54] *Ibid.*, 58.
[55] *MD*, Section 6.
[56] *Ibid.*
[57] *FC*, 21.
[58] *MD*, Section 7.
[59] *Ibid.*
[60] *Ibid.*
[61] *Ibid.*
[62] Garrigou-Lagrange, *Interior Life*, 5-6.
[63] *MD*, Section 7.
[64] Therese of Lisieux, *The Story of a Soul*, trans. John Beevers (Broadway, NY: Doubleday, 1957), 148.
[65] *MD*, Section 8.
[66] *MD*, Section 7. Quoting the Second Vatican Ecumenical Council, Pastoral Constitution on the Church in the Modern World, *Gaudium et Spes*, 24.
[67] *Ibid.*
[68] *Ibid.*, 8.
[69] Catherine of Siena, *Dialogue*, 211.
[70] *MD*, Section 9. Quoting the Second Vatican Ecumenical Council, Pastoral Constitution on the Church in the Modern World, *Gaudium et Spes*, 13.
[71] *CCC*, Paragraph 390.
[72] *Ibid.*, 392.

73 *MD*, Section 9.
74 *Ibid.*
75 *Ibid.*
76 *CCC*, Paragraph 398.
77 *Ibid.*, Paragraph 399.
78 *MD*, Section 9. Quoting *Gaudium et Spes*, 13.
79 *Ibid.*
80 *CCC*, Paragraph 400. Quoting Romans 5:12.
81 *Ibid.*
82 *MD*, section 13.
83 *Ibid.*
84 *Ibid.*, 10.
85 *Ibid.*
86 *Ibid.*
87 *Ibid.*
88 *Ibid.*
89 *Ibid.*
90 *Ibid.* Quoting *Gaudium et Spes*, 24.
91 *Ibid.*
92 *Ibid.*, 11.
93 *Ibid.*
94 *Ibid.*
95 *Ibid.*
96 *Ibid.*
97 *Ibid.*
98 John Paul II, Encyclical Letter *Redemptoris Mater: On the Blessed Virgin Mary in the Life of the Pilgrim Church.* 25 March 1987 (Hereafter cited as *RM*), 18.3.
99 *MD*, Section 11.
100 *Ibid.*, 12.
101 *Ibid.*
102 *Ibid.*
103 *Ibid.*
104 *Ibid.*
105 *Ibid.*
106 *Ibid.*, 13.
107 *Ibid.*
108 *Ibid.*
109 *Ibid.*
110 *Ibid.*, 14.
111 *CCC,* Paragraphs 375-376.
112 *MD*, Section 14.
113 *Ibid.*
114 *Ibid.*
115 *Ibid.*
116 *Ibid.*
117 *Ibid.*

[118] Augustine of Hippo, *The Confessions*, 2nd ed., trans. Maria Boulding, ed. John E. Rotelle (Hyde Park, NY: New City Press, 2012), II,4,9.
[119] *MD*, Section 15.
[120] *Ibid.*
[121] *Ibid.*
[122] *Ibid.*
[123] *Ibid.*
[124] *Ibid.*, 16.
[125] *Ibid.*
[126] *Ibid.*
[127] *Ibid.*
[128] *Ibid.*
[129] *Ibid.*, 17.
[130] *Ibid.*, 11.
[131] *Ibid.*, 17.
[132] *CCC*, Paragraph 358.
[133] *MD*, Section 11.
[134] *Ibid.*, 17.
[135] *CCC*, Paragraph 1265.
[136] *MD*, Section 18. Quoting *Gaudium et Spes*, 24.
[137] *Ibid.*
[138] *Ibid.*
[139] *Ibid.*
[140] *Ibid.*
[141] John Paul II, Encyclical Letter *Dominum et Vivicantem: On the Holy Spirit in the Life of the Church and the World*. 18 May 1986 (Hereafter cited as *DV*), 43.1. Quoting *Gaudium et Spes*, 16.
[142] *MD*, Section 18.
[143] *Ibid.*
[144] *Ibid.*
[145] *Ibid.*
[146] *Ibid.*, 19.
[147] *Ibid.*
[148] *Ibid.*
[149] *Ibid.*
[150] *Ibid.*
[151] *Ibid.*
[152] *Ibid.*
[153] *Ibid.*
[154] *Ibid.* Quoting *Redemptoris Mater*, 18.3.
[155] *Ibid.*
[156] *Ibid.*
[157] *Ibid.*, 20.
[158] *Ibid.*
[159] *Ibid.*
[160] *Ibid.*
[161] *Ibid.*
[162] *Ibid.*

163 *Ibid.*
164 *Ibid.*, 21.
165 *Ibid.*
166 *Ibid.*
167 Teresa of Calcutta, Paul Murray, *I Loved Jesus in the Night* (Brewster, MA: Paraclete Press), 76.
168 *MD*, Section 31.
169 *Ibid.*
170 *Ibid.*, 22.
171 *Ibid.*, 22. Quoting *Lumen Gentium*, 64.
172 *Ibid.*, 23.
173 *Ibid.*
174 *Ibid.*
175 *Ibid.*
176 *TOB*, 45.
177 *Ibid.*, 57.
178 *MD, Section* 23.
179 *Ibid.*
180 *Ibid.*
181 *CCC*, Paragraph 409.
182 *MD*, Section 23.
183 *Ibid.*
184 Peter Williamson, *Catholic Commentary on Sacred Scripture,* (Grand Rapids, MI: Baker Academic, 2009), 174.
185 *MD*, Section 24.
186 Peter Williamson, *Catholic Commentary on Sacred Scripture,* (Grand Rapids, MI: Baker Academic, 2009), 176. Quoting *TOB*, 310.
187 Mary Hayden Lemmons, *"Prophetic Femininity in the Bible, the Church, and Nature,"* Women as Prophet in the Home and the World: Interdisciplinary Investigations. (Lanham, ML: Lexington Books, 2016) 92.
188 *MD*, Section 24.
189 *Ibid.*
190 *Ibid.*
191 *Ibid.*
192 *Ibid.*
193 Peter Williamson, *Catholic Commentary on Sacred Scripture,* (Grand Rapids, MI: Baker Academic, 2009), 178.
194 *MD*, Section 25.
195 *Ibid.*
196 *Ibid.*
197 Mary Hayden Lemmons, *"Prophetic Femininity in the Bible, the Church, and Nature,"* Women as Prophet in the Home and the World: Interdisciplinary Investigations. (Lanham, ML: Lexington Books, 2016), 80.
198 *MD*, Section 25.
199 *Ibid.*

²⁰⁰ Pope Benedict XVI, *Mass for the Inauguration of the Pontificate, 24 April 2005: Imposition of the Pallium and Conferral of the Fisherman's Ring for the Beginning of the Petrine Ministry of the Bishop of Rome.*
²⁰¹ *FC*, 3.
²⁰² Cardinal Suenens, *Baudouin, King of the Belgians: The Hidden Life*, trans. Sr. Helen M. Wynne, (Belgium: F.I.A.T. Publications, 1996), 70.
²⁰³ *MD*, Section 26.
²⁰⁴ John Paul II, Encyclical Letter *Ecclesia de Eucharistia: On the Eucharist in its Relationship to the Church*, (Hereafter cited as *EE*), 17.
²⁰⁵ *CCC*, Paragraph 1324.
²⁰⁶ *MD*, Section 26.
²⁰⁷ *Ibid.*
²⁰⁸ *Ibid.*
²⁰⁹ *MD*, Section 27. Quoting *Lumen Gentium*, 10.
²¹⁰ *Ibid.*
²¹¹ *Ibid.*
²¹² *Ibid.* Quoting *RM*, 362-367.
²¹³ *Ibid.*
²¹⁴ David Van Biema, Dr. Rick Warren, Fr. James Martin, SJ, Susan van Houte, Fr. Brian Kolodiejchuk, "Mother Teresa at 100." *Time*, 2010, 20.
²¹⁵ "Mother Teresa of Calcutta (1910-1997), Biography." Vatican. Accessed April 7, 2023. https://www.vatican.va/news_services/liturgy/saints/ns_lit_doc_20031019_madre-teresa_en.html
²¹⁶ David Van Biema, Dr. Rick Warren, Fr. James Martin, SJ, Susan van Houte, Fr. Brian Kolodiejchuk, "Mother Teresa at 100." *Time*, 2010, 24.
²¹⁷ *Ibid.*, 35-37.
²¹⁸ *MD*, Section 27.
²¹⁹ *Ibid.*, 28. Quoting *Gaudium et Spes*, 10.
²²⁰ *Ibid.*
²²¹ *Ibid.*
²²² *Ibid.*, 29.
²²³ *Ibid.*
²²⁴ *Ibid.*
²²⁵ *Ibid.*
²²⁶ *Ibid.*
²²⁷ *Ibid.*
²²⁸ *Ibid.*
²²⁹ *Ibid.*
²³⁰ *Ibid.*
²³¹ *Ibid.*, 30.
²³² *Ibid.*
²³³ *Ibid.*
²³⁴ *Ibid.*, 31.

www.ingramcontent.com/pod-product-compliance
Lightning Source LLC
Chambersburg PA
CBHW070640160426
43194CB00009B/1515